SWINBURNE

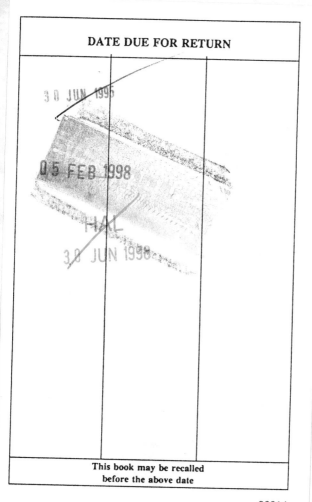

Swinburne, *c.* 1865
From the painting by G. F. Watts, R.A.

SWINBURNE

A Critical Biography

By

JEAN OVERTON FULLER

1968

CHATTO & WINDUS

LONDON

Published by
Chatto & Windus Ltd
40 William IV Street
London W.C.2

*

Clarke, Irwin & Co. Ltd
Toronto

SBN 7011 1310 3

© Jean Overton Fuller 1968

Printed in Great Britain by
Cox and Wyman Ltd
London, Fakenham and Reading

This book
is affectionately dedicated to
TIMOTHY D'ARCH SMITH
friendship with whom was
its inspiration

Contents

CONTENTS

Illustrations

Thanks are due to the following for permission to reproduce photographs for the illustrations: The Trustees of the National Portrait Gallery (Frontispiece); Mrs. Hilda Mason (2, 4, 6); Chatto & Windus Ltd (3); Mrs. Mary Lefroy (5)

Acknowledgements

My first acknowledgement, which I have great pleasure in making, is to the directors of Messrs. Chatto & Windus, Swinburne's own publishers, for testifying to their faith in my ability to write his biography by giving me a contract in advance and placing at my disposal all the papers in their possession dealing with their relations with the poet.

I have had frequent recourse to Professor Lang's edition of *The Swinburne Letters*, and my next acknowledgement must be to the Oxford University Press for permission to quote from this.

With regard to libraries, the main part of my research has been done at the British Museum and I am indebted to the Principal Keeper of Printed Books and the Keeper of Manuscripts for permission to consult books which are kept in the Private Case and manuscripts which are reserved from public use. I would also like to thank specially Miss Olorenshaw of the Manuscript Department for her help on many occasions. For books on loan I am indebted to the University of London Library. Long hours spent in the Bibliothèque Sainte Geneviève, in Paris, have stood me in good stead with regard to the French literature which was so important an influence on Swinburne.

My friend Dame Irene Ward, D.B.E., M.P., elucidated for me the Northumbrian references in poems and letters of Swinburne which I showed her, and only confinement to hospital for a surgical operation prevented her from driving me herself to all the places he mentioned.

I have to thank the *Daily Telegraph*, *The Times Literary Supplement* and the *Wandsworth Boro' News* for printing my appeals for personal reminiscences of Swinburne, and I am indebted to Miss Shirley Toulson for the suggestion that I should write to the last named. Amongst those who replied was Mrs. Rosemary Bailey, whose grandfather, Lord Redesdale, was Swinburne's first cousin once removed. It was an unexpected pleasure to be able to entertain at my home a blood relative of the poet.

I owe both the photograph of Swinburne, 1866 and the one of Mary Leith, née Gordon, to the response to my appeals. Mrs. Mary E. Lefroy sent me the latter, which is particularly important as being the only picture, of which I know, of the woman who had so great an influence on Swinburne's life. The 1866 photograph of Swinburne I had enlarged by Barr of Camberwell from a tiny print sent me by Mrs. Hilda Mason, widow of the son of 'Bertie',

13

ACKNOWLEDGEMENTS

famed through Swinburne's poems. Both Mrs. Mason and Mrs. Lefroy sent me useful background information. Mrs. Mason provided further pictures.

I must also make special mention of Mrs. Enid Yglesias, of Putney Hill, who was the only person able to recount to me a living fragment of conversation which she herself had had with Swinburne. Mrs. Yglesias also made suggestions with regard to further enquiries I could make in Putney which were very fruitful.

Others who responded to my appeal are, alphabetically, Mrs. Joyce Davis, Mr. A. F. Minchin, Mr. W. J. S. Neale, Major-General A. L. Ransome, C.B., D.S.O., M.C. (a friend of Swinburne's sisters, Miss Alice and Miss Isabel Swinburne), Mr. William Reader, Mr. F. Gordon Roe, F.S.A., F.R.Hist.S., Mrs. Aileen Skrimshire, and Dr. H. Gordon Smith, M.D.

Amongst persons acting in their official capacities, I have to thank the Headmaster and Headmaster's secretary, Mr. F. Porter, of Eton College; Mr. Edmund V. Corbett, F.L.A., the Borough Librarian of Wandsworth (West Hill District) Library; Mr. Sidney C. Hutchinson, Secretary of the Royal Academy of Arts; Major-General F. J. Brill, R.A., of the Ministry of Defence; and Mr. J. C. Chapman, Chief Clerk of Trinity College, Cambridge, all of whom sent me, in reply to my enquiries, details from their records.

I am indebted to Somerset House for copies of the death certificate and will of Swinburne, the birth and marriage certificates and will of Mary Leith, the birth and death certificates of Simeon Solomon and the birth, marriage and death certificates of Clara Watts-Dunton.

I have to thank Mr. Peter Fryer for directing me to one reference.

My late mother gave the manuscript a very careful reading and made many helpful suggestions.

It is a pleasure to thank my friend Mr. Timothy d'Arch Smith for his gift of a copy of the original edition of *A Song of Italy*, published by John Camden Hotten, for letting me have on long loan several very rare books from his own collection, for placing at my disposal his bibliographical knowledge, and for reading my manuscript more than once and making a special scrutiny of my footnotes and bibliographical references.

J.O.F.

Note on References and Abbreviations

THE following frequently occurring references given in the footnotes are to be understood as beneath:

Chatto, where no title follows, means the Chatto & Windus edition of Swinburne's Poems.

Chatto, *The Tragedies*, means the Chatto & Windus edition of *The Tragedies* of Swinburne.

Gosse, where no other title follows, means his biography of Swinburne.

Lafourcade, where *La Jeunesse* is not specified, means his biography of Swinburne written in the English language. This is not a translation or abridgement of his two-volume work in French, but a different book.

Leith, excepting where the title of one of her other works follows, means Mary Leith's book *The Boyhood of Algernon Charles Swinburne*.

Lang means Professor Cecil Lang's edition of Swinburne's *Letters*.

Full titles and other particulars of these works are given in the Bibliography.

I

Wight and Northumbria

ALGERNON CHARLES SWINBURNE was born in London, but his
childhood home was the Isle of Wight. Neither place was ancestral
territory. His father's family was one of the oldest in Northumberland,
and his mother's had had their seat for centuries in Sussex.

The poet was born at 5 a.m. on April 5, 1837. This was eleven weeks
before Queen Victoria ascended the throne. His father, Charles
Henry Swinburne, was a Captain, later an Admiral, in the Royal Navy,
while his mother, Lady Jane Henrietta Swinburne, was the fourth
daughter of the third Earl of Ashburnham. Shortly after Algernon was
born his parents rented, in the Isle of Wight, at Bonchurch near Ventnor,
the large, gabled house, set amid lawns and trees, called East Dene.

Their choice of this residence may have been partly determined by
its proximity to Northcourt, on the south-western side of the island.
This was the home of Lady Swinburne's sister, Lady Mary Gordon,
and her husband, Sir Henry Gordon, who was Captain Swinburne's
first cousin. Curiously ingrown families of this sort, in which everybody
seems to be related to everyone else, and which constitute complete
worlds in themselves, are features of Swinburne's novels.

His father being so much at sea, Algernon saw him only at intervals.
Yet he wrote:[1] 'I can remember no earlier enjoyment than being held
up naked in my father's arms and brandished between his hands, then
shot like a stone from a sling through the air, shouting and laughing
with delight, head foremost into the coming wave, which could only
have been the pleasure of a very little fellow.'

Algernon was his parents' first child, but had for playmates four
younger sisters. In this he resembled Shelley, who was also the eldest
child and likewise had four younger sisters. In each case a sixth child,
a brother, arrived but not until the poet's childhood was nearly over.
In both cases, habituation to being the leader of a little troup of gentler
and smaller companions may have accounted for a girlishness in his
manner noted when he began to meet other people. Swinburne's juniors
were Alice, Edith, Charlotte Jane, Isabel and Edward.

[1] Lang, Vol. III, p. 12.

17

A frequent addition to their society, making practically a fifth sister, three years younger than Algernon, was his cousin Mary Charlotte Julia Gordon, daughter of Sir Henry and Lady Gordon, born on July 9, 1840. This cousin, Mary Gordon, was to become far the most important person in Swinburne's life; and it is to her memoir, *The Boyhood of Algernon Charles Swinburne*, published under her married name of Leith late in her life and after his death, that we owe almost all the details we have concerning the poet's early childhood. Some of Mary's earliest memories were of:[1] 'seeing Algernon and his eldest sister walking on ahead of the rest over the rough grass of the Bonchurch Down – he with that springy, dancing step which he never entirely lost; while I, a much younger and very unsteady-footed child, stumbled along after them'.

Sometimes she would see him on a Shetland pony, which he called York, led by a servant. She knew him as 'Cousin Hadji'. How he acquired this nickname has never been explained, but his mother, in her letters to him, addressed him as Hadji to the end of her life. His name for her was 'Mimmy', and for his father, 'Pino'.

When the Gordons stayed with the Swinburnes, the children said their Catechism together, and Mary formed part of Lady Swinburne's little class. Lady Gordon and Lady Swinburne were both Anglicans, rather high church and very serious. Algernon's reading, when it came to his turn to read a text, was, his cousin Mary noticed, particularly beautiful. She noticed, also, that Algernon was privileged to have a book at meals, usually a fat Shakespeare. Needless to say, this was Bowdler's expurgated edition.

On some afternoons, the children would paint. Scraps were cut out of illustrated papers for them to fill in with water-colours. The governess would read them stories. On one occasion, she warned them that one of the stories contained something about drowning puppies. Algernon said vehemently, 'If it's anything about cruelty, don't read it!'

Often, the two families met at the home of Mary's paternal grandparents. The garden, rambling in terraces down to the sea, is described in the *Dedication* to Lady Gordon of one of Swinburne's later works:[2]

> Between the sea-cliffs and the sea there sleeps
> A garden walled about with woodland, fair
> As dreams that die or days that memory keeps
> Alive in holier light and lovelier air

Leith, pp. 5–6.   [2] *The Sisters*, 1892.

Than clothed them round long since and blessed them there
With less benignant blessing, set less fast
For seal on spirit and sense, than time has cast
For all time on the dead and deathless past.

Beneath the trellised flowers the flowers that shine
    And lighten all the lustrous length of way
From terrace up to terrace bear me sign
    And keep me record how no word could say
    What perfect pleasure of how pure a day
A child's remembrance or a child's delight
Drank deep in dreams of, or in present sight
Exulted as the sunrise in its might.

The shadowed lawns, the shadowing pines, the ways
    That wind and wander through a world of flowers,
The radiant orchard where the glad sun's gaze
    Dwells, and makes most of all his happiest hours,
    The field that laughs beneath the cliff that towers,
The splendour of the slumber that enthralls
With sunbright peace the world within their walls,
Are symbols yet of years that love recalls.

When he became old enough to attend a preparatory school, Algernon
was sent to Brooke Rectory. Here, Mary came with her mother to see
him, and he showed them his room proudly and told them that everything in it was his.

But his mother helped to prepare him. Part of her education had been
in Florence, and she was able to teach French and Italian to her children.
In old age, he wrote to her:[1] 'Do you remember our Goldoni readings
when I was a little chap? *You* got me the modern language prize at Eton,
you know.'

It was because of her that he was able to boast that he knew Alfieri
before Spenser. Together, while he was still quite small, they read
Alfieri's *Rosamunda*.[2]

The soft and sheltered bays of the Isle of Wight were not, however,
the only scenic influence upon Swinburne's childhood. The Isle of Wight,
since the Romans came to it and called it Vectis, had little history; but

[1] Leith, p. 219.
[2] Lang, Vol. VI, p. 142.

every autumn the Swinburnes and the Gordons went to stay with Sir
John Swinburne, the poet's grandfather, at Capheaton, Northumberland; that is to say very close to the Border, and the Border was redolent
with history, history in which the Swinburne family had played a part.
This country was to inspire a great part of Swinburne's poetry. He not
only came to exult in the bleak moors across which the wind drove, and
the wild seas which beat up its beaches; he felt a patriotism for it, expressed in his poem *Northumberland*:[1]

> Between our eastward and our westward sea
> The narrowing strand
> Clasps close the noblest shore fame holds in fee
> Even here where English birth seals all men free –
> Northumberland.
>
> The sea-mists meet across it when the snow
> Clothes moor and fell, . . .
>
> O land beloved, where nought of legend's dream
> Outshines the truth,
> Where Joyous Gard, closed round with clouds that gleam
> For them that know thee not, can scarce but seem
> Too sweet for sooth,
>
> Thy sons forget thee not . . .

Swinburne seldom refers to his father, but he recorded one charming
recollection of him, which relates to one of the family holidays in
Northumberland:[2]

> Once when I was a little boy – years before Eton, I think – my
> father came once into my bedroom at Mounces . . . took me out of
> bed, wrapped (or happit) me in a blanket and carried me through
> the garden, across the road, through the copse and down the bank
> to see the place where I had bathed that morning before breakfast,
> in a clear pool at the bottom of a waterfall – and where there was
> now neither waterfall nor pool, but one unbroken yellow torrent
> roaring like continuous thunder.

[1] Chatto, Vol. VI.
[2] Lang, Vol. VI, pp. 133–4.

It was, however, his grandfather who really captured the poet's imagination. He later wrote:[1]

> My father, Admiral Swinburne, is the second son of Sir John Swinburne, a person whose life would be better worth writing than mine. Born and brought up in France, his father (I believe) a naturalised Frenchman (we were all Catholic and Jacobite rebels and exiles) and his mother a lady of the house of Polignac (a quaint political relationship for me as you will admit), my grandfather never left France till called away at 25 on the falling in of such English estates (about half the original quantity) as confiscation had left to a family which in every Catholic rebellion from the days of my own Queen Mary to those of Charles Edward had given their blood like water and their lands like dust for the Stuarts. I assume that his Catholicism sat lightly upon a young man who in the age of Voltaire had enjoyed the personal friendship of Mirabeau; anyhow he had the sense to throw it to the dogs and enter the political life from which in those days it would have excluded him. He was (of course on the ultra-liberal side) one of the most extreme politicians as well as one of the hardest riders and the best art-patrons of his time. Take these instances; 1) he used to tell us that he and Lord Grey had by the law of the land repeatedly made themselves liable to be impeached and executed for high treason; and certainly I have read a speech of his on the Prince of Wales which if delivered with reference to the present bearer of that title would considerably astonish the existing House of Commons. 2) It was said that the two maddest things in the North country were his horse and himself; but I don't think his horse can have been the madder . . .

His cousin Mary, in her memoir of Algernon, has pointed out that he was in error in supposing that he had French blood in his veins. His grandfather often talked of his French connections, and Algernon must have misunderstood the nature of them. In fact, Algernon's great grandmother was not 'a lady of the house of Polignac' but Christiana Dillon, daughter of Robert Dillon.[2]

Nevertheless, Swinburne's belief that he had a vein of French blood is important, for, together with his grandfather's great library of French works (particularly of the eighteenth century) at Capheaton, it must have contributed to the eagerness with which he was later to interest himself

[1] Lang, Vol. III, pp. 10–11.
[2] Leith, p. 4, n.

in French writers. It is important to realize that the influence of French literature upon Swinburne's work is almost as great as the influence of English.

It is of course to the holidays at Capheaton that Swinburne owed his interest in the songs and ballads of the Border and the legends of Mary Stuart.

2

Eton

SWINBURNE entered Eton when he was twelve years old, at the beginning of the summer half of 1849. He was an Oppidan, and boarded at Joynes's; Joynes was his tutor. His first cousin once removed, Algernon Bertram Mitford, who later became Lord Redesdale, had already been at the school for three years, and although, as a Colleger, he could not do much for his younger relative, Admiral and Lady Swinburne sent for him when they brought their own Algernon, and confided him to his care. Years later, Lord Redesdale wrote:[1]

> What a fragile little creature he seemed as he stood there between his father and mother, with his wondering eyes fixed upon me! Under his arm he hugged his Bowdler's Shakespeare, a very precious treasure, bound in brown leather with, for a marker, a narrow strip of ribbon. . . . He was strangely tiny. His limbs were small and delicate; and his sloping shoulders looked far too weak to carry his great head, the size of which was exaggerated by the touzled mass of red hair standing almost at right angles to it. Hero-worshippers talk of his hair as having been a 'golden aureole'. At that time there was nothing golden about it. Red, violent, aggressive red it was, unmistakable, unpoetical carrots.

In the *Life* of Swinburne by Sir Edmund Gosse, his first biographer, this passage appears twice, once in the text and once in the Appendix, where the long letter from Lord Redesdale, from which it comes, is given in full. There is a curious discrepancy between the citations, for while in the Appendix the description of Swinburne's hair is given as above, in Gosse's text the last words appear as 'unmistakable red, like burnished copper'.[2] At first sight, this looks as though Gosse had outraged editorial fidelity by writing 'burnished copper' for 'unpoetical carrots'. In Lord Redesdale's *Memories*, however, the words 'burnished copper' appear where the same paragraph is used.[3] It seems that Lord Redesdale himself, whether or not on a hint from Gosse, repented his

---

[1] Gosse, p. 319.   [2] Gosse, p. 12.   [3] Redesdale, p. 69.

own boldness and substituted a conventionally poetic phrase for one more alive and graphic.

Lord Redesdale goes on to describe Swinburne's voice, as 'exquisitely soft . . . with a rather sing-song intonation', which he had evidently caught from his mother.

It was at Eton, Lord Redesdale says, that Swinburne first read Shakespeare in an edition which had not been expurgated by Bowdler; also Marlowe and the other major dramatists of the sixteenth and seventeenth centuries. Dickens he certainly quoted. Lord Redesdale dismisses the legend that Swinburne possessed, while in his Eton days, a knowledge of Greek beyond that usual in an intelligent boy; on the other hand, he confirms Swinburne's early familiarity with French and Italian.

During the holidays of his first year at Eton Swinburne was taken by his parents to the Lakes, where, in September, they visited Wordsworth. A Miss Elizabeth Sewell, who was present, wrote:[1] 'He was so very nice to Algernon, especially at last, that I could have cried, as Algernon did when we went away.' Wordsworth supposed Algernon might have read *We are Seven*, and said there was nothing in his writings which could do him harm, and some things that could do him good. He did not think Algernon would forget him. Six months later Wordsworth died, and (so Swinburne later told Gosse) when he learned of it at Eton, it 'darkened the April sunshine' for him.

Sometimes Swinburne and his cousin Mitford would walk together in Windsor Forest or the Home Park, Swinburne with blown hair, reciting.[2] 'Other boys would watch him with amazement, looking upon him as a sort of inspired elfin – something belonging to another sphere. None dreamt of interfering with him – as for bullying, there was none of it.'

Not all recollections were so sympathetic. Lord St. Aldwyn, when applied to by Gosse, replied that Swinburne was 'a horrid little boy with a big red head and a pasty complexion, who looked as though a course of physical exercise would have done him good'.[3] According to Lord Redesdale, he was, although pale, not pasty: 'His skin was very white – not unhealthy, but a transparent tinted white, such as one sees in the petals of some roses.'

To quote Redesdale again: 'He carried with him one magic charm – he was absolutely courageous . . . in the matter of horses he was absolutely without terror. He, unskilled though he was, would ride anything as

[1] Gosse, p. 15.   [2] Gosse, p. 322.   [3] Gosse, p. 14.

24

fearless as a Centaur.' This is what one might call the bright side of Swinburne's days at Eton. Remembering the school in later years, he wrote: 'I should like to see two things there again [,] the river – and the block.'[1] Sometimes it is the block, the flogging block, which seems to have marked his memory more than the river. In after years, he was to write:[2]

> Every fresh cut well laid on
> The bare breach of Algernon
> Makes the swelled flesh rise in ridges
> Thick as summer swarms of midges;
> Every stroke the Master deals,
> Every stripe the schoolboy feels,
> Marks his breech with fresh red weals;
> How he blubbers, how he bellows!
>
> On those broad red nether cheeks
> That their own blood scores and streaks,
> That the red rod streaks and dapples
> Like two great red round streaked apples . . .

This, if it were a single poem of its kind, might be all very well; but it is not; it is one of very many. Flagellation was to haunt his poetry, his novels and his letters; all his life he was to be drawn back to it, as it were, longingly. Birching was not the punishment for misconduct only, but for mistakes in lessons. Swinburne, having a facility for languages and a good ear, was never whipped for a false quantity, but made up for it in mathematics. But it was not only by getting his sums wrong that he came to be birched. A 'swishing' was an occasion for heroism, since the ability to take it without 'singing' was the test of a boy's metal. Although Algernon was to grow to five feet four and a half inches, his large head and great shock of hair made his body look puny. Because this laid him open to the charge of unmanliness, he needed, and by bad behaviour provoked, occasion to show that he could take punishment. The opportunity was so much the greater because the punishment of the junior boys was public, and they could therefore compare notes on each other's comportment beneath the birch. There was competition in it.

[1] Lang, Vol. I, p. 256.
[2] *Algernon's Flogging* in *The Flogging Block*: British Museum: MSS. Ashley 5256. (Reserved from public use.)

Swinburne was fond of comparing himself with Shelley, his predecessor at Eton, but while Shelley was tormented by the boys' teasing, one
does not hear of his having been birched. But then Shelley hardly ever
referred to his days at the school, and it is from the recollections of his
contemporaries that one gains the impression he was unhappy there.
This, Swinburne regretted. Years later, in connection with an edition of
Shelley's poems containing lines from *The Boat on the Serchio* which
had not appeared in earlier editions, Swinburne wrote to William
Michael Rossetti, who was responsible:[1]

> The new lines in the 'Serchio' are delightful – to me especially
> in person as showing that S. had kindly memories of Eton when all
> was said and done, like the rest of us ... After reading the new
> verses I am more than ever amazed at Shelley's neglect of swim-
> ming – the one poem alluding to Eton pleasures being a river poem,
> my one really and wholly delightful recollection of the place and
> time being that of the swimming lessons and play in the Thames.
> I would have wagered that Shelley of all verse-writing men and
> Eton boys would have been the one at least to match me in the
> passion for that pursuit. I suppose he took it out afterwards in
> boating – whereas I never can be *on* the water without wishing to
> be *in* it.

One thing, however, they had in common. Shelley was known as 'Mad
Shelley'; Swinburne was known as 'Mad Swinburne'. When, late in life,
Swinburne was invited by the headmaster to write an ode in honour of
the four hundred and fiftieth anniversary of the College, Shelley's was
the only name he mentioned in *Eton: an Ode:*[2]

> Shelley, lyric lord of England's lordliest singers, here first heard
> Ring from the lips of poets crowned and dead the Promethean word
> Whence his soul took fire ...'

The formal ode which Swinburne composed for this occasion was, as
might be expected, stately and laudatory:

> Four hundred summers and fifty have shone on the meadows of
> Thames and died
> Since Eton arose in an age that was darkness and shone by his
> radiant side
> As a star ...

[1] Lang, Vol. II, p. 84.   [2] Chatto, Vol. VI.

That these lines expressed only a part of his feeling about the College, and that he had recollections of it that would have been unsuitable for incorporation in the tribute desired, he revealed in a companion poem, entitled pointedly *Eton: Another Ode*. This he did not publish, but it is preserved in manuscript at the British Museum, though reserved from public use on account of its flagellant character:[1]

> Tell me, S——, does shame within burn as hot (Swish! Swish!)
>   as your stripes my lad.
> Burn outside, have I tamed your pride? I'm glad to see how it
>   hurts you – glad –
> Swish! . . .

Swinburne had from childhood certain peculiar physical mannerisms such as, when excited, stiffly pulling down his arms from his shoulders and vibrating his hands, or, if seated, jerking his legs and twisting his feet, his expression at such times becoming rapt and radiant. His mother took him to a specialist, who told her the motions came from 'an excess of electric vitality' and that it would be dangerous to interfere with them.

Gosse, to whom we owe this information, continues:[2]

> Through the summer of 1853 Swinburne had increasing trouble with Joynes of a rebellious kind, and in consequence of some representations he did not return to Eton, although nothing had been said during the previous half about his leaving, and although at the last he seemed to be doing particularly well. When he left school he was within a few places of the headmaster's division.

Gosse does not give his source for this information, but as he came to know Swinburne well later in the latter's life the source may well be Swinburne himself. In the summer of 1853 Swinburne would only just have turned sixteen and this does seem unusually young for a boy to leave his public school, and it may well be that his rebelliousness, combined with his compulsive mannerisms and peculiar attitude to punishment, embarrassed the authorities to the extent that they suggested to his parents it would be better they took him away.

[1] British Museum: MSS. Ashley 5271.
[2] Gosse, pp. 26–27.

3

Culver Cliff

SWINBURNE now wanted to enter the army. When he left Eton, the Crimean War had already started, and according to a letter he wrote to his cousin Mary it was the action at Balaclava on October 25, 1854, which inspired him with a desire to enter the cavalry. One would have thought that Tennyson's account of how six hundred men rode to their death in obedience to an order they all knew had been given by mistake, would have put anybody off entering the army. Presumably what excited Swinburne's admiration was the blindly self-sacrificial heroism of the men. Algernon's martial ambition was thwarted by his father: Captain Swinburne would not allow his son to enter the army, as he considered that his inferior physique unfitted him for the life of a soldier.

It was this frustration, with the implied criticism of his manly qualities, which goaded Algernon to a desperate exploit near their home in the Isle of Wight. As he described it in the same letter to Mary:[1]

> It was about the middle of the Christmas holidays, and I went out for a good hard tramp by the sea till I found myself by the foot of Culver Cliff; and then all at once it came upon me that it was all very well to fancy or dream of 'deadly danger' and forlorn hopes and cavalry charges, when I had never run any greater risk than a football 'rooge'; but here was a chance of testing my nerve in face of death which could not be surpassed. So I climbed a rock under the highest point, and stripped, and climbed down again, and just took a souse into the sea to steady and strengthen my nerve, which I knew the sharp chill would, and climbed up again, thinking how easy it would be to climb the whole face of the cliff naked – or at least how much more sure one would feel of being able to do it – if one did not mind mere scratches and bruises; but to that prehistoric sort of proceeding there were obviously other objections than the atmosphere of mid-winter. So I dressed and went straight at it. It wasn't so hard as it looked, most of the way, for a light weight with a sure foot and a good steady hand; but as I got near the top I remember thinking I should not like to have to climb down again. In a minute or two more I found that I must,

[1] Leith, p. 13.

as the top part (or top storey) of the precipice came jutting out aslant above me for some feet. Even a real sea-gull could not have worked its way up without using or spreading its wings. So of course I felt I must not stop to think for one second, and began climbing down, hand under hand, as fast and as steadily as I could, till I reached the bottom, and (equally of course) began to look out for another possible point of ascent at the same height.

At his second ascent:

I was most of the way up again when I heard a sudden sound as of loud music, reminding me instantly of 'the anthem' from the Eton College organ, a little below me to the left. I knew it would be almost certain death to look down, and next minute there was no need: I glanced aside, and saw the opening of a great hollow in the upper cliff, out of which came swarming a perfect flock of 'the others', who evidently had never seen a wingless brother so near the family quarters. They rose about me in a heaving cloud – at least, I really don't think the phrase exaggerates the density of their 'congregated wings' – and then scattered.

This sense of himself as being, by his real nature, a sea-gull, here surrounded by his own kind in their habitat, is one to be found again and again in Swinburne's writing. At last he reached the top of the cliff, or almost so:

I swung in the air by my hands from a ledge on the cliff which just gave room for the fingers to cling and hold on. There was a projection of rock to the left at which I flung out my feet sideways and just reached it; this enabled me to get breath and crawl at full speed (so to say) up the remaining bit of cliff. At the top I had not time to think what a sell . . . it would be if I were to roll back over the edge after all, when I became unconscious . . . I found a sheep's nose just over mine, and the poor good fellow-creature's eyes gazing into my face. . . .

Presumably it was the sheep's breath on his face which had recalled him to consciousness; at its seeming solicitude he gave such a shout of laughter that it scuttled off, and he made his way home. His mother, when he told her, was horrified, and demanded to know why ever he had done such a thing. When he told her she assured him: 'Nobody ever thought you were a coward.'

She had been less against his going into the army than was his father, and so it was his father who bore the brunt of Algernon's resentment.

Years later, when corresponding with W. M. Rossetti about Shelley, Swinburne was to write:[1]

> I think you are rather hard upon him as to the filial relation . . . I have no more doubt that it may be said for Sir Timothy [Shelley] that his son was what Carlyle calls 'an afflictive phenomenon' than that I was the same to my father before, during and since my Oxford time; but I do not think you make allowance for the provocation given (as well as received) by a father, who may be kindly and generous, to a boy or man between seventeen and twenty-one or so, with whom he has no deep or wide ground of sympathy beyond the animal relation or family tradition. You will allow me to say that I am sure you can never have felt at that age the irreparable, total and inevitable isolation from all that had once been closest to the mind and thought, and was still closest to the flesh and the memory, the solitude in which one passes from separation to antagonism of spirit (without violent quarrels or open offense,[2] but by pure logical necessity of consequence) the sense that where attraction gradually ends repulsion gradually begins, which many besides Shelley, and as affectionate and faithful by nature and temperament as he, *have* felt at that age.

Swinburne never had the violent breach with his father that Shelley did. Though there is the oblique evidence of Swinburne's fiction, later to be discussed, that his father had flogged him as much as had the authorities at Eton, they always remained in some sort of relation. Indeed, Captain (later Admiral) Swinburne never ceased to manifest an attitude of paternal concern and responsibility with regard to Algernon, though it is equally obvious that he was perturbed by his character, as it developed.

He was still too young to go up to Oxford, and it was therefore decided to fill in the next two and a half years by having him privately tutored. This was carried out at Capheaton, where the Rev. John Wilkinson, perpetual curate at Cambo, his grandfather's parish, was engaged to prepare him for Oxford.[3] It seems indicative of strain at home that it should have been arranged for his tutoring to take place at his grandfather's, in Northumberland.

Northumberland neighbours who now began to play a role in Alger-

[1] Lang, Vol. II, pp. 82–83.

[2] Swinburne sometimes uses the French spelling of words which have practically the same form in both languages.

[3] Gosse, p. 29.

non's life were Sir Walter and Lady Trevelyan. They lived at Wallington, near by. Lady Trevelyan, a friend of Ruskin and of the Scottish
painter and poet, William Bell Scott, looked with a sympathetic eye on
Algernon's early essays in the art of writing verse. She was apparently
a woman of great charm, and Algernon would ride on his pony from
Capheaton to Wallington to read her his compositions and to talk. One
has the impression he spent much of his time out on the moors, where:

> ... the hillside winds resume
> The marriage song of heather-flower and broom

The lines are from *Thalassius*.[1] Not written until later in life, it is a
poem of idealized autobiography, in which he tells how he was cradled
and taught by the elements. Describing an evening spent on the Northumbrian coast, he tells in the same poem of a prophetic feeling which
came over him:

> And one bright eve ere summer in autumn sank
> As stardawn standing on a grey sea-bank
> He felt the wind fitfully shift and heave
> As towards a stormier eve;
> And all the wan wide sea shuddered; and earth
> Shook underfoot as toward some timeless birth,
> Intolerable and inevitable; and all
> Heaven, darkling, trembled like a stricken thrall.
> And far out of the quivering east, and far
> From past the moonrise and its guiding star,
> Began a noise of tempest and a light
> That was not of the lightning; and a sound
> Rang with it round and round
> That was not of the thunder; and a flight
> As of blown clouds by night,
> That was not of them; and with songs and cries
> That sang and shrieked their soul out at the skies
> A shapeless earthy storm of shapes began
> From all ways round to move in on the man,
> Clamorous against him silent; and their feet
> Were as the winds are fleet,
> And their shrill songs were as wild birds' are sweet.

[1] Chatto, Vol. III.

But far more uninhibitedly eloquent of the days during which
Swinburne ran wild in Northumberland are passages from his later
semi-autobiographical novel, *Lesbia Brandon*:[1]

> Being by nature idle and excitable he made himself infinite
> small diversions out of the day's work, and was by no means
> oppressed by the sense of compelled inaction. Well broken in to
> solitude and sensitive of all outward things, he found life and
> pleasure enough in the gardens and woods, the downs and the
> beach. Small sights and sounds excited and satisfied him; his mind
> was as yet more impressible than capacious, his senses more
> retentive than his thoughts. Water and wind and darkness and
> light made friends with him ... For months he lived and grew on
> like an animal or a fruit ... Riding and reading and wandering,
> he felt no want in life; three men only kept him company now and
> then, the clergyman, the land-steward, and the head-groom ...
> but for places rather than persons he has a violent and blind
> affection. Small pools in the pouring stream roofed with
> noiseless leaves out of the wind's way; hot hollows of short
> grass in the slanting down, shaped like cups for the sun to fill;
> higher places where the hill-streams began among patches of
> reeds, extorting from the moist moorland a little life; dry corners
> of crag whence light trees had sprung out of the lean soil,
> shadowing narrow brown nooks and ledges of burnt-up turf
> slippery with the warm dust of arid lands; all these attracted and
> retained him; but less than the lower parts about the sea. In a
> few months' time he could have gone blindfold over miles of
> beach.

The days Swinburne spent at Capheaton, with his paternal grandfather, were amongst the most formative of his life, but he also owed
something to the great library of his maternal grandfather, the Earl of
Ashburnham, whom he visited sometimes at Ashburnham Place, Sussex.

In the summer of 1855, Algernon was taken abroad for the first time,
by his uncle, General Ashburnham. They went to Germany and
travelled up the Rhine on a steamer from Cologne to Wiesbaden.
Swinburne wrote long letters to his mother, giving detailed descriptions
of all the places they visited, frequently comparing the scenery to that
of Northumberland:[2] '... The country ... is very beautiful, very like
Mounces on a larger scale ... the streams are exactly like those of

[1] British Museum: MSS. Ashley A 4386. ff. 6–7.
[2] Leith, pp. 40–41.

Mounces and the water just the moss-water colour. One place was so like the Tyne just below Keeldar.'

And again: 'He and I walked yesterday to the loveliest place on earth – a sort of mixture of the prettiest parts of Mounces and Capheaton...' Mounces was his grandfather's shooting estate, near Capheaton.

On the way back, as they crossed the Channel, they were caught in a violent storm. This experience provided Swinburne with one of his most dramatic storm poems, though it was not written until his old age: *A Channel Passage, 1855*:[1]

> Stern and prow plunged under, alternate: a glimpse,
>   a recoil, a breath,
> And she sprang as the life in a god made man would
>   spring at the throat of death.
> Three glad hours, and it seemed not an hour of
>   supreme and supernal joy,
> Filled full with delight that revives in remembrance
>   a sea-bird's heart in a boy.
> . . .
>
> And the rage in the roar of the voice of the waters
>   were heard but when heaven breathed free.
> Far eastward, clear of the covering of cloud, the sky
>   laughed out into light
> From the rims of the storm to the sea's dark edge
>   with flames that were flowerlike and white.
> The leaping and luminous blossoms of live sheet
>   lightning . . .

Nobody, so far as I know, but Swinburne has compared the patterns made by lightning to flowers; the bold image shows how this boyhood experience had power to move him almost until he died. This poem was not written until 1904.

For some reason Swinburne's preparation for Oxford was completed not by the tutor at Capheaton but, according to his cousin Mary, by another tutor, in Gloucestershire.[2]

[1] Chatto, Vol. VI.   [2] Gosse, p. 33.

4

Oxford:
Old Mortality and the Pre-Raphaelites

SWINBURNE went up to Oxford on January 18, 1856. He entered Balliol, and had the good fortune to be there in Benjamin Jowett's time. Jowett had become Regius Professor of Greek the previous year, so that Swinburne had the benefit of his tuition from the beginning.

An early impression of Swinburne, as an undergraduate of nineteen, comes from a man who entered Balliol in October of the same year:[1]

> A slight girlish figure, below the middle height, with a great shock of red hair, which seemed almost to touch his narrow sloping shoulders. He had the pallor which often goes with red hair. There was a dainty grace about his appearance, but it was disappointing that, like some figure in a Pre-Raphaelite canvas, where he would not have been out of place, there was a want of youthful freshness in his face. He walked delicately, like Agag, with a mounting gait, as if picking his steps. He had a pleasant musical voice, and his manner and address, slightly shy and reserved, had a particular charm of refinement and good breeding.

He remained much in his rooms, according to the same informant, never appeared at wine-parties or at breakfasts, and took no part in outdoor activities.

Swinburne had through his father an introduction to Manuel John Johnson, keeper of the Radcliffe Observatory,[2] and another student, G. Birkbeck Hill, records on May 9, 1856, 'Last night I dined at the Observatory, and met a Balliol friend of mine – Swinburne – with his father, Captain Swinburne.' Through Hill, Swinburne made other friends. Chief of these was John Nichol, who had come up a year earlier and was four years his senior. Nichol is important, for he was to remain permanently Swinburne's friend. His father was Regius Professor of Astronomy at the University of Glasgow, and he, the younger Nichol,

[1] Donald Crawford, quoted in Gosse, p. 34.
[2] Lafourcade, p. 58.

had been for four years a student of the University of Glasgow before coming to Oxford.[1] No very intimate picture of Nichol ever emerges, but he was a republican and an agnostic, and he helped Swinburne with the logic that formed part of his course.[2]

Republicanism, despite the fact that he was an aristocrat, Swinburne had in his background as the result of his association with his grandfather in Northumberland; but his mother had taught him the Christian faith, and it is believed that it was his conversations with Nichol which caused him to renounce it. An essay written while he was at Oxford, entitled *The Limits of Experience*, gives some idea of the steps by which he arrived at his agnostic attitude. In it he points out:[3]

> That much which is with us a matter of real and universal acceptance – much which has come to be regarded as intuitive and as it were indispensable to our existence and faculty of thinking – is indeed mere matter of experience and previous acquaintance removed beyond the limit of consciousness or memory, is an evident truth.

This 'much' includes the moral and religious ideas taught one by one's parents when one was too infantile to have any later memory of being instructed. In other words, one might infer, what one took to be intuitional knowledge might be but opinion transmitted. It was a counsel of wariness, not necessarily nihilistic.

In November 1856, Nichol founded a society for the purpose of affording its members 'such intellectual pastime and recreation as should seem most suitable and agreable'. They called it the Old Mortality Society, because there was not one of the founders who was completely sound in health. Swinburne, naturally, was one of them. Later, to have been a member became a mark of distinction, for, curiously, there was not one of them who did not attain to some eminence, in scholastic or other fields. Subsequent members included Walter Pater, J. A. Symonds and Lord Bryce, to whom we owe a reminiscence of one of its meetings that took place in Swinburne's rooms. Swinburne read them Browning's preface to the edition of Shelley's (supposedly newly discovered) letters, which later turned out to have been forged.

Lord Bryce also recalls that Swinburne read them several of

---

[1] Cassidy, pp. 34–35.   [2] Lafourcade, p. 61.

[3] A. C. Swinburne, *Two Unpublished Manuscripts* (San Francisco, 1927), quoted in Cassidy, p. 36.

Browning's poems, including *The Statue and the Bust*.[1] This is interesting, for it is a poem in which the balance of feeling runs against Christian morality, and the illicit lovers are rebuked, in the poet's final summing up of their case, for having been too faint hearted to run away together, though one of them was married.

Nichol was an enthusiast for Italian liberty, a cause which was at that time in its doldrums. It was nearly a decade since the massive but unsuccessful, popular risings of 1848, and the days of Garibaldi were not yet. Mazzini, the idealist of the cause, had been an exile in England since 1850, trying in such ways as he could to keep it alive. From Nichol, Swinburne learned to care for Italian liberty and admire Mazzini. His *Ode to Mazzini*, apart from his schoolboy work at Eton, may well be his earliest poem. Hill remembers Swinburne reading it to him in March, 1857.[2] An irregular Pindaric, it moves already with a certain pace and surety:[3]

> Dost thou not hear, thro' the hushed heart of night,
> The voices wailing for thy help, thy sight,
> > The souls that call their lord?
> > 'We want the voice, the sword,
> We want the hand to strike, the love to share
> > The weight we cannot bear;
> The soul to point our way, the heart to do and dare.
> > We want the unblinded eye,
> > The spirit pure and high,
> And consecrated by enduring care:
> > For now we dare not meet
> > The memories of the past;
> They wound us with their glories bright and fleet,
> > The fame that would not last,
> > The hopes that were too sweet;
> > A voice of lamentation
> Shakes the high places of the thronèd nation,
> The crownless nation sitting wan and bare
> > Upon the royal seat.'

Swinburne must, at about this time, have composed a poem, *The Temple of Janus*, which he entered for the 1856 Newdigate prize; but it did not win.

[1] Gosse, p. 40.   [2] Lafourcade, p. 61.   [3] Bonchurch, Vol. 1.

Nichol did not return to Oxford during the Hilary and Summer terms. There is a letter from Swinburne, dated February 11 (1857), beginning:[1]

Balliol College

My dear Nichol

I am sorry to hear that we are not to have you back this term, which I had rather counted upon. Our society does, however, manage to keep above water, as yet, but how long it will go on without you, I don't know.

The body of the letter is almost entirely concerned with the poetry of Elizabeth Barrett Browning, which he admired exceedingly. After giving his opinion that *Aurora Leigh* is her great work, he goes on to write:

Have you seen the additional poems in the last edition of Mrs. Browning's? Some, I think, are very beautiful. I have scandalised Grenfell, I am afraid, by asserting that she is the greatest woman who ever lived, except Sappho and Deborah!

In the summer vacation Swinburne journeyed to Scotland to visit Nichol. On the way up he stopped at Capheaton, and it would seem that it was at this time that he made the acquaintance of William Bell Scott, while the latter was staying again with Lady Trevelyan at Wallington. Scott then recollected having, on one of his previous visits, in 1854, seen Swinburne riding on a small pony, with his big tomes strapped to his saddle, on his way from Capheaton to Cambo.[2]

Nichol came, apparently, as far as Edinburgh to meet Swinburne; then they stayed for a few days at Nichol's home in Glasgow, and afterwards set out together on a sightseeing tour of the islands, of which Nichol wrote to a friend:[3]

Swinburne has been with me for a fortnight or so, and we have just returned from a trip to Skye ... Swinburne has gone on before by the main road to secure beds, but how to find the inn was the mystery ... Swinburne says we ran a Muck once or twice, and were like to have made a Mull out of the affair, but on the whole it was a Rum go.

While Swinburne and Nichol were exploring Scotland, Oxford had been dignified by the arrival of three picturesque figures. Dante Gabriel Rossetti, with whose name the Pre-Raphaelite Movement will always

[1] Lang, Vol. 1, pp. 8–9.   [2] Lafourcade, p. 52.
[3] William Knight, *Memoir of John Nichol*, Glasgow, 1896, pp. 155–6.

be primarily associated, had come up to see the newly-built Union Society Debating Hall, and the bare walls and ten undecorated bays looked to him so inviting that he offered to fill these spaces with murals, for nothing. The authorities accepted, and to help him in the task he brought a number of other painters, including the youngest wave of the Pre-Raphaelite Movement, William Morris and Edward Jones (it was not until later that the latter assumed the hyphenated form, Burne-Jones). Swinburne was soon to call him Ned Jones, while the painter was to address the poet, in correspondence, as 'Dear Carrots'.

The painters took rooms opposite Queen's College, in the High, and worked daily at the Union. It was what came to be called the Jovial Campaign, and was, indeed, marked by much good humour and high spirits, even horse-play. They emptied bucketfuls of water upon each other's heads from the tops of ladders, to roars of laughter and curses, and sang as they worked.[1]

Swinburne entered their lives on November 1, 1857,[2] when at Birkbeck Hill's rooms he met Jones and Morris. Swinburne later explained that it was after this and through them that he met Rossetti, or, as he always called him, Gabriel, who almost instantly asked him to pose for him; though the intended fresco was never executed. Swinburne had red hair of exactly the shade Rossetti loved to paint, and though he did not immortalize him on the walls of the Union he later used him as a model. Swinburne watched the work in the Union grow, and as he shared the fun he absorbed the Pre-Raphaelite principles. He saw take shape upon the walls figures from Arthurian romance: Lancelot and Guinevere, Tristram and Yseult.

It was Tristram and Yseult who mainly claimed him. He produced seven out of an intended ten cantos under the title *Queen Yseult*. Swinburne had not at that time read Malory; he seems to have seen the *Tristan* of François Michel but to have followed in the main the *Sir Tristrem* attributed to Thomas of Ercildoune.[3] In writing in trochaic tercets he copied Morris (who like Rossetti was a poet as well as a painter), having in November heard Morris read *The Willow and the Red Cliff*, a poem in this verse-form. The feeling is, however, his own, and the poem is psychologically revealing. When first Tristram sees Yseult, having been sent by King Mark of Cornwall to fetch her to be his bride:[4]

[1] Doughty, *A Mid-Victorian Romantic*, pp. 225–7.   [2] Lafourcade, p. 66.
[3] Lafourcade, *La Jeunesse*, pp. 45–46.
[4] Bonchurch, Vol. I.

> ... he thought it well and meet,
> Lain before that lady sweet,
> To be trodden by her feet.

This, perhaps, in romantic parlance, is conventional. But when we get to King Mark's castle at Tintagel, Tristram cannot find the way to her room and it is she who comes for him:

> ... she raised him tenderly,
> Bore him lightly as might be,
> That was wonderful to see.
>
> So they passed by trail and track,
> Slowly in the night all black,
> And she bore him on her back.
>
> As they twain went on along
> Such great love had made her strong,
> All her heart was full of song.
> ...
>
> Smiling ...
> Did she walk beneath his weight
> ...
>
> Till she stood on the strewn floor
> Right within the chamber door,
> With the weight of love she bore.

Then, at last, she sets him down and covers him with her kisses. What is curious is the relatively passive role of the lover, who needs to be carried upon his mistress's back. This forms no part of the legend of Tristram and Yseult. The distinguished French Swinburne scholar, Georges Lafourcade, writes:[1]

> Mais il faut plutôt reconnaitre ici l'épisode bien connu du page Eginhard porté dans les bras d'Emma sous l'oeil courroucé de Charlemagne. Il importait de signaler cette audacieuse transposition à la légende de Tristan d'une tradition du XII siècle se rapportant à Charlemagne; Swinburne avait pu le rencontrer dans William de Malmsbury.

That the idea of a young man being carried by a girl exists in a different legend takes nothing away from the extraordinary character of Swin-

[1] Lafourcade, *La Jeunesse*, Vol. II, pp. 46–47.

burne's decision to use it. He imported it, an alien element, because it appealed to him. In English literature I can think of only one thing at all comparable, and that is Shelley's *Revolt of Islam*, in which Cythna snatches up Laon and sets him on her horse, to ride away with him; but she had a reason, which was to rescue him from their enemies: she had a horse and he had not. Swinburne's Yseult had no such pretext for assuming the aggressive role and picking her lover up. Even if he could not find the way through the courtyards of the castle, she could have led him, without carrying him, to her bed-chamber.

His repetition of the word 'weight', and his insistence upon the strength that was required to bear it, indicates his enjoyment of an inversion of the usual sexual roles.

He goes on to tell of Tristram's exile and meeting in Brittany with Yseult of the white hands, so called to distinguish her from Yseult of the golden hair, in Tintagel. Rendered tender by the identity of name, he drifts into marriage but cannot bring himself to consummation of the nuptial rite:

> . . . he stood away and said:
> 'Lo, an evil rede were read
> If I had her maidenhead.
>
> 'One that I love more than her
> Dwells across the water fair,
> Yseult of the golden hair.

It occurs to him, now, as a reason for not taking her, that others would mock her, remembering that the other Yseult was his mistress. Naturally, his bride is perplexed that he does not come to her.

> Spake the snow-hand maidenly,
> 'Tristram, for thy courtesy,
> Think thou no scorn to kiss me.'
> . . .
> Sidelong to him crept she close,
> Pale as any winter rose
> When the air is grey with snows.
> . . .
> Soft as lighteth bird on bough
> Thrice he kissed her, breathing low,
> Kissed her mouth and maiden brow,

> And in under breath said he
> When his face she could not see,
> 'Christ, look over her and me.'

> Low sweet words of love she said
> With her face against his head
> On the pillows of the bed.

Affected, despite himself, he bares her throat and shoulder and kisses her again; but:

> Praying in his heart he spake,
> That for Mary's maiden sake
> Christ would keep his faith awake.

A modern poet following an ancient legend is, to some extent, bound by its traditional form, but Swinburne dwells lingeringly, indeed lovingly, upon the void bridal night, conceiving it sublime that the bridegroom should pray to Christ for strength to resist his bride's charms, though:

> She lay out before him there,
> All her body white and bare,
> Overswept with waves of hair.

Though excited by books of an advanced nature, Swinburne was obviously still very much under the influence of the conventional Victorian belief that women had no sexual desire, and one must forgive a young and very inexperienced man of nineteen for not realizing the intense cruelty of the behaviour he ascribes to the bridegroom, tantalizing by his proximity and kisses, and yet denying. Swinburne must have thought kisses were all a modest woman could enjoy, and therefore been unaware of the irony, not to say the improbability, of his next lines:

> So her love had all it would,
> All night sleeping as she could,
> Sleeping in her maidenhood.

Perhaps many an inexperienced young man in the Victorian era could have made the same mistake. It is when one takes it in conjunction with the behaviour attributed to Tristram in his relations with the first Yseult, whom he did love, but who had to carry him on her back to her bedchamber, that an unusual absence of masculine aggression seems to appear. He did not finish the poem, and one does not know how he intended to end the story.

He wrote another fragment on the same theme, under the title *Joyeuse Garde*, from Joyous Gard, the old name for Bamborough Castle, Northumberland, associated by legend with the idyll of the lovers; but it is in a different verse-form and so cannot have been intended to be part of *Queen Yseult*.

The members of the Old Mortality now produced a magazine, called *Undergraduate Papers*. It was only destined to run for three issues, but the first number, which appeared on December 1, 1857, carried an essay by Swinburne on Marlowe and Webster, and the first canto of *Queen Yseult*.

In the Christmas vacation he wrote to Nichol, from the Isle of Wight, a letter full of the magazine, but expressing some doubts about *Queen Yseult*. Apart from the first canto, which dealt only with Tristram's parents' story and could stand by itself, he now felt it was 'too imperfect, feeble and unfinished to publish for a year or two'. Presumably the same hesitation as to its quality deterred him from completing it. Nevertheless, he continued to Nichol, he had received much encouragement when he had read the poem to Morris and the others:[1] 'They all, however, praise the poem far more than I (seriously speaking) believe it deserves. Morris says it is much better than his own poem, which opinion I took the liberty to tell him was absurd.'

Another college friend, Edwin Hatch, came to visit him during the vacation, and together they called on Tennyson, at Farringford, on the western side of the island, near Alum Bay. The Laureate invited them to dinner, and, in a letter to a friend, commended Swinburne's good manners in not having pressed on him his own verses.[2]

[1] Lang, Vol. 1, p. 13.
[2] Letter to R. J. Mann, quoted in *Alfred Lord Tennyson*, 1898, ed. Hallam (and in Lang, Vol. I, pp. 14–15, n.).

5

Oxford and Navestock
Rosamund and *The Queen Mother*

IN June 1858 Swinburne took Moderations and passed with second-class
honours. Bolder than Nichol, who had departed without taking one, he
decided to proceed to an Honours Degree. With regard to subject,
however, he made a very strange choice. He chose, for his Honours
course, to read Law; and he read Literae Humaniores (Classics and
Philosophy) only for the earlier 'Little' examination. With his knowledge
of Greek and Latin, and his interest in ideas, one would have thought
Literae Humaniores the Honours course for which he was cut out.
Perhaps the decision was provoked by personal difficulties with Jowett.
One knows from later papers that Jowett disapproved of Swinburne's
giving so much time to poetry.

On February 17, 1858, Swinburne had written to Hatch:[1] '*Rosamund*
is about my favourite poem, and is now verging on a satisfactory com-
pletion.' But *Rosamund* was destined to be written three times in all;
that first draft, though Morris had approved it, was consigned to the
flames so that the poem might be composed afresh; and the perfecting
of so long a work in blank verse could easily, in itself, have occupied a
term. There may have been little time left for his scholastic studies.

Though the Pre-Raphaelite painter-poets had left Oxford at Christmas, there is still, in *Rosamund*, a considerable Pre-Raphaelite influence
discernible. It is the story of Rosamund Clifford, the mistress of King
Henry II, and the setting is largely Woodstock, near Oxford, where she
lived. It may have been walks out to Woodstock which inspired Swinburne with thoughts of her, or, more probably, a recorded visit to
Godstow, where, according to legend, she died a nun. There is a letter
from Birkbeck Hill, dated May 3, 1857, saying:[2]

> Tomorrow I believe that Old Mortality intends to take a pic-nic
> up the river and make merry. We shall go to Godstow and dream
> of the fair Rosamund there, I suppose, and the old days of the
> nunnery.

[1] Lang, Vol. I, p. 16.   [2] Lafourcade, *La Jeunesse*, Vol. II, p. 236.

Swinburne was probably of the party, though he made no use (as did Tennyson in his later *Becket*) of the story that she died there.

The first scene is set at Woodstock, and takes place between Rosamund and Constance, her maid. Vaguely uneasy, as though the wet and reluctant spring presaged some ill, Rosamund says:[1]

> I never loved white roses much; but see
> How the wind drenches the low lime-branches
> With shaken silver in the rainiest leaves.

The observation of raindrops in the cups of flowers and in leaves is something which fascinated Swinburne. Later in the poem Rosamund's rival, Eleanor, the Queen, recalls her earlier and happier days, when she would walk:

> . . . with a few dames about the white pear-trees –
> Spring was it? Yea, for the green sprang thick as flame
> And the birds bit the blossom and sang hard –
> Now sat and tore up flowers to waste, wet strips
> Of hyacinth, rain-sodden bells –

Some critics have accused Swinburne of writing from literature rather than life, and of lacking the capacity to observe nature closely; yet I can call to mind no other poet who has noted birds biting and tearing up petals, as they certainly do, in apparent wantonness, since they do not eat them. Hyacinths, like croci and geraniums, are special sufferers, and this passage comes not from books but from observation in a garden.

The psychological drama is less satisfactory. Rosamund is beautifully created in her rose-like quality, gradually becoming aware, in the first scene, that, as a red rose, representing the fulfilment of love, she has to to be on her guard against the disapproving jealousy of her maid; but there is something over self-conscious about her declaration that she is Helen of Troy, Guinevere and the personification of the love that is in every great story. It would have been better said for her, by one of the other characters. Put into her own mouth, it makes her sound arrogant, and one is the more surprised that in the dénouement, when Queen Eleanor makes her way to Woodstock and holds out poison, commanding her to drink it, she is so overcome that she does so. Such meekness seems out of character. Nevertheless, the poem is a considerable achievement, a lyric to the accompaniment of roses and rain:

[1] Chatto, *The Tragedies*, Vol. i.

> Hark, the rain begins,
> Slips like a bird that feels among shut leaves;
> One – two; it catches in the rose-branches
> Like a word caught.

At the same time, Swinburne was immersing himself in the work of Victor Hugo, with which he had first become acquainted while still at Eton. From Capheaton he wrote now, in the summer vacation, to Hatch, concerning *Les Contemplations*, which had appeared in 1856:[1]

> I am glad you begin to read V. Hugo aright. My sisters are already among his faithful worshippers – Edith above all. Get her to speak of him some day, and see the effect of my training. Cérige (Book V of *Contemplations*) is our great favourite here.

Cérigo (in Hugo's work the name ends in an *o* not an *e*) is the island, formerly known as Cythera, associated with the birth of Venus. Once green with the myrtles sacred to the goddess, it is now, says the French poet, a bare rock, parched and bald beneath the sun; exhausted. Yet, upon the horizon, Venus shines over the water. In the second part of the poem, full of the sense (which certainly would be approved by an astrologer) that:[2]

> Les astres sont vivants et ne sont pas des choses

The island and the star are made to seem, at the end, like the exhausted body and the eternal spirit of love.

In November 1858 Swinburne failed to pass his Little examination in Classics. Apparently under the impression that his associates in Oxford distracted him from pursuing his studies, Jowett took the unusual course of sending him to read quietly under the supervision of the curate of Navestock, near Romford, in Essex.

W. H. Hutton, who had access to the correspondence which passed between the curate on the one hand, and Captain Swinburne and Jowett on the other, has written,[3] Mr. Jowett deplored the influence of Pre-Raphaelite artists, and considered no good – scholastically – could come of him [Swinburne] 'unless he can be hindered from writing poetry.'

From Navestock, we find Swinburne writing to tell Scott, in December, that he had, on a visit to London, seen Rossetti and read *Rosamund*

[1] Lang, Vol. I, p. 22.   [2] *Les Contemplations*, Vol. I, p. 107.
[3] Lafourcade, p. 75.

to him, and looked at Rossetti's own new work; he had got Blake's *Dante* and *Job*, and he was writing a seemingly interminable play about Catherine de Medici. He continues:[1]

> Have you seen Victor Hugo's *Légende des Siècles*? It is the greatest book that has been published there or here for years. The mediaeval poems in it – for instance 'Ratbert' – simply whip creation into mush and molasses.
>
> Item – I have got the immortal Whitman's *Leaves of Grass* and there are some jolly good things in it, I allow. Do lend yours to Lady Trevelyan. Also entreat her to abstain from Hugo's 'Ratbert' till I come and read it to her.

In his preference for *Ratbert*, the story of a Neronic type of orgy culminating in the striking down, as if by a divine hand, of the presiding tyrant, Swinburne shows his taste for the gory. Certainly Hugo, in his Jeremiad style, wrote many poems in which prophetic vengeance is called down upon kings and their licentious courts – for Hugo, as for the Puritans of the Commonwealth, riches, kings and luxury went with licence, and were together attacked – yet, Swinburne could have found in *La Légende des Siècles* poems of greater sublimity than *Ratbert*.

The play about Catherine de Medici which Swinburne was writing was *The Queen Mother*.[2] Composed in five acts of blank verse, it is built upon a Shakespearean, or rather Elizabethan model, although its language betrays touches of Browning's breeziness and of the Pre-Raphaelites' romanticism. The long hours Swinburne had spent watching the artists at their work shows in such words as are given to the king to speak to the girl he loves:

> Eh, sweet,
> You have the eyes men choose to paint, you know:
> And just that soft turn in the little throat
> And bluish colour in the lower lid
> They make saints with.

The king is Charles IX of France, Catherine's son, and the girl is Denise, his mistress. She is straight and true in spirit, but the Queen Mother, from whom Charles has become estranged, thinks she can use her to mend the breach between them and to gain his sanction for the massacre of the Huguenots. Denise, in innocence, persuades Charles to make up his quarrel with his mother, but when she learns the purpose for

[1] Lang, Vol. I, p. 28.   [2] Chatto, *The Tragedies*, Vol. I.

which Catherine desired a reconciliation she is appalled, and tells the king that he must not, even at his mother's bidding, authorize so terrible a crime against humanity. From scene to scene, the weak king vacillates pitiably between the counsels of the two women who rule his life. Catherine then contrives to make Denise appear guilty of a crime and has her imprisoned, and the order for the massacre is given.

Certainly, there are shades of Shakespeare's *Macbeth* in Catherine's:

> do but think
> This thing shall be no heavier then, being done,
> Than is our forward thought of it.

and of Lady Macbeth in Catherine's premonition that she will never be cleansed of the blood.

> It is man's blood that burns me deep and bites,
> No crying cleans it. If one kill a dog,
> The spot sticks on your skirt . . .

Yet there is real horror and suspense in the scene in which Catherine, all the orders given, waits in her palace through the earlier part of the evening for the hour at which the butchery is to begin.

Nevertheless, it is the heroism of Denise which dominates the play. The enormity of the impending outrage, and the knowledge that, even at the eleventh hour, she is the one person who could persuade the king to revoke the order, gives her such blazing force that her gaoler, at her command, simply hands over the keys (Rosamund could have done with some of this strength), and she rushes from the prison towards the palace. It is too late, for the soldiers have already begun moving into the marked houses to murder, pursuing through the streets the victims who try to escape. Seeming like one of these in the throng, Denise is killed by a shot from an arquebus wantonly fired from the balcony by the king himself.

The tremendous courage she has shown gains her the reluctant respect of Catherine, who speaks the last lines of the play:

> For this girl slain,
> Her funeral privacy of rite shall be
> Our personal care . . .

Later, Swinburne wrote to Scott:[1]

[1] Lang, Vol. I, p. 41.

On the whole I like *Rosamund* better than the five-acter. But I rejoice that you approve of Denise.

During some part of the Christmas vacation Swinburne went up to Northumberland and, presumably after a stay at Capheaton, called upon Scott at Scott's home in Newcastle. The painter began a portrait of Swinburne, which was not destined to be finished until later. Together they made an expedition to Bamborough Castle. Then they took a boat and were rowed out to Grace Darling's island. Swinburne, with his adoration of the sea, was in his element, but Scott was sick, and later wrote:[1]

> ... he [Swinburne] and Commander Jermin set out with me to visit Grace Darling's lighthouse and the scene of her heroical exploit previous to my painting it for Wallington Hall. It was a rough day. I was, as usual, very ill, while he and of course the sailor were enjoying the tossing of the waves.

Swinburne, happy, saw three blue herons standing upon a ledge; he tried in vain to draw Scott's attention to them, and many years later they figured in his greatest epic, *Tristram of Lyonesse*. Everything which he saw on this visit, the castle of Joyous Gard, Grace Darling's lighthouse, and the said three herons, was destined to remain with Swinburne and to grow in his memory.

Saying good-bye to Scott, Swinburne returned to London by sea, sailing from the Tyne to the Thames. From Navestock, on his return, he wrote to Scott on February 25, 1860:[2]

> I had a very good voyage south, and saw Ned Jones in my passage through London. We were delayed a day off Shields and could not get over the harbour-bar, which was our only mishap.

At Navestock, Swinburne read *Rosamund* to the Rev. William Stubbs, in whose care he had been placed, and to Mrs. Stubbs. Stubbs criticized some of the amatory passages, and evidently expected the young poet to tone them down. Instead, Swinburne fixed him with a long, silent stare, then turned with a scream and bolted up the stairs. He resisted Mrs. Stubbs when she knocked on the door to suggest he came down for supper. Sounds of tearing paper distressed the clergyman and his wife. In the morning, Gosse tells us, Swinburne told them he had lit a fire in the empty grate, torn up and burned the whole of *Rosamund*; but

[1] Lang, Vol. I, p. 34.   [2] Lang, Vol. I, p. 33.

afterwards, repenting, had written it out again from memory, which occupied the entire night.

Swinburne now read in the *Guardian* for February 8, 1860, that a prize of £50 was offered for the best poem on *The Life, the Character and the Death of the heroic seaman Sir John Franklin*. It was as his entry for this (not, as Gosse supposed, misled by the similarity of the subject, for the Newdigate prize of 1858, for which the theme set was *The Discovery of the North West Passage*) that Swinburne composed his poem *The Death of Sir John Franklin*. This is the first poem written by Swinburne in a style not obviously influenced by something he had read, and gives a sensitive description of the arctic scenery amidst which Franklin and his men must have sailed in their search for the North West Passage (from the Atlantic to the Pacific round the 'top' of America):[1]

> Out in some barren creek of the cold seas
> Where the slow shapes of the grey water-weed
> Freeze midway as the languid inlets freeze.

His description of an iceberg seen at the noon of the sunless mid-winter is a powerful piece of imaginative visualization:

> Among the thousand colours and gaunt shapes
> Of the strong ice cloven with breach of seas
> Where the waste sullen shadow of steep capes
> Narrows across the cloudy coloured brine
> And by strong jets the angered foam escapes,
> And a sad touch of sun scores the sea-line
> Right at the middle motion of the noon . . .

The *terza rima* in which the poem is written is an unusual metre in English. Swinburne may have noticed the success with which Shelley used it in the *Ode to the West Wind* and *The Triumph of Life*, but the poem is not otherwise Shelleyan.

It did not win.

In April or May 1860, Swinburne went to Oxford to sit for his 'Littles', and this time passed them. In the summer vacation of 1860 he went to Northumberland again, and he was there when, on September 26, his grandfather Sir John Swinburne died at Capheaton, in his ninety-ninth year. After the funeral, Algernon moved to the Trevelyans' home at

[1] Bonchurch, Vol. I.

Wallington. He had loved the old man more than he had ever been able to love his father, and his loss was the greater in that he had no such sympathetic link with his cousin, the new baronet, and so never again stayed at Capheaton. On all future visits to Northumberland, instead of going to the house that he had loved, he stayed with the Trevelyans.

Swinburne should now, normally, have returned to Oxford in October, and begun reading for 'Greats'. Gosse asserts (though Lafourcade questions the assertion) that he did in fact return, and took rooms in Broad Street, and that it was here he wrote the three acts of a comedy called *Laugh and Lie Down*, of which he was later to write:[1]

> I was delighted with the name . . . but I shall take good care that this one never sees the light.

It contains a scene in which a page-boy, Frank, declares his love to a courtesan, Imperia, and beseeches her to beat him:[2]

IMPERIA: Come, come, you are not old enough.

FRANK: I have bled for your sake some twenty times a month,
Some twenty drops each time; are these no services?

IMPERIA: I tell you, if you use me lovingly,
I shall have you whipt again, most pitifully whipt,
You little piece of love.

FRANK: God knows I care not
So I may stand and play to you, and you kiss me
As you used to kiss me, tender little side-touches
Of your lip's edge i' the neck.

IMPERIA: By my hand's hope,
Which is the neck of my Lord Galeas,
I'll love your beard one day; get you a beard, Frank;
With such child's cheeks.

FRANK: Madam, you have pleasant hands,
What sweet and kissing colour goes in them
Running like blood!

IMPERIA: Ay, child, last year in Rome
I held the Pope six minutes kissing them
Before his eyes had grown up to my lips.
Alas!

[1] Lang, Vol. II, p. 343.   [2] Lafourcade, pp. 82–83, and Cassidy, *Swinburne*, p. 59.

FRANK: What makes you sigh still? You are now
So kind the sweetness in you stabs mine eyes
With sharp tears through. I would so fain be hurt
But really hurt, hurt deadly, to do good
To your most sudden fancy.
    ...

IMPERIA: Nay, live safe
Poor little red mouth. Does it love so much?
I think when schooltime's off then thou wilt be
No such good lover. Dost thou know, fool Frank,
Thou art a sort of pleasant thing to me
I would not lose for ten kings more to kiss?
Poor child! I doubt I do too shamefully
To make thy years my spoil thus: I am ashamed.
Would not thy mother weep, Frank, cry and curse
That an Italian harlot and dyed face
Made out of sin should keep thee for a page
To be kissed and beaten, made so much
Her humour's jesting-stock, so taught and used
As I do here.

Here we have the earliest lines in which Swinburne's interest in flagellation is evident; but there is a further degree of self-revelation in Imperia's speech, wherein it appears that, for him, tenderness and torment, kissing and beating, go together.

The remainder of the plot contains elements still odder. Frank presents his younger brother, Frederick, to Imperia, telling her Frederick is a girl dressed as a boy. Imperia, believing this to be true, or else that Frederick is a hermaphrodite, tells him to dress as a girl, but later makes them change clothes. They do. Now it is Frank who is dressed as a girl. Another of Imperia's suitors embraces him, and he plays up marvellously to the role he has been given. What Swinburne intended afterwards to do with the curious characters he had invented cannot be known. Perhaps the reason the play is unfinished is that he lacked the courage to write down what was forming in his imagination.

Lafourcade asserts that 'le point de vue n'est nullement celui d'un homosexuel'.[1] I am not so certain. Swinburne adknowledges a debt to Fletcher for the title, and most of the names are to be found in Fletcher, Frank being there a girl; but the plot is Swinburne's own. There is in Elizabethan comedy much transvestism (the fact that Shakespeare's

[1] Lafourcade, *La Jeunesse*, Vol. II, p. 131.

Twelfth Night is prescribed for the study of schoolchildren has blinded us to the sexual character of the imbroglio which follows on Viola's dressing as a boy), and Swinburne had read much Elizabethan comedy; but coupled with his tendency to reverse the usual masculine and feminine roles, this strange early fragment shows that in his student days his mind was already running on ambiguity of sex.

Gosse avers that Swinburne's 'late hours and general irregularities'[1] caused his landlady to make a complaint to Balliol College. A landlady's complaint, unless of a very serious order, seems slender ground for sending a student down, even unofficially. He was not expelled, or even rusticated, but in later life wrote as though he had been. He left without taking an Honours degree, and, if he had indeed returned for any part of the Michaelmas term, left before the end of November. Perhaps the authorities, warned by the awful example of a near-by college in having expelled Shelley, afterwards recognized to be a genius, intimated to him in some more tactful manner that it would be better he should leave.

[1] Gosse, p. 63.

6

Tragedy at the Rossettis

In December 1860, at his father's expense (£50),[1] Swinburne published *The Queen Mother and Rosamund*. It was, he told Gosse long afterwards, of all stillborn books the stillest. He gave some copies as presents to friends, and his publishers made the usual distribution to the Press, but there the circulation ceased. Not a single copy was sold, and there were, apparently, no reviews.

Admiral Swinburne had taken a villa in Mentone for the winter, and Swinburne went there with the rest of the family. He must have been in depressed spirits, and on January 19, 1861, wrote from there to Lady Trevelyan in terms which would astonish those to whom the Riviera seems a region of the greatest beauty. For Algernon, it was:[2]

> A calcined, scalped, rasped, flayed, broiled, powdered, leprous, blotched, mangy, grimy, parboiled country, *without* trees, water, grass, fields – *with* blank, beastly, senseless olives and orange-trees like a mad cabbage gone indigestible ... females with hunched bodies and crooked necks carrying tons on their heads and looking like death turned seasick.

The family must have passed through Paris, for later in the same letter he writes: 'I am in love with Paris – you know I never saw it before.'

It seems, in view of these last words, that Gosse was in error in dating Swinburne's first visit to the French capital at the Easter vacation of 1858. There is, however, no reason to doubt the substantial truth of an episode concerning this visit related to him by Swinburne.[3] Admiration for Victor Hugo had led Swinburne to a detestation of Napoleon III, 'Napoleon the little', by whom Hugo had been exiled for his anti-monarchical writings. In Paris, driving along the Champs Elysées in an open carriage, the Swinburnes found themselves facing the carriage of the Emperor. Admiral and Lady Swinburne stood up and bowed to him, and the Emperor took off his hat to them as he passed. It was, for their son, a crisis of principle. Gosse, hearing the story many years later, asked

---

[1] Lafourcade, p. 86; *La Jeunesse*, p. 27.
[2] Lang, Vol. 1, p. 38.   [3] Gosse, pp. 54–55.

him whether he had taken off his own hat. Swinburne replied with ecstatic emphasis: 'Not wishing to be obliged to cut my hand off at the wrist the moment I returned to the hotel, I – did – *not!*'

In Mentone his spleen mounted, and he wrote, in late January, to Bell Scott:[1]

> This country is more like hell than you can imagine – calcined, burnt, jaw-broken hills – dolorous gorges, hideous stone terraces – beastly olives and orange trees and not a decent bit of wood in the country. As for grass – it ought to sell £10 a blade.

His destestation of Mentone was to be, for years to come, a family joke. He left his parents and sisters there and made a short tour of Italy – Genoa, Turin, Milan, Venice – by himself. From Italy he wrote no letters, or if he did they have not been preserved.

Back in England, Swinburne lived, for the first time, in London. He had extracted an allowance from his not very pleased father, believed to be £400 a year. On this he took rooms at 16 Grafton Street, near the Tottenham Court Road, so as to be near the British Museum. The library would obviously be useful to him from the point of view of the research required in connection with poems and dramas with historical themes.

He also became a member of the Hogarth Club, and it may have been through this that he became acquainted with Monkton Milnes (later Lord Houghton), another member. The first indication of this connection is a short note from Swinburne, dated May 4 (1861), replying to and accepting an invitation from Milnes to 'come tomorrow'.[2]

A month later, on June 5, Swinburne breakfasted at Milnes's house in Upper Brook Street, together with Coventry Patmore, Aubrey de Vere and Richard Burton, the translator of *The Arabian Nights*, who had strange travels of which to boast. In August, Swinburne was Milnes's guest for a fortnight at his house at Fryston, Yorkshire, and Burton was there again. It was well known among Milnes's acquaintances that he delighted to fill his house with strongly divergent types. The fragile poet and the tough explorer were delighted to admire each other's qualities. They had a common interest in the mysterious – and in erotica. This their host had, also, in abundant measure, his library at Fryston being known to contain a large number of erotic and scatological works. Swinburne seems to have come up partly in the hope of being allowed to borrow or see Milnes's copies of the works of the Marquis de Sade;

[1] Lang, Vol. 1, p. 42.   [2] Lang, Vol. 1, p. 44.

but, though Milnes must have mentioned his possession of these, he was not yet ready to hand them over to the perusal of a young man in his early twenties.

On October 15 Swinburne wrote Milnes from London a long letter in which he reminded Milnes of a promise one day to allow him to read de Sade, to do which he was becoming mad with curiosity.[1] In the same month he composed *Charenton* (the name of the asylum in which de Sade died), a eulogy of the Marquis based upon what he had gathered of his works at second hand. Sir William Hardman, who met Swinburne at Rossetti's wrote: 'Swinburne is a strange fellow, young and beardless, with a shock of red hair . . . although almost a boy, he upholds the Marquis de Sade as the acme and apostle of perfection, without (as he says) having read a word of his works . . . He has a curious kind of nervous twitching, resembling or approaching St. Vitus' Dance.'[2]

In Swinburne's same letter of October 15 he mentions that he is working on *Chastelard* (this is the first we hear of this play about Mary Queen of Scots), and that he has been posing for Rossetti:

> Rossetti has just done a drawing of a female model and myself embracing – I need not say in the most fervent and abandoned style – meant for a frontispiece to his Italian translations. Two mornings of incessant labour on all hands completed the design; and the result will I suppose be, as everybody who knows me already salutes the likeness with a yell of recognition, – that when the book comes out I shall have no refuge but the grave.

The model was probably Fanny Cornforth, the sensual and good-natured woman who posed for Rossetti, while sharing an occasional bed with him. She possessed the red hair for which Rossetti had an almost fetishistic passion. Rossetti, as one knows from what he was later to do, was perplexed that Swinburne, for all the erotic poetry that he wrote, had never had relations with a woman; he may, therefore, have thought that in posing him with Fanny, so that their lips touched, he was giving him an introduction, as it were, which would help him to grow up. Swinburne may have felt the contact embarrassing, but one has the impression he made the most of it in his letter to Milnes.

It was, however, Mrs. Rossetti whom Swinburne preferred. The three Pre-Raphaelite painters had all married since he met them in Oxford; Burne-Jones, who lived near him in Russell Place, had married

[1] Lang, Vol. 1, p. 46.   [2] S. M. Ellis, *A Mid-Victorian Pepys*, pp. 78–9.

Georgiana Macdonald, Rossetti himself had married Elizabeth Siddal, and Morris had married Jane Burden. Behind the latter two marriages lay a drama which held the seeds of tragedy.

Elizabeth Siddal had been Rossetti's companion for ten years before the wedding. She had been discovered by another painter, Deverell, when he entered the milliner's shop, near Leicester Square, kept by her mother. She had the red hair and ethereal look which made her the Pre-Raphaelites' dream. She was the *Viola* in Deverell's *Twelfth Night*, *Sylvia* in Holman Hunt's *Valentine rescuing Sylvia from Proteus* (but he later took out her face), Millais's *Ophelia* (posed floating in a bath of water) and Rossetti's *Beata Beatrix*.

She was romantic; but she was consumptive. Her youth was consumed by Rossetti; under his tutelage she learned to paint and to write poetry. He had perhaps always been occasionally unfaithful, but, as her health weakened and her attraction for him waned, he came (partly at Ruskin's urging) to feel under an obligation to marry her.

It was during the Jovial Campaign at Oxford that the painters made the acquaintance of black-haired Jane Burden, daughter of a groom living over a livery stable at 65 Holywell.[1] Georgiana Burne-Jones said that Elizabeth Siddal's beauty was that of a painting, Jane Burden's that of a statue; she was indeed Junoesque, with a 'neck like a column'. Rossetti as well as Morris became attracted to her. Perhaps because he felt the attraction threatened his resolve to marry Lizzie (as she was always called), Rossetti encouraged Morris to take the plunge and to marry Janey. The step caught four lives in a clamp of unhappiness. On May 23, 1860, Rossetti took Lizzie to the altar; but poor Lizzie's long years of waiting were crowned by the shell of a victory.

She had not been with Rossetti at Oxford, but now, in Rossetti's studios at Chatham Place, near Blackfriars, Swinburne came to know her. With him she brightened up. Simple things amused her, as when, in a theatre, a person catching sight first of her red hair and then of Swinburne's, farther down the row, exclaimed, 'There's another of 'em!' Their same coloured red heads were often bent together over a book. Swinburne was later to write:[2] 'her sense of humour, her fine appreciation and exquisite relish of poetic comedy and dramatic invention or satire, could not be surpassed, and would have sufficed to confute the charge that no woman can enjoy the finest effects or creations of satiric humour – and good humour – as men do'. The charge he had in mind was probably

[1] Grylls, *Portrait of Rossetti*, p. 68.   [2] Lang, Vol. VI, p. 132.

that made by Byron, and occasioned by the dislike of his mistress, the Countess Guiccioli, for the satiric passages in *Don Juan* because they suggested cynicism about love.

Swinburne had discovered Lizzie's aptitude for the appreciation of comedy by reading the Elizabethans to her. Later he was to write:[1]

> Except Lady Trevelyan, I never knew so brilliant and appreciative a woman – so quick to see and so keen to enjoy that rare and delightful fusion of wit, humour, character-painting, and dramatic poetry – poetry subdued to dramatic effect – which is only less wonderful and delightful than the very highest works of genius. I used to come and read to her sometimes, when she was well enough, at Chatham Place, and I shall never forget her delight in Fletcher's magnificent comedy of 'The Spanish Curate', I read her – of course with occasional skips, though there really is not much need for a Bowdler – the superb scenes in which that worthy and his 'old honest sexton' figure – and I can hear the music of her laughter to this day, when after disclaiming all knowledge or recollection of an imaginary old friend they suddenly wake up to the freshest and keenest recollection of him on hearing that he has left each of them a handsome legacy. She thought it 'better than Shakespeare'; and though I could not allow that, I do think it is better than anything except Shakespeare's best ... I won't enlarge on the deeper and sadder side of my brotherly affection for her, but I shall always be sorrowfully glad and proud to remember her regard for me – not undeserved, certainly, if the warmest admiration and the greatest delight in her company could deserve it. She was a wonderful as well as a most loveable creature.

On the evening of February 10, 1862, Rossetti, Lizzie and Swinburne dined together at the Sablonière restaurant, near Leicester Square. Lizzie, who had bought a new cloak the day before, seemed tired but in gay spirits. At eight o'clock the party broke up, and Rossetti and Lizzie went straight home. Later Rossetti went out again, by himself, to speak at the Working Men's Club. When he returned, about half past eleven, the room reeked with laudanum and he could not wake Lizzie. He fetched their doctor, and also several friends, including Ford Madox Brown; the efforts of the doctor, who applied a stomach pump, were useless. In the early hours of the morning, she died. Swinburne, unaware of all that had passed since he saw them at dinner, arrived in the morning, as had

[1] Lang, Vol. VI, pp. 93–94.

been arranged, to sit for Rossetti, and found himself in a scene of the utmost gloom.

Swinburne had to attend the inquest, which was held on February 12, at Bridewell Hospital. Rossetti, of course, was the principal witness. Swinburne, when called, testified that husband and wife had been on good terms. 'They dined with me on Monday. I saw nothing in particular in the deceased except that she appeared a little weaker than usual.' The doctor gave evidence that 'she died from the effects of laudanum which must have been a very large dose'. The jury brought in a verdict that the deceased 'accidentally took an overdose of laudanum'.

The funeral was on February 17, and it is believed that Swinburne was present when Rossetti buried the poems he had written to Lizzie with her in her coffin; Swinburne, who had listened to the poems being read, regretted their disappearance from the world in what seemed to him a useless gesture. On March 13 he wrote to his mother:[1]

> I am sure you will understand how that which has happened since I last wrote to you has upset my plans and how my time has been taken up. Till last week when I was laid up with a bad turn of influenza I have been almost always with Rossetti ...
>
> I would rather not write yet about what has happened – I suppose none of the papers gave a full report, so that you do not know that I was almost the last person who saw her (except her husband and a servant) and had to give evidence at the inquest. Happily there was no difficulty in proving that illness had quite deranged her mind, so that the worst chance of all was escaped.

These lines are part of the evidence for supposing that, at any rate amongst Rossetti's friends, it was believed Lizzie had committed suicide. Only if the verdict might have been one of suicide could it have been 'happy' to be able to prove that she was at the time of unsound mind.

It seems that Madox Brown afterwards told several people that there had been a note attached to Lizzie's nightgown, or on the floor, and that Rossetti gave it to him. After reading it, he destroyed it. It read 'Take care of Harry.' Harry was a brother of Lizzie's, who was feeble minded. The destruction was intended to protect Lizzie's reputation and also Rossetti's; its preservation could have spared Rossetti the still uglier rumour, later to be put about by Violet Hunt, that he had murdered Lizzie.

[1] Leith, pp. 102–3.

TRAGEDY AT THE ROSSETTIS

Swinburne, though he was to be for ever Lizzie's champion, stood by
Rossetti. His letter of March 13 to his mother ends:

> Rossetti and I are going to live together as soon as we move – of
> course he could not stay in the old house, and asked me to come
> with him. Luckily I had put off deciding on a lodging as it would
> have been a great plague to change again. In the autumn we get
> into a house at Chelsea – in Cheyne Walk, facing the trees and
> river – with an old garden. The house is taken (like every other
> nice one) for the Exhibition season, so we must make shift some-
> where till then.

As it would be half a year until the house in Cheyne Walk became free,
Rossetti went to stay with his mother. Much later Swinburne wrote
concerning Lizzie's death:[1]

> The anguish of her widower, when next we met, under the roof
> of the mother with whom he had sought refuge, I cannot remem-
> ber, at more than twenty years' distance, without some recrudes-
> cence of emotion. With sobs and broken speech . . . he appealed to
> my friendship, in the name of her regard for me – such regard he
> assured me, as she had felt for no other of his friends – to cleave to
> him in this time of sorrow, to come and keep house with him as
> soon as a residence could be found.

Swinburne had already met Rossetti's younger brother and sister,
William Michael Rossetti and Christina Rossetti; now, having occasion
to visit the Rossetti home in Albany Street, in order to see Gabriel, he
came to know them better. Both were to become important to him in the
future years, William Michael as a literary man with whom he could
discuss editorial and critical questions, Christina as a poet and an
inspiration.

William Michael and Christina were beneficial in Swinburne's life.
A more sinister influence was on the way. In the summer, Swinburne at
last persuaded Milnes to let him read de Sade.

[1] Gosse, p. 85.

7

De Sade

DE SADE'S two great novels, *Justine ou les Malheurs de la Vertu* and *Juliette ou les Prospérités de la Vice*, are intended by their author, as he indicates in his sub-titles, to point the immoral moral that vice pays and virtue does not. Justine and Juliette are sisters, brought up together at a convent school. As their story opens, they learn that their father's ruin has left them not only orphaned but unprovided. Since no more money is coming for their keep, the convent authorities show them the door and leave them mistress of their own actions.

It is from this point that their ways diverge. Juliette, undismayed, recalls that she was once given the address of a brothel; she feels sure she will be taken in there, and decides to go to it. She invites Justine to come too, to try her fortune; but seeing that Justine only weeps, Juliette, after trying for a moment to dry her tears, sets forth alone.

Justine is concerned above all things to preserve her virtue. She calls upon a woman who had assiduously flattered her parents in their prosperous days, but finds herself not received as before. No help is offered her. She next tries her mother's dressmaker and asks to be taken into her employ (and this is the only attempt at entering a skilled employment which Justine ever makes), but again finds her assistance not required. Thirdly, she seeks out the parish priest; he offers her board and lodging at his home, but as he does so he kisses her in a manner a shade unfitting for a man of the Church. Shocked beyond measure, Justine not only withdraws; she insults him with the utmost violence for seeking to exploit the misfortune which brought her to his door. Affronted, the priest ejects her. Justine ends her first night on her own resources still chaste, but miserable, in a dingy furnished room.

The landlady, seeing that she has nothing but the few coins with which she came, gives her in the morning the address of a gentleman in the neighbourhood. She goes to his house, and the speech she makes him is almost a model of how not to apply for a job. She mentions, first, her shame in asking for work, since she was not lowly born, and secondly the repulses which she has met. She omits to say what kind of work she is qualified or willing to do, except that it must be compatible with her honour. He makes it plain his only interest in her would be sexual.

After some further misadventures Justine is at last given a home, without threat to her chastity, by a homosexual; but it turns out that he wants her to murder his mother. From this point on her misfortunes, which at the beginning had been merely drab, slide into phantasmagoric horror, and when she finally loses her virginity it is by multiple rape in an obscene monastery. Her humiliations are at their nadir when she is rescued by a richly dressed lady, who happens to cross her path; the rich lady is Juliette.

For all its author's grim intent, *Justine* just misses being a funny book. It also just misses being a morality, of an unusual and salutary order. It does not, in truth, make its author's intended point, that virtue always gets the worst of it, if by virtue is meant wisdom and goodness in any deeper sense. Justine's concern with her chastity is spiritually self-regarding; taking it as her due that everyone should give her disinterested help, she is demanding; this she fails to notice when constantly complaining. Even though it is very much exaggerated (and in later editions de Sade elaborated the horror to the detriment of the artistry), there is a certain poetic justice in the fate which overtakes her. This she never perceives.

The companion volume does not, for sheer artistic architecture, compare with *Justine*. It tells, of course, the road by which Juliette came to her riches. Juliette regards Justine as stupid (not without a grain of reason), and herself as intelligent because ready to experience every pleasure. Only, some of her pleasures are very odd, as are those of the members of the secret society to which she is introduced by her first big patron. Most of them have reached a state of satiety such that only flagellation can revive their ardour. This they are fully as willing to suffer as to inflict. It is a point of principle with them that each one should be self-regarding; therefore, when one of them gives help to another, they say, 'Do not thank me; I do it for my pleasure'. In this they contrast to their advantage with Justine, who always expected gratitude for anything she did for anybody. De Sade has been reproached with the unkindness with which he treats the sentiment of gratitude; but the fact is that the expectation of gratitude can amount to emotional blackmail, and this may be the reason for his hostility towards it. The characters in *Juliette* can never be under an obligation to one another. Oddly enough, these apostles of pleasure rank friendship even higher than satisfaction.

'What's left if you cannot count upon your friends?' asks one of them pathetically. When adverse fortune strikes them, they are stoic, and never complain.

The ethics, however, apply only between equals in intelligence (or iniquity).

One very curious feature of the book is that the secret society impudently named *La Société des Amis du Crime*, to which Juliette is introduced, has an initiation rite which could be that of an esoteric order. At the inauguration of a new President, the members each in turn kiss the President at the base of the spine. This is the old Templar Rite.[1] (I am insufficiently a de Sade scholar to know whether this has been pointed out before; it is not mentioned in any of the de Sade studies I have consulted.) One knows that after the dissolution of the Knights Templar by Phillippe le Bel in 1307, and the subsequent martyrdom of the Grand Master, the order went underground and turned into a number of secret esoteric orders; but the possibility that the secret societies for personal indulgence which flourished in the very different cultural climate of the eighteenth century could be remnants of the old Templar order, gone to seed as it were, the sacred side having dropped out, though disturbing, would explain many things. Not least, it would explain the tendency of de Sade's characters to debate fine points of philosophy in their moments of respite, and the very real sense, by which they all seem possessed, of a mission to teach Juliette, as one who by her natural intelligence was worthy to receive teaching.

When one has picked out the few points of interest, *Juliette* remains a pornographic book, crude, obsessive, ill-constructed, repetitious and much too long. Not only is it revolting, it is almost inconceivably dull.

Swinburne began with *Justine*, in the second edition: its effect upon him was overpowering. Nevertheless, in the exceedingly long letter which he wrote on August 18, 1862, to Milnes immediately after reading it, he affected to be disappointed and to take the work lightly:[2]

> I have just read 'Justine ou les Malheurs de la Vertu'. As you seemed anxious to know its effects on me I mean to give you a

[1] ... *et cil qui le rechoit en bout de l'eschine*, Philippe IV of France, called le Bel, in his letter of September 14, 1307, accusing the Templars and describing their rites. See *Le Dossier de L'Affaire des Templiers*, ed. Lizerand, p. 26; also my own earlier book *The Magical Dilemma of Victor Neuburg*, Chapter 12, *Templars and the Tradition of Sheikh el Djebel*, pp. 195-202.

[2] Lang, Vol. 1, pp. 53-8.

candid record, avoiding paradox or affectation. I would give anything to have, by way of study, six or seven other opinions as genuine and frank as mine shall be.

At first, I quite expected to add another to the gifted author's list of victims; I really thought I must have died or split open or choked with laughing. I never laughed so much in my life. I couldn't have stopped to save the said life. . . . I regret to add that all the friends to whom I have lent or shown the book were affected in just the same way. One scene . . . I never thought to survive. I read it out and the auditors rolled and roared. Then Rossetti read . . . and I wonder to this minute that we did not raise the whole house by our screams of laughter.

This is intended as a take-down of the book which has, in all serious-ness, been described as the most shocking ever written; but the fact is that *Justine* is, in an odd way, funny. Nevertheless it is probable that Swinburne, in order to show his immunity to its influence, exaggerates the mirth with which it was received; unless, indeed, the laughter to which he refers was partly nervous or hysterical. Swinburne continues:

Of course the book must be taken on its own grounds; well, assuming every postulate possible, I lament to say it appears to me a most outrageous *fiasco*. I looked for some sharp and subtle analysis of lust – some keen dissection of pain and pleasure – 'quelques taillades dans les chairs vives de la sensation': at least such an exquisite relish of the things anatomised as without explanation would suffice for a stimulant and be comprehensive at once even if unfit for sympathy. But in *Justine* there seems to me throughout to be one radical mistake, rotting and undermining the whole structure of the book. De Sade is like a Hindoo mythologist; he takes *bulk* and *number* for greatness. As if a crime of great extent was necessarily a great crime; as if a number of pleasures piled one on another made up the value of a single great and perfect sensa-tion of pleasure.

This is true enough; though it is, in a way, the numerical piling up which lightens the recital, for, since the horrors are listed rather than described, one is not obliged to imagine them.

Adopting the second person, Swinburne continues as though it were to de Sade, instead of to Milnes, that he was writing:

Take the simplest little example of your way of work. You have, say, a flogging to describe. You go in for *quantity* in a way quite regardless of expense. You lay on some hundreds of cuts, behind and before; you assert that they drew blood; probably they did; that the recipient wept and writhed; which is not unlikely; that the inflictor enjoyed himself and was much excited in his *physique*; which is most probable of all. Well? You have asserted a great deal ... let the sense of it bite ... and sting your reader. Assertion is easy work. Shew us how and why these things are as they are. I on my part assert that you never do this once. ... I boast not of myself; but I do say that a schoolboy, set to write on his own stock of experience, and having a real gust and appetite for the subject in him, may make and has made more of a sharp short school flogging of two or three dozen cuts than you of your ... interminable afflictions; more of the simple common birch rod and daily whipping-block than you of your loaded iron whips. ...

This is perhaps the most unfortunate tribute to Eton ever penned. The fact is that Swinburne's *Flogging-Block* poems are infinitely more painful to read than anything in de Sade, because one believes in them, as one certainly does not believe in the further reaches of de Sade's imagination. At the same time, one regrets that the element in de Sade's work that Swinburne seized upon was precisely that out of which Krafft-Ebing was later to coin the word Sadistic.

Later in the same letter, one comes upon a very sinister little revelation:

As to your horrors – ask people what they remember, as little children, to have said, heard of, thought of, dreamed of, done or been tempted to do. Nothing in your books but will find its counterpart or type. (I remember when I was seven a most innocent little girl of six telling me of a bad dream that made her unhappy: in that dream there was the whole practical philosophy of Justine embodied ...

The little girl may well have been his cousin Mary, even though she was three years the younger. But of her character, more later.

Swinburne continues his humorous castigation of de Sade:

Tenez, my friend, Arch-Professor of the Ithyphallic Science as you are, will you hear the truth once for all? You take yourself for a great pagan physiologist and philosopher – you are a Christian ascetic bent on earning the salvation of the soul through mortification of the flesh. You are one of the family of St. Simeon Stylites. ... You belong to Christian Egypt; you smell of nitria;

DE SADE

you have walked out of some Nile monastery; you are twin
brother to St. Maccarius; you are St. Anthony and his pig rolled
into one. It matters little that you have forgotten your own
genealogy...

This is in a way shrewd – and remarkable, seeing that it was written in
the days before the advent of modern psychology.

Swinburne concludes the long account of his first reaction to de Sade
by assuring Milnes that he has sustained no damage:

> I drop my apostrophe to M. de Sade, having relieved my mind
> for good and all of its final judgement on a matter of some curiosity
> and interest to me. I should like to know (if you forgive me for
> writing such a farrago on the chance of its finding you désoeuvré
> for half an hour) whether you agree or not. I have said just what I
> think in the first words that came uppermost. I am very glad *not*
> to have waited (as you advised) some 29 years on the chance of
> being alive then to read *Justine*. You see that whether it drives
> curates and curates' pupils to madness and death ... it has done
> decidedly little damage to my brain or nerves ...

As turning to a healthier subject, at the end, Swinburne asks whether
Milnes has seen his review, in the *Spectator*, of Victor Hugo's *Les
Misérables*, and whether he has seen the latest edition of Walt Whitman's
Leaves of Grass:

> for there is one new poem in it – 'A Voice from the Sea' – about
> two birds on the sea-beach, which I really think the most lovely
> and wonderful thing I have read for years and years.

Swinburne was anxious to assure Milnes that he had not been affected
by de Sade; yet the new influence may have been in part responsible for
the violent metaphor with which Swinburne, in his review of *Les
Misérables*, took Hugo to task for the injection into that novel of too
much moralizing:[1]

> ... and indeed we may reasonably grudge the time and labour – still
> more the faith and hope and fervent vigour of mind – lavished on
> social subjects, and all kinds of actual wrongs and remedies; such
> of us at least as regard a good work of art as the first of all good
> deeds for an artist, and would consider a fresh Hamlet or a new
> Ruy Blas cheaply purchased by the hanging without trial of a
> dozen innocent men...

[1] Bonchurch, Vol. XIII.

It is true that he could have found a similar idea in Gautier, or in Baude-laire, whose *Fleurs du Mal* he had already reviewed for the *Spectator*.

Fortunately, he had also, in Blake, a healthier influence. Alexander Gilchrist, a friend of the Rossetti brothers, had died leaving a two-volume work on Blake unfinished. Gabriel Rossetti, in particular, had an affinity for Blake, and he and William Michael, a man of scholastic bent, decided to complete the second volume themselves, and to see it through publication in memory of their friend and of the poet. They asked Swinburne if he would contribute an appreciation of the *Prophetic Books*. In a letter which is his first to William Michael, Swinburne replied that he did not think he could fit what he had to say into the existing framework, but would write a separate 'small commentary'.[1] This was to grow to such proportions as to occupy him for several years and to bring him into continual consultation with the Rossetti brothers over points of Blake scholarship.

In October the house on Cheyne Walk became vacant for Gabriel Rossetti and Swinburne to move into. Swinburne, however, can have done little more than transfer some of his effects to it at this moment, for at the beginning of November he accepted an invitation from Milnes to stay at Fryston, in Yorkshire. Here he recited his newly composed poem *Faustine*, and, as he wrote to William Michael, helped Milnes to decipher 'a *priceless* autograph of the Marquis de Sade'. He added in a postscript:[2] 'The handwriting I flatter myself with thinking not unlike that of this note.'

In December Swinburne went to Northumberland again, and from Wallington went to Newcastle to see Scott. Scott writes:[3]

> It was close on the Christmas of 1862 when we were preparing for a Tynemouth holiday. Swinburne suddenly appeared early in the forenoon having posted to Morpeth from Wallington early that morning. Why so early?

Swinburne had not a clear answer, but seemed to be full of something. The Bell Scotts stayed to talk with him until it became necessary for them to take a later train to Tynemouth, and eventually Swinburne went with them. They all walked down to the beach and there Swinburne declaimed, to the sea, stanzas from the *Hymn to Proserpine* and the *Laus Veneris*.

[1] Lang, Vol. I, p. 60.   [2] Lang, Vol. 1, p. 63.
[3] Lafourcade, *Le Jeunesse*, Vol. I, pp. 208–9.

It must have been on this visit to Tynemouth that Swinburne wrote to Milnes from Wallington on December 27. He calls him 'Mon cher Rodin'. Rodin was a sadistic schoolmaster encountered by Justine in the course of her misadventures. Still in French, Swinburne gives Milnes a wonderful description of the sea at Tynemouth, but links with the Marquis his sensations on seeing the cruelty of the waters:[1]

> Il est dommage que ce digne et cher marquis n'ait pas imaginé des supplices de mer. J'ai vu la semaine passée un effet admirable de bourrasque sur les grèves de la côte du nord. En contemplant les grandes lames blanches et roussâtres de cette mer houleuse, et les rochers crenelés qui soufflaient l'écume par mille bouches et milles narines de pierre, j'ai trouvé des supplices à faire bonder un cadavre.

A thousand mouths and nostrils of stone! He continues in English:

> ... By the by for heaven's sake send me your chapter of school-master's autobiography. What is the good man's honoured *name* to be? Mine is getting done and you shall have it in return as we covenanted. It will be very pretty I expect – two victims each, you will please remember. Mine are brothers. I want to see your style of flagellant fiction infinitely.

Now one sees why he was addressing Milnes as 'Rodin'. This is the first indication of an overtly flagellant correspondence between Swinburne and Milnes, and of a covenant between them each to produce a flagellant work. Swinburne signs his letters:

> Ever your affectionate
> Frank Fane

There is in the British Museum a short unpublished flagellant manuscript in Swinburne's hand entitled 'Frank Fane'. This I have examined. It is on two leaves, both showing chain-lines but no watermark. It could be of this date, but Frank Fane, in this composition, has no brother. Reggie and Fred Fane are two brothers who appear in the *Reginald's Flogging* contributed by Swinburne, under the pseudonym *Etonensis*, to the *Whippingham Papers*, an anthology of flagellant verse and prose later produced. This *Reginald's Flogging* is in a different metre from, and has nothing in common with, the *Reginald's Flogging* which exists only in Swinburne's hand and forms part of *The Flogging Block*, an unpublished epic held in the Manuscript Department of the British Museum

[1] Lang, Vol. I, pp. 66–67.

but reserved from public use, which I have also examined. In *The Flogging Block*, which I will describe later, Reginald's full name is Reginald Loraine, or, in one of the eclogues, Reginald Swinburne, but in *The Whippingham Papers* it is Reginald Fane. Swinburne's flagellant manuscripts are a vast and tangled jungle, in which he rings the changes upon a limited number of Christian and surnames in a manner suggesting connections between one piece and another, sometimes falsely. It seems probable that the particular piece to which he referred in this letter to Milnes has escaped the collectors. Milnes's composition under the covenant might perhaps be *The Rodiad*.[1]

In his next letter to Milnes, of January 2, 1863, Swinburne again addresses Milnes as 'Cher M. Rodin' and makes further reference to 'Ce bon M. de Sade' and to the flogging romances. However, there is other subject matter. Victor Hugo had written to thank him for having reviewed *Les Misérables* in the *Spectator*.

A point missed by Swinburne is that Hugo could not read English and had obviously misunderstood what Swinburne had written about him and his work in the *Spectator*. He must have shown the text to some friend

---

[1] Professor Wilson Knight seems to be in error when, in his book *Lord Byron's Marriage*, p. 164, he ascribes authorship of *The Rodiad* to George Colman the younger. This was drawn to my attention by Mr. Timothy d'Arch Smith, who referred me to the *Centuria Librorum Absconditorum* by Pisanus Fraxi (pseudonym of Henry Spencer Ashbee), London, 1879, pp. 471–4. Following up this reference, I read:

THE RODIAD ... published by John Camden Hotten in 1871, at 12s. 6d.; issue 250 copies of which about 200 were in 1873 sold to a bookseller of New York. The date 1810 is certainly false, as are the names of authors and publishers. The poem could not have been earlier than 1820, because at p. 27, line 4, we find:

I read his bill of penalties and pains

and again at p. 61, line 3:

Cut up with red hot wire adulterous Queens

which obviously refer to the queen CAROLINE scandal: and her trial only took place in 1820. Nor was the poem written by either the elder or younger Colman (the name, be it remarked, is misspelt, an *e* being erroneously inserted), but by one of the clients of the notorious Sarah Potter, alias Stewart, from whom it was obtained by a well-known London collector; he lent the MS. to Hotten who printed it without permission. ...

Mr. d'Arch Smith, who lent me his copy of *The Rodiad*, tells me that, apart from Fraxi's definitive information, paper and print prove its later issue.

who, either through ignorance or kindness, gave him a mis-translation of the sentences referring to the preoccupation of the novel with social questions. This explains what so surprised Swinburne, that Hugo should not take amiss the criticism he had made on this head. He wrote to Milnes:[1]

> Je viens de recevoir une lettre charmante de Victor Hugo qui veut bien m'adresser des remerciments au sujet de mes articles sur *Les Misérables*. Vous croyez bien que j'en ai encore la tête toute échauffée. Si j'eusse su qu'il devrait les lire, j'aurais craint de lui avoir déplu en m'attaquant aux philanthrope; j'ai aussi un peu nargué en passant la vertue publique, et la démocratie vertueuse. Il me parait cependant plus que satisfait.

Hugo had in fact written, from Hauteville House in Guernsey, where on account of his republican principles he lived as an exile from France:

> J'ai connu, seulement à mon retour en cette île, vos deux excellents articles sur *Les Misérables*. Je suis heureux que ce livre a appelé l'attention d'un esprit tel que le vôtre, et que vous soyez, vous aussi, sollicité par les questions sociales; préoccupa-tion suprême de notre siècle. Je vous félicite de votre talent, Monsieur. . . .

Swinburne was naturally enchanted. To Milnes, he continued:

> C'est sans doute un plaisir innocent, mais c'en est toutefois un assez grand, que d'avoir su plaire . . . au maître qu'on a toujours vénéré.

Hugo's condescension in thanking him for the reviews in the *Spectator* made Swinburne his admirer for life.

The sombre influence of de Sade had, however, yet to run its course. At the end of January, Swinburne went down to Bournemouth, to be near his sister Edith, who was seriously ill, and started a letter to Milnes:[2]

> My dear M. Rodin,
> Having had to come down hither in something of a hurry owing to sickness in the family, I have unluckily left the MSS. of our incipient fictitious-biography in Grosvenor Place. Can I write to a maiden aunt rising seventy – 'Be kind enough to look over a large portfolio in my bedroom containing autograph studies and sketches in verse and prose, all totally unfit for publication, ranging in date from 1854 to 1862, and forward the more offensive specimens to M. Rodin . . .

[1] Lang, Vol. 1, p. 69.   [2] Lang, Vol. 1, p. 70.

Casting one's mind back to his undergraduate play *Laugh and Lie Down*, one realizes that Swinburne was already well on the road to writing *The Flogging Block*. This must have been so from his days at Eton. Constituted as he was, Swinburne did not need the Marquis de Sade to explain to him that pleasure and pain are sometimes connected. But if he insisted upon reading de Sade's works because he was the way he was, he was the more vulnerable to their influence. In a certain sense de Sade brought him out; but whether that was a catharsis or whether it merely increased his morbidity is open to argument.

8

Love's Cross Currents

SWINBURNE'S first novel may be dated in an approximate manner by reference to a letter about it which, more than forty years later, he wrote to his sister Isabel, in which he said '. . . the letters are dated just about the time I wrote them or perhaps a year earlier'.[1] The year's letters of which the novel consists begin in January 1861. If this was a year earlier than the writing, then composition would have been in 1862. There is, however, a point which has not been noted before, and that is that a fragment which seems to have been a preliminary try-out for the novel contains the development of ideas concerning the possible 'supplices de mer' neglected by de Sade, of which Swinburne wrote to Milnes after watching the sea at Tynemouth. That letter having been written on December 27, 1862, I would suppose that the try-out was done immediately afterwards and the main body of the novel written in 1863. After forty years, Swinburne's memory could easily have slipped a little, and that the body of the work is written on paper bearing an 1862 watermark proves nothing, as the author could have been using up paper purchased earlier.

The try-out is known as the *Kirklowes* fragment, from its having *Kirklowes* written across the top, though this was probably intended as the title of the first chapter only. It is the name of a farm in Westmorland, and the hero is called, as in the completed work, Reginald Harewood. Westmorland is a thin disguise for Northumberland and Reginald is Swinburne himself, with certain incidents and circumstances of his life slightly changed about. He has a father who continually birches him, and a sister to whom he is excessively devoted. Reginald is:[2]

> a boy who used up enormous quantities of birch; on whom no rule grammatical or moral took the least hold, till it was well beaten in; the seat of the intellect or conscience being to appearances by no means in the head. He had an animal worship of his sister's beauty and seldom rebelled against her: she in return was decidedly fond of him, but there was no weakness in her affection.
> She was by nature untender, thoughtful, subtly apprehensive,

[1] Lang, Vol. VI, p. 194.   [2] *Lesbia Brandon* (Appendix).

71

greedy of pleasure, curious of evil and good; had a cool sound head, a ready, rapid, flexible cleverness. There was a certain cruelty about her which never showed itself in a harsh or brutal way, but fed with a soft sensual relish on the sight or conceit of physical pain. It was a nervous passion derived from her mother's weak blood and retained in the strong body given her by her father. She was a mixture of two breeds: of a sensual blood and quick nerves, but also of a steady judgement and somewhat cold heart. At bottom, she had no moral qualities at all.

He explains that she knew, for instance, that murder was a theological sin, but except for the prohibition had nothing against it. Her instinct was not moral:

> ... she could not disapprove of anything except by rote. This character of mind was born with her and grew up quietly, as her body grew in beauty. She was curiously beautiful; her features were clear, tender, regular; she had soft and subtle eyes... drowned and vague under heavy white eyelids and curled lashes. She had the sign given by Lavater as typical of faces not to be trusted; eyebrows and hair of a different colour. The hair was saffron coloured, thick and sinuous, the neck large, polished and long. The shape of her cheeks and temples was of a singular perfection, which could only be understood when the hair was fastened up from the sides of the head.

The description is so detailed and so particular that it must be that of an actual woman whom Swinburne had observed. If one wants to know who she was, one will store every one of the details in one's memory, so as to recognize them if they recur in other works. For though she is his sister in this fragment, it is not necessary to suppose that the model was one of his real sisters. The fragment continues:

> ... But her liking was for her brother Reginald; her interest for his affairs within doors and without... Each of Redgie's floggings was a small drama to her: she followed with excitement each cut of the birch on her brother's skin, and tasted a nervous pleasure when every stroke drew blood; she analysed the weals, and anatomised the tears of the victim. ... It is certain that Helen felt real and acute enjoyment at the sight of her brother horsed and writhing under the rod; there was in her senses a sort of reversed sympathy with the pain of Reginald's tingling flesh. When the flogging was over she would comfort and coax him, being really grateful to him for the pleasant excitement she had gone thro': but it never entered her head to intercede for him, or his to appeal to her.

Helen marries a dull husband, and also acquires an admirer, whose destruction she watches with excitement when a boat in which he has put to sea capsizes and he is dashed by the waves upon the rocks. The scene, with its sadistic overtones, has affinities with Swinburne's description, in his letter to Milnes, of the sea at Tynemouth and his thoughts concerning it:[1]

> Lying down and grasping the rims of rock, she stooped and peered upon the pale-coloured sea, crossed now with slow serpentine streaks of moving foam. All under and round the rock it came in with a bubbling and gurgling noise, distinct from the kiss of the rain. . . .
> Helping herself with hands and knees, Helen crawled down the slant back of the great rock, and watching her time, when the recoil of the water left a little space between that and the next rock, leapt down . . . her eyes shone and smiled; . . . Meeting Reginald . . . she took him round with her arms and kissed him, laughing.

This is after watching the man thrown dead upon the shingle beneath. Perhaps, having written it, Swinburne felt it was too horrid, for he abandoned this beginning and started again.

In the new manuscript, which he called *A Year's Letters*, later changing the title to *Love's Cross Currents*, Reginald's ghoulish sister Helen is dropped from the cast of characters, though his sadistic father is developed. Moreover, he has been changed from a farmer into being, like Swinburne's own father, a Captain in the Royal Navy.

But to understand the plot of *Love's Cross Currents* one has to go back two generations and to understand the relationships of the Cheyne family. The weakness of the novel is that the opening pages, in which these are explained, are hard to follow, and as it is essential to understand them a reader who makes out a genealogical tree saves himself much trouble later. There are three elder Cheynes, two brothers and a sister; these are Lord Cheyne, John Cheyne and Helena Cheyne, who by marriage becomes Lady Midhurst. Lord Cheyne marries and has a son, Edmund, who succeeds him and is the Lord Cheyne of the action of the story. John Cheyne marries and has two children, Clara and Frank. Lady Midhurst has a daughter Amicia, who marries, first, the Captain Harewood by whom she has Reginald, and, after a divorce from him, a Mr. Stanford, by whom she has a daughter called, after herself, Amicia. This Amicia, half-sister to Reginald (and nothing whatever like the

[1] *Lesbia Brandon* (Appendix), pp. 178–80.

original Helen), marries Lord Cheyne, that is Edmund, her mother's cousin, and thus becomes the Lady Cheyne of the story. It is in the inter-relationships of all the cousins that the story consists; and in their domination by Lady Midhurst, quite the most powerful character in the family, whose jealous devotion to her two grandchildren, Redgie and Amicia (Lady Cheyne) motivates her every action.

Redgie had first met his mother's cousins Clara and Frank when he was a schoolboy. Although they were his mother's cousins, he was older than Frank, and so was able to over-awe Frank by boasting of the frequency with which he was birched, or to use his word 'swished', both by his father and at school, and of the nonchalance with which he was accustomed to receive this punishment.

Though Frank is Redgie's junior, Frank's sister, Clara, is Redgie's senior. She marries a Mr. Ernest Radworth, a worthy man and very dull.

Except for the *Prologue*, in which these matters are explained, the book consists of letters supposed to have been written by the characters to each other. The form has the advantage of mystery. The author does not have to play God and know all that the characters do. The letters can be presented as though they were merely a bundle of documents in an unsolved case. As with letters written in real life, they do not explain situations which are known to the recipient as well as to the writer; the reader, a third party, can only guess at the meaning behind some of the phrases and form his own conclusions. It is a detective story in relation-ships.

The first letter is from Lady Midhurst to Clara, from which it may be gathered that she wants Clara to stop Frank from paying to Amicia (Lady Cheyne) such attentions as cause gossip; she says for his sake, but it is obviously for Amicia's. It also seems to be intimated that Lord Cheyne is found by his wife rather dull, for which reason she needs protecting.

A few days later, we find Lady Midhurst writing to Amicia, asking her to invite Redgie to stay, so as to get him away from Clara:

> Clara Radworth must be at least six years older than he is. I believe she has taken to painting already. If there was only a little bit of scandal in the matter! but that is past praying for. It is a regular quiet amicable innocent alliance; the very worst thing for such a boy in the world.

There one has the situation. Both her grandchildren are in trouble, the one with Frank and the other with Clara; and she is trying to use Clara to get Frank from Amicia, and Amicia to get Redgie from Clara.

To Reginald, whom she loves the best, she writes not in a roundabout but in a direct manner:

> It is a great deal worse for a man than for a woman to get talked about in such a way as you two will be . . . I have no doubt you are riding with Clara at this minute; . . .

Since they ride on horseback together, perhaps it is Clara who has taken over, in a modified key, the role that was Helen's in the original try-out. Lady Midhurst's objections are not merely prudish:

> If she were only the least bit cleverer than she is I would never say a word. Indeed, it would be the best training in the world for you to fall into the hands of a real and high genius. But you must wait. Show me Athénais de Montespan and I will allow you *any* folly on her account; but with Louise de la Vallière I will *not* let you commit yourself. You will say C.R. is more than this last; I know she is; but not enough.

The next letter is from Redgie himself to another young man, perhaps one of the friends he made at Oxford, mentioning his cousin Clara:

> I wish I could sit a horse half as well; she is the most graceful and the pluckiest rider you ever saw. I rode with her yesterday to Hadleigh, down by the sea, and we had a gallop over the sands; three miles good, and all hard sand; . . .

With a date of only six weeks later, there is a most extraordinary letter from Redgie to Clara, urging her, not indeed to join him, but to leave her husband, since she has nothing in common with him:

> It is too monstrous and shameful to see things as they are and let them go on . . . You told me once I knew you to the heart and ought to give up dreaming and hoping – but I might be sure, you said, of what I had . . . It is not for myself – I am ashamed to write even the denial – that I summon you to break off the hideous sort of compromise you are living in. What you are doing insults God, and maddens men who see it. Think what it is to endure and to act as you do! I ask you what right you have to let him play at husband with you? You know *he* has no right; why should you have. . . . I say you cannot live with him always . . . Say why you go, and then go at once.

There is a reply to this from Clara, saying she is not 'a woman of the Sand breed', the prophetess of a 'new morality', and will not desert her husband. Reginald, though he is disappointed, thinks the letter a good one, and sincerely admires the self-sacrificial sentiments expressed in it. He sends it to Lady Midhurst, his grandmother, to show her that she has misjudged Clara.

Lady Midhurst's reply to Reginald is a masterpiece. She tells him Clara sent her the mad letter she had received from him, and asks him why he thinks Clara should have found it necessary to do this save to make ostentatious demonstration of her virtue and to lull suspicion. It was a move:

> to raise herself in my judgement . . . There was no call for her to refer to anybody. She is old enough . . . to manage by herself for herself . . . How could I help her . . . Do you see? it was no bad stroke; just the kind of sharpness you know I always gave her credit for. . . .
> And now for her letter to you.

Lady Midhurst then takes Clara's letter to Reginald to pieces, phrase by phrase, showing the falsity of the sentiment, and asks him why he thinks she said at the end that he was not to show anybody the letter – seeing that it was written to be shown as evidence of her impeccability – if not to put it into his head to show it.

Meanwhile Lady Midhurst's other grandchild, Amicia, continues to give cause for concern. Lady Midhurst writes to her with brisk cynicism:

> . . . Married ladies, in modern English society, *cannot* fail in their duties to the conjugal relation. Recollect that you are devoted to your husband, and he to you. . . . Here is a bit of social comedy in which you happen to have a part to play; act as well as you can, and in the style now received on the English boards.
> . . . I wish to Heaven there were some surgical process discoverable by which one could annihilate or amputate sentiment. Passion, impulse, vice of appetite or conformation, nothing you can define in words is so dangerous. Without sentiment one could do all the good one did either by principle or by instinct, and in either case the good deed would be genuine and valuable. Sinning in the same way, one's very errors would be comprehensible, respectable, reducible to rule. But to act on feeling is ruinous. Feeling is neither impulse nor principle – a sickly, deadly mongrel breed between the two – I hate the very word sentiment. The

animalist and the moralist I can appreciate, but what, on any ground, am I to make of a sentimentalist?

In other words, Lady Midhurst would rule out every tender emotion, every affectionate attachment, and leave us nothing between animal impulse and desiccated principle. It is the negation of the whole pulsating beauty of life. But she is not concerned with beauty; she is the anti-romantic, not puritan, but concerned only with keeping households together, and with the preservation of a traditional order within which her grandchildren are to live. So individual is her character, one feels that Swinburne must have had for it, though he denied it expressly, a living model, and it is interesting to review the woman who could have furnished it.

One need not doubt who was the model for Reginald's father, as he comes out in a letter he writes to his son:

> ... You must be very well aware that for years back you have disgracefully disappointed me in every hope and every plan I have formed with regard to you ... It is poor comfort to reflect that, as far as I know, you have not yet fallen into the more open and gross vices which many miserable young fools think it almost laudable to indulge in. This can but be at best the working of a providential accident, not the outcome of any real self-denial or manly self-restraint on your part. Without this I count all fortuitous abstinence from sin worth very little ...

> ... At school you were incessantly under punishment; at home you were constantly in disgrace. Pain and degradation could not keep you right; to disgrace the most frequent, to pain the most severe, you opposed a deadly strength of sloth and tacit vigour of rebellion. So your boyhood passed; I have yet in my ear the remark of one of your tutors – 'Severity can do little for the boy; indulgence nothing'. What the upshot of your college career was you must remember only too well, and I still hope not without some regret and shame. Absolute inert idleness and wilful vanity, after a long course of violated discipline in small matters, brought you in time to the dishonourable failure you had been at no pains to avoid.

One cannot help wondering whether this is not in part at least a literal transcript of a letter Swinburne had received from his own father, and, as such, very revealing.

The novel moves to its dénouement when the entire Cheyne family go down to Portsmouth for the yachting. There has been a letter from Amicia to Frank in which she reproaches him because, for the first time, she has to lie to her husband; and now, in an unfortunate accident, Lord Cheyne is drowned.

Lady Midhurst, for all her scorn of sentiment, has qualities of character which command our respect in the letter which she writes to Amicia:

> ... As for comfort, my dearest child, what can I say? I have always hated condolence myself: where it is anything, it is bad – helpless and senseless at best. A grievous thing has happened; we can say no more when all comment has been run through. To us for some time – I say to us, callous as you are now thinking me – the loss and misfortune will seem greater than they are. You have the worst of it. Nevertheless, it is not the end of all things. . . . Have as little as you can to do with fear, or repentance, or retrospection of any kind. . . . Stoicism is not an exploded system of faith. It may be available still when resignation in the modern sense breaks down. . . . Courage, taking the word how you will, I have always put at the head of the virtues. Any sort of faith or humility that interferes with it, or impairs its working power, I have no belief in.
>
> But, above all things, I would have you always keep as much as you can of liberty. Give up all for that; sacrifice it to nothing – to no religious theory, to no moral precept.

Here, surely, Swinburne has gone beyond his model, if model he had for this grandmother, and speaks in his own voice.

Subsequent letters reveal that Amicia is pregnant, which is possibly significant in view of her distant relations with her husband during the weeks before his death. It seems to be accepted that Frank, who becomes Lord Cheyne (unless the child she is to bear should disinherit him) must not see Amicia, and a possible marriage for him is considered. He cannot bear the prospect, he confides in a letter to his sister, as between the girl and himself there rises up:

> an invincible exquisite memory of a face . . . pale when I saw it last, as if drawn down by its hair, heavily weighted about the eyes with a presage of tears, sealed with sorrow, and piteous with an infinite unaccomplished desire. The old deep-gold hair and luminous grey-green eyes shot through with colours of sea-water in sunlight, and threaded with faint keen lines of fire and light about the pupil . . .

then that mouth of hers and the shadow made on the chin by the underlip – such sad perfect lips, full of tender power and faith, and her wonderful way of lifting and dropping her face imperceptibly, flower-fashion, when she begins or leaves off speaking. I shall never hear such a voice in the world, either. I cannot, and need not now, pretend to dissemble or soften down what I feel about her. I do love her with all my heart and might. And now that . . . she has fallen miserable and ill . . . If I can never marry the one woman perfectly pleasant to me and faultlessly fit for me in the whole beautiful nature of her, I will never insult her and my own heart by marrying at all.

It has been pointed out that the description is that of Lizzie Rossetti. She was not the woman of Swinburne's own great passion; yet the passage is evidence of how her face and personality haunted him.

Amicia's child is delivered and is a boy, and so becomes Lord Cheyne, in place of Frank. So Lady Midhurst wins; at the end of a year in which several situations threatened, order has been preserved in the family and there will be a regular line of descent through Amicia. In the reader's mind, however, there lingers a suspicion that Frank begat the child by which he is disinherited.

The novel, which is sophisticated, subtle and mature, is a remarkable achievement for a young man who was only twenty-five when he wrote it. On the technical side it is infinitely subtler, as on the human it is infinitely deeper, than the better known novel in letters, *Les Liasons Dangereuses* by Laclos, with which it is sometimes compared.

9

Cheyne Walk, Paris and *Chastelard*

ON his return to London early in 1863, Swinburne took up residence with Rossetti at Tudor House, 16 Cheyne Walk. The strangeness of this household may have been exaggerated, but not much. The red-haired Fanny Cornforth was much present, but although still luscious she was losing her bloom, and tended to become a housekeeper rather than a model. She was still Rossetti's mistress, but he was in love with the black-haired Janey Morris, who sometimes came to pose for him. Not even for Janey, however, could Rossetti forego a model with red hair. In the street he passed a girl with hair exactly the right shade of red; he stopped her, introduced himself and asked her to pose for him. She was Alexa Wilding, and she was at Cheyne Walk the next day.[1]

In the garden Rossetti installed pets, which he purchased as the fancy took him. They included armadillos, hedgehogs, mice and dormice, a Canadian marmot, an ordinary marmot, a racoon, squirrels, wombats, wallabies, kangaroos, two owls (named Jessie and Bobbie), and peacocks. What with the peacocks and the red-haired people whom Rossetti collected, it can hardly have needed his now developing craze for Nankin-blue faience to supply the place with colour.

The peacocks were objected to by the neighbours because of the screech with which they greeted the dawn, and the armadillos because they burrowed. One disappeared, and later came up through the floor of the basement kitchen of an adjacent house, amid astonished servants. The cook, on seeing the scaley, armour-plaited, dog-sized monster emerge, is alleged to have exclaimed, 'If it isn't the Devil, there's no saying what it is!'[2]

The story that Swinburne came sliding down astride the banisters with nothing on may be apocryphal; but Lafourcade believes that he did, at least, pass from one room to another naked, causing Rossetti annoyance.[3]

Bernard Falk, in his memoir[4] of the young Pre-Raphaelite painter Simeon Solomon, asserts that at Cheyne Walk Solomon and Swinburne,

[1] Grylls, *Portrait of Rossetti*, pp. 113–14.
[2] Pedrick, *Life with Rossetti*, pp. 84–85.
[3] Lafourcade, *La Jeunesse*, Vol. I, p. 213.   [4] *Five Years Dead*, pp. 311–31.

both without a stitch of clothing on, chased each other round the house to the desperation of Rossetti, who kept calling out at them to stop. Falk's informant was, it appears, Solomon himself, and as Solomon was given to exaggeration I suspect that this story may be, like that of Swinburne's sliding nude down the banisters, untrustworthy. Nevertheless, there are so many stories about life at Cheyne Walk in which Swinburne figures in a state of nudity that one is inclined to think some at least of them must be true.

What is certain is that during the early part of 1863, Simeon Solomon wrote Swinburne a very long letter, in which he made it quite plain that he was a homosexual and thought Swinburne was one too. One does not know how Swinburne replied to this, and I shall hold over quotation from it, and discussion of Solomon himself and Swinburne's relations with him, until a later chapter dealing with a period in which the correspondence between them came to be continual. At this time there was probably not much more between them than a certain amount of mutual fooling on Rossetti's terrain at Cheyne Walk.

Into this household, Christina and William Michael Rossetti would sometimes step with caution. The rent of the house was £100, and to help defray it, it had been suggested that George Meredith, the novelist, and William Michael become co-tenants. Meredith, being conventional, gave residence only a very short trial before deciding that conditions did not suit him, but he kept on one room as an occasional study; this was on the ground floor right. Swinburne had his on the ground floor left, and while he worked could look out on the Thames, which must have seemed considerably nearer to the window than today, as there was then no embankment. He had also a bedroom upstairs. Rossetti, likewise, had a bedroom upstairs, the ground floor back being his studio, looking out on to the garden and the animals. William Michael, prudently, never took up residence but just called. Fanny Cornforth, though not domiciled at this address, was present much if not most of the time. This was unpleasant to Swinburne, for whom Fanny's terrestrial face, as compared with the etherial face of Lizzie was: 'as a clot of dung in the gutter at nightfall to the splendour of the evening star'.[1] Whether or not Fanny was sensitive to Swinburne's attitude to her, her humiliation as a woman was complete when Rossetti, who had used her as the model for his Lady Lilith, took her face out and painted in that of Alexa Wilding.

James MacNeil Whistler, who loved to paint the Thames in ghostly

[1] Lang, Vol. VI, p. 50.

blue mists, lived in Queen's Road, a few steps from Cheyne Walk. He and Rossetti had been in correspondence the previous year,[1] though it is thought that it was Swinburne who first made Whistler's acquaintance and brought the two painters face to face. Whistler, in his journal, describes an evening when he called at Cheyne Walk:[2] 'The wombat was brought to the table with the coffee and cigars, while Meredith talked brilliantly and Swinburne read aloud pages from *Leaves of Grass*. But Meredith was witty as well as brilliant and the special target of his wit was Rossetti, who as he had invited two or three of his patrons did not appreciate the jest.' In the course of the evening, they lost sight of the wombat. It was expected that it would reappear, but it did not. There was an unhappy sequel to the evening when the cigar box was again opened and the dead body of the wombat found inside. The lid must have been closed on it without anybody's noticing.

Swinburne spent much of his time in Whistler's studio, and became a favourite with Whistler's mother, who lived with him. He also came to know Whistler's friend, the French painter, Alfonse Legros. It is a curious fact that Swinburne numbered more painters than poets amongst his personal friends and acquaintances. The influence of this can be seen in his tendency to describe the two arts in terms of one another.

In March 1863 Swinburne went to Paris with Whistler, who took him to the studio of the French painter, Édouard Manet. Years later, Swinburne wrote to the French symbolist poet, Stéphane Mallarmé:[3]

> ... c'était au printemps de 1863 – que je fus conduit chez M Manet par mes amis MM. Whistler et Fantin; lui sans doute ne s'en souvient pas, mais moi, alors très jeune et tout à fait inconnu (sinon à quelques amis intimes) comme poète ou du moins comme aspirant à ce nom, vous croyez bien que ce fut pour moi un souvenir qui ne s'envolerait facilement.

Fantin was the French painter Fantin Latour.

In the studio Swinburne saw a sketch of Tannhäuser in the Venusberg. This could not have been the inspiration of the *Laus Veneris*, as it had been composed earlier, at least in good part; the sketch was probably shown him by the painters because Whistler knew he was interested in the theme. Swinburne's inspiration was probably Wagner's opera, which was also the inspiration of the sketch.

[1] Lafourcade, p. 110. [2] Lafourcade, *La Jeunesse*, Vol. I, p. 213.
[3] Lang, Vol. III, p. 42.

It must have been in the same spirit that, later in the year, Baudelaire sent Swinburne a copy of his study *Wagner et Tannhäuser*; that the letter mentioning this, and his appreciation of Swinburne's review of *Les Fleurs du Mal*, which he sent by the hand of a M. Nadar, was never delivered was unfortunate, yet not the tragedy some have imagined. Swinburne understood from the receipt of the booklet itself, on Wagner and Tannhäuser, with its inscription, *Bon souvenir et mille remerciements*, that his review in the *Spectator* had been appreciated. Moreover, as he later wrote,[1] 'C[harles] B[audelaire] and I had some friendly intercourse in the way of exchanging messages and review articles.'

The messages were most likely conveyed by Whistler's friend, the painter Legros, who was a personal friend of Baudelaire, and who was always crossing the Channel.

While he was in Paris this time, Swinburne saw the Greek statue *Hermaphroditus* in the Louvre, and wrote the poem which bears the subscription *Au Musée du Louvre, Mars 1863*. Having toyed already in his Oxford days with the idea of hermaphroditism, Swinburne was bound to be interested in the sculpted form:

> Turning the fruitful feud of hers and his
> To the waste wedlock of a sterile kiss.

as he wrote in his poem *Hermaphroditus*.

The word 'sterile' is curious, since there is no means of knowing whether the creature, if it existed in flesh and blood, would be sterile or otherwise. It is probable, however, that Swinburne owed the word not to his inspection of the statue but to his recollection of a literary work inspired by it, *Fragoletta*, by Henri de Latouche. In this, the statue plays a major part, for it is the sight of it (or rather of the well-known Italian copy) in the art gallery of Naples which gives to the heroine a clue as to her own condition. She repulses the hero, leaves her native Italy and dons man's clothes, but later meets and falls in love with his sister; knowing, however, that she cannot consummate the relationship, she evades becoming engaged to her, as the girl's family, supposing Fragoletta to be a man, had expected, and, in an incoherent explanation, refers to 'les dangers steriles'.[2] (The Swinburne scholar Randolph Hughes asserts that Fragoletta is a physical hermaphrodite, in contradistinction from a Lesbian woman, but I can find no warrant for this assumption in the text of Latouche. The dénouement, in which Fragoletta, having

[1] Lang, Vol. III, p. 201.   [2] Latouche, p. 259.

been killed in a duel, is revealed upon the removal of her man's clothes for the laying out of the body, as purely female, seems to make exactly the opposite point.)[1]

That Swinburne had read Latouche's novel is certain, for he wrote a poem called *Fragoletta* which he placed next to *Hermaphroditus* when both poems were later published in a collection (*Poems and Ballads*).[2] He was also to include the name of 'Fragoletta' in a list of peculiar women in a later and more famous poem, *Dolores*. In his poem entitled *Fragoletta*, Swinburne writes:

> Being sightless, wilt thou see?
> Being sexless, wilt thou be
> Maiden or boy?

Why 'sightless'? Latouche's heroine was not blind. It is the statue which is here the real subject. Writing of Fragoletta, he thinks of the statue, just as writing of the statue he thinks of Fragoletta. The sculptor's and the novelist's creation had fused in Swinburne's mind.

It may be remembered that the statue of *Hermaphroditus* (the Italian copy of it) was Shelley's inspiration for *The Witch of Atlas*, and, in part, for the *Epipsychidion*.[3] It was also the inspiration of Théophile Gautier's poem *Contralto*. That Gautier's poem refers to the statue in the Louvre is revealed in the opening:

> On voit dans la musée antique,
> Sur un lit de marbre sculpté,
> Une statue énigmatique
> D'une inquiétante beauté.
>
> . . .
>
> Pour faire sa beauté maudite,
> Chaque sexe apporta son don,
> Tout homme dit: 'C'est Aphrodite!'
> Toute femme: 'C'est Cupidon!'

That Swinburne had read Gautier's poem is obvious from a borrowing from one of the later verses:

[1] Hughes, *Lesbia Brandon* (Appendix), p. 396 and p. 405.
[2] Chatto, Vol. I, pp. 79–88.
[3] See my recent biography, *Shelley* (Cape, 1968).

Sexe douteux, grâce certaine,
On dirait ce corps indécis
Fondu, dans l'eau de la fontaine,
Sous les baisers de Salmacis.

. . .

This becomes, in Swinburne's *Hermaphroditus,*

Love stands upon thy left hand and thy right,
    Yet by no sunset and by no moonrise
    Shall make thee man and ease a woman's sighs,
Or make thee woman for a man's delight.
To what strange end hath some strange god made fair
    The double blossom of two fruitless flowers

. . .

Beneath the woman's and the water's kiss
The moist limbs melted into Salmacis,

. . .

Few pieces of marble, indeed, can have inspired greater quantities of imaginative literature.

Hermaphroditism as a metaphysical concept enters into Balzac's *Seraphita,* which Swinburne had read while at Oxford, as is clear from a phrase in a letter to Bell Scott in February 1860, describing the book he was sending him: 'and the Seraphic individual is a lusus naturae, hermaphrodite, quasi-eunuch or – something'. (My own understanding of Balzac's *Seraphita* was that the she-he was an angel, but no matter.)

Back in London, Swinburne resumed residence with Rossetti at Cheyne Walk. His brief connection with the *Spectator,* which he appears to have owed to Milnes, had come to an end, partly because he was annoyed by the paper's meanness in requiring the return of volumes sent him to review[1] and partly, perhaps, because they were annoyed at his having played a practical joke on them in sending them articles on the work of two non-existent French poets, complete with quotations from their poetry. Apart from a number of shorter poems, he must therefore mainly have been working, in his study overlooking the Thames, on *Chastelard.*

If it was finished, save for some touches, in the spring or summer of

[1] Lang, Vol. I, p. 72.

85

1863, *Chastelard* had been begun at Oxford. On and off, Swinburne had been working at it for a long time. Chastelard was a Frenchman in the train of Mary Stuart, who, when she sailed from France to become Queen of Scots, formed part of her escort. From the pages of the historian Brantôme, Mary's future biographer, who also formed part of this escort and therefore knew Chastelard personally, Swinburne gathered a primary impression of the young man, who was in love with the Queen and wrote poetry in the style of Ronsard and the Pléiade, and who was later executed for having been found, twice, secreted in the Queen's bed-chamber. The discovery that in France the subsequent execution of Mary Queen of Scots had been looked upon as a judgement, a kind of divine or poetic retribution, upon the woman who had allowed her lover to lose his head, fired Swinburne's curiosity.

Pursuing his researches, he found in John Knox's *History of the Reformation*, Volume IV, this significant passage:

> ... the Queene would ly upoun Chattelettis shoulder, and some-tymes prively she wold steall a kyss of his neck ... the familliaritie was so great, that upoun a nycht he privilie did convoy him self under the Quenis bed; but being espyed, he was commanded away. But the bruyte arising, the Quene called the Erle of Murray, and bursting forth in a womanlie affectioun, charged him, 'That as he loved hir, he should slay Chattelett, and let him never speak word.' The other, at the first, maid promesse so to do; but after calling to mynd the judgementis of God pronunced against the scheddaris of innocent bloode, and also that none should dye, without the testimonye of two or thre witnesses, returned and fell upon his kneis befoir the Quene, and said, 'Madam, I beseak your Grace, cause me not tack the bloode of this man upoun me. Your Grace has entreated him so familiarlie befoir, that you have offended all your Nobilitie; and now yf he shalbe secreatlie slane at your awin commandiment, what shall the world judge of it? I shall bring him to the presence of Justice, and let him suffer be law acording to his deserving.' 'Oh,' said the Quene, 'ye will never let him speak?' 'I shall do,' said he, 'Madam, what in me lyeth to saiff your honour.'

It was upon the implication of these lines that Swinburne pivoted his drama. It opens in a room of the palace of Holyrood, the curtain rising to discover the Queen's four women, Mary Beaton, Mary Seyton, Mary Carmichael and Mary Hamilton, who, as if joined by their common Christian name, seem like a kind of chorus. Mary Beaton sings:[1]

> Le navire
> Est à l'eau;
> Entends rire
> Ce gros flot
> Que fait luire
> Est bruire
> Le vieux sire
> Aquilo.
>
> . . .

The second Mary says:

> I know the song; a song of Chastelard's
> He made in coming over with the Queen.
> How hard it rained!

The song, though it is in the style of the Pléiade, is by Swinburne, and, it has been remarked, is of a higher quality than the few lines of Chastelard which have been preserved. It is curious how, with Swinburne, rain is so often the accompaniment of ominous romance. He has been called the poet of the sea; but he is also the poet of rain to set a mood of expectancy.

The two states of water are united in a superbly evocative picture of Mary's arrival at the grey, unwelcoming shore of her future kingdom, as, in speaking to Chastelard, she recalls it:

> Do you not mind at landing how the quay
> Looked like a blind wet face in waste of wind
> And washing of wan waves? how the hard mist
> Made the hills ache? your songs lied loud, my knight,
> They said my face would burn off clouds and rain
>
> . . .

As a counterpoint to the story of Chastelard and the Queen, Swinburne has invented a love of Mary Beaton for Chastelard. Dreaming of the Queen, and in a dim light half expecting her, Chastelard mistakes Mary Beaton for her and embraces her. It is the old trick in the dark, but more credible than in Shakespeare's *Measure for Measure*. It is only for

[1] Chatto, *The Tragedies*, Vol. II.

a moment, during which she has not the strength to break away or speak,
that he is under the illusion:

> . . . I can feel your hair
> Touch me – I may embrace your body too?
> I know you well enough without sweet words.
> How should one make you speak? This is not she.

Mary Beaton is overcome with shame that she did not disclose her
identity at once. As a gentleman, he assures her she has no cause to be
ashamed, and that he does not, as she thinks, hold her in contempt
because of what has happened. She asks him, now, for one kiss, in
courtesy:

> Even the same lips you kissed and knew not of
> Will you kiss now, knowing the shame of them,
> And say no one word to me afterwards,

He can hardly refuse; and the kiss is seen and reported to the Queen.

Very dignified, she says she is not angered; and the episode seems to
have no direct effect upon the scene between herself and Chastelard
which follows. This, though confidential, contains sinister presage in
a dream she has had, of which she tells him:

> . . . I was deep asleep;
> And thinking *I must dream now, or I die,*
> *God send me some good dream lest I be slain,*
> Fell fancying one had bound my feet with cords
> And bade me dance, and the first measure made
> I fell upon my face and wept for pain:
> And my cords broke, and I began the dance
> To a bitter tune; and he that danced with me
> Was clothed in black with long red lines and bars
> And masked down to the lips, but by the chin
> I knew you though your lips were sewn up close
> With scarlet thread all dabbled wet in blood.

She is puzzled. He says: 'An evil dream I hold it for, sweet love.'

Yet neither of them see what she, with the foreknowledge of the unconscious, has seen in the language of sleep's symbols, that she will grant
him the favour he asks, and that, having granted it, she will, to secure
his silence, tie his lips with his blood.

They talk of other things. Darnley, with others, comes in, and, as though the reported kiss in the dark had been working with her, beneath the skin, she makes public suddenly her decision to marry him. The drama moves forward to the time of her wedding. Here, as Swinburne avows, he has falsified history by making Mary's marriage to Darnley take place two years earlier than it did, in order to bring it within the drama of *Chastelard*. Invention where truth is unknown is one thing, but the violation of known fact, in a work which purports to probe with insight the character of the principal *dramatis personae* is another. Mary was, in history, at the time of the affair with Chastelard, an unattached widow, and it seems unnecessary for Swinburne to have made the night on which Chastelard was discovered in her bedroom her wedding-night.

In any case, his discovery by her jealous servitors put her in an awkward position, since she could hardly say, even though it were the case, that he was there by her invitation. She could, however, have 'pardoned' him. This is where the real drama, as Swinburne saw it, begins.

Throughout the whole of the fourth act the Queen oscillates between the promptings of her different advisers and those, equally variable, of her own heart. She speaks with her half-brother, Murray, and, her repute and safety suddenly all to her, insinuates, snake-like, that Chastelard must not be brought to trial:

> If Chastelard have trial openly,
> I am but shamed.
>
> . . .
>
> . . . men might feign belief of him
> For hate of me; it may be he will speak;
>
> . . .
>
> You will not mind me: let him be removed;
> Take means to get me surety: there be means.

Murray, the repugnant truth dawing upon him, asks:

> So, in your mind, I have to slay the man?

With much reluctance he consents, goes out; then comes back and says he will not do it.

Darnley comes in, roughly determined upon Chastelard's execution.

He has brought the warrant for her to sign. She sues to him in the name of pity not to press this on her but consent she free the man. One might think she had repented her cruelty of a moment past, then one reflects that if Chastelard were discharged he would have no need to speak in his defence. It is not kindness but another trick to find a way out of the trap she is in.

Her apparent tenderness arouses Darnley's suspicion; to allay it, she has to sign, but, coming out in her true colours, urges him to have the execution carried out instantly. She seems to have her way, but then she demands the warrant back. Perhaps her heart has asserted itself at last. She sends again for Murray and tells him she has decided to reprieve Chastelard. Even against other adverse advice, she gives him the reprieve to take to Chastelard in his cell.

In the fifth act, in a supreme gesture of meanness, she repents her reprieve and goes to his cell to get it back from him. Her care is needless. He is soliloquizing. Asking only to die in her service, he has been puzzled, not pleased, by the paper. The anticlimax of a life dragged out elsewhere, after this, seems to him dishonouring. But he does not believe in it. He expects a visit:

> I wonder will she come
> Sad at her mouth a little, with drawn cheeks
> And eyelids wrinkled up? or hot and quick
> To lean her head on mine and leave her lips
> Deep in my neck? For surely she must come
> . . .

> . . . she will come to get her warrant back:
> By this no doubt she is sorely penitent,
> Her fit of angry mercy well blown out
> And her wits cool again.

One realizes with incredulity that he anticipates and approves her taking back the reprieve. In another moment she is at the cell door, and is let in by the gaoler. Embarrassed, she speaks of noble concepts, of the superiority of death with honour to life with shame:

> But look you, sweet, if this my warrant hold
> You are but dead and shamed . . .
> . . .

> . . . I know
> I should be nobler, bear a better heart:
> But as this stands – I pray you for good love,
> As you hold honour a costlier thing than life–
> . . .
>
> . . . give you me that again.

He shows her, having with a touch of sadism of his own let her run on for so long, that the warrant is already torn up, and by his own hand. She gasps:

> God help me, sir!
> Have you done this?

Her shock of relief, and of admiration for him, is so great, that she falters:

> Suppose you need not die?

He steadies her, and says it must be so. She says:

> Shall I kiss now? I pray you have no fear
> But that I love you.

In a sudden heat of passion, she almost throws herself upon him, crying:

> What if we lay and let them take us fast,
> Lips grasping lips? I dare do anything.

The prison guard, and others of the execution party enter, and he is taken away.

In the final scene, the execution is witnessed from an upper window, Mary Carmichael looking out and describing what takes place to Mary Beaton. All being at a distance, we are deprived of hearing Chastelard's authentic last words, which were, '*O cruelle Dame! Marie!*' Perhaps the utterance would have interfered with Swinburne's conception of him as a voluntary victim. Instead, we are given a rather horrid description by the window-watcher of the last moments:

> Something he says, if one could hear thus far:
> She leans out, lengthening her throat to hear
> And her eyes shining.

The implication is that the Queen derives a lover's excitement from witnessing her lover's decapitation.

91

Perhaps the nastiest touch, however, is the presence at her side of a 'big man with broad shoulders', with whom she talks. The description applies, one knows, to Bothwell. It is as though Chastelard's frail silhouette were already eclipsed by a heavier.

Rossetti, consulted privately, had doubts as to the wisdom of publication. Perhaps at his suggestion the play, and a number of Swinburne's poems, were forwarded to Ruskin for an opinion. On July 5, 1863, Ruskin replied that he did not think they should be published, 'for they would win him a dark reputation'.[1]

[1] Lafourcade, pp. 112–13.

Northcourt and *Atalanta*

SWINBURNE was always liable to the occasional convulsive movements which, while he was still a child, had troubled his mother. It was while he was visiting Whistler's studio[1] one day that he suffered, so far as is known for the first time, an epileptiform fit, in which he lost consciousness and fell. Whistler's mother, who was present, helped to bring him round. She and Whistler, and Rossetti when he was informed, were most concerned, apparently more so than Swinburne himself; and it was they who consulted a doctor or persuaded Swinburne to receive a doctor's visit. His friends connected the seizure, like the earlier convulsive movements, with cerebral excitement, and the doctor advised a period of rest in the country. That is why, on August 8, we find Swinburne writing to Rossetti from the Isle of Wight:[2] 'I am half living in the sea here, rough or smooth; and generally swimming, riding and croquetting myself into a rampant state of muscular Christianity.'

He was staying at East Dene, with his parents.[3] His sister Edith, whose illness had taken him to Bournemouth the previous year, now fell ill again and, after some weeks of anxiety to all the family, died on September 25, 1863. The rest of the family, perhaps to give themselves a break, now went for a holiday on the Continent. Only Algernon remained behind.

He went to stay with his aunt and cousin, Lady Mary Gordon and Mary Gordon her daughter, at their home, on the western side of the island, Northcourt. While there, he rode over to Farringford, hoping to see Tennyson again, but on arriving found that Mrs. Tennyson was ill and both she and the Laureate 'invisible'. He did not, at first, intend to make his stay there long. On October 11 he wrote to William Michael Rossetti:[4] 'Till I return, which will be in two or three weeks, my direction will be "Northcourt, Shorwell, Isle of Wight."'

[1] Gosse, p. 99.   [2] Lang, Vol. I, p. 86.
[3] Not in Cornwall, as according to Gosse, who confuses this period of rest in the country, prescribed by the doctor, with Swinburne's holiday in Cornwall of the following year.
[4] Lang, Vol. I, p. 89.

The next we hear from him is on December 15, again to W. M. Rossetti:[1]

> ... I don't wonder you were doubtful how to direct; but the truth is having settled down here for quiet with no company but some of my nearest relations and older intimates I have shrunk from moving week after week, perhaps not wisely. But I think after being hard hit one is more afraid of any change than any monotony: and so I let myself be kept beyond the date I had thought of, readily and rather thankfully: especially as one can neither do nothing or *retremper* oneself with riding and walking, one's only choice in a place like this. I wish I could send Gabriel a photograph of it: the old gardens and hall would be in his style: and of all such houses it it is about the quietest.

In this quietness, Swinburne wrote what is generally considered to be his greatest work, *Atalanta in Calydon*. But he had other aids and inspirations than silence. In a letter to his sister Alice, of December 31, he wrote:[2]

> .... My greatest pleasure just now is when Mary practises Handel on the organ; but I can hardly *behave* for delight at some of the choruses. I care hardly more than I ever did for any minor music; but *that* is an enjoyment which wants special language to describe it, being so unlike all others. It crams and crowds me with old and new verses, half remembered and half-made, which new ones will hardly come straight afterwards: but under their influenec I have done some more of my Atalanta which will be among my great doings if it keeps up with its own last scenes throughout.
>
> I repay Mary to the best of my ability but cheaply, by blundering over Greek verbs with her. She keeps her energy fresh by her versatility.

Mary, in her editing of this letter, has deleted all but the initial of her name, though M—— can, in the context, be no one but herself. Swinburne repaid her not merely by teaching her Greek verbs, he helped her write a story, *The Children of the Chapel*, of which more later. He also rode with her, and she asserts in her memoir that it was as they rode together between Newport and Shorwell that he recited to her, for the first time, the most celebrated of the choruses of *Atalanta*, that beginning:

[1] Lang, Vol. I, p. 90.   [2] Leith, p. 61.

When the hounds of spring are on winter's traces,
  The mother of months in meadow or plain
Fills the shadows and windy places
  With lisp of leaves and ripple of rain; . . .

If one is asked the sources Swinburne may have drawn upon for *Atalanta*, the obvious answer would be the *Iliad* Book IX, the *Meleager* of Euripedes, and Ovid's *Metamorphoses* Book VIII. In the same way, one might say that Shelley's source for *Prometheus Unbound* was Aeschylus. It is a partial truth; yet the hero is partly Byron and partly himself, the rocks to which he was chained were those of the Alpine ravines through which Shelley had recently passed, while the wonderful apostrophe to Spring which opens the second act was surely inspired by the lovely spring weather and the circumstances which permitted him to write out of doors. Correspondingly, it was not in Greece but on the wet bushes of the Isle of Wight that Swinburne observed the 'ripple of rain'. And, as the year turned, it was surely all about him that he saw what he put into the lines:

And in the green underwood and cover
  Blossom by blossom the spring begins.

The full streams feed on flower of rushes,
  Ripe grasses trammel a travelling foot,
The faint fresh flame of the young year flushes
  From leaf to flower and flower to fruit.

Atalanta dominates the drama only as Shakespeare's *Julius Caesar* is dominated by the eponymous hero. She does not appear much; it is Althaea who is on stage almost all the time, and who, like Brutus, is the real tragic character. She is the mother of Meleager. At his birth she had dreamed that she brought forth a burning brand, and a prophecy was made that he would live no longer than the brand burning in the fire should remain unconsumed. She snatches the burning wood, plunges it in water, crushes the flame out with her foot and hands, and preserves the charred piece where fire can never come near it.

The goddess Artemis, displeased by the King's neglect of her altars, sends a boar against Calydon, which lays waste the land. The people are unable to destroy it. Those who have tried to do so have been killed by it. Huntsmen from all over Greece come to Calydon to hunt the boar together, and amongst them is the maiden Atalanta.

The opening of the poem finds Althaea in great distress. First she rails against the goddess:

> First Artemis for all this harried land
> I praise not, and for wasting of the boar
> That mars with tooth and tusk and fiery feet
> Green pasturage and the grace of standing corn
> And meadow and marsh with springs and unblown leaves,
> Flocks and swift herds and all that bite sweet grass,
> I praise her not; what things are these to praise.

Her deeper vexation, however, is that her son Meleager rides about with Atalanta. Her objection to this is difficult to understand, since nothing is alleged contrary to Atalanta's honour. The chorus declare:

> . . . this maiden hath no touch of love.
> . . .
>
> She is holier than all holy days or things,
> The sprinkled water or fume of perfect fire;
> Chaste, dedicated to pure prayers, and filled
> With higher thoughts than heaven; a maiden clean,
> Pure iron, fashioned for a sword; and man
> She loves not; what should one such do with love?

Althaea's reply is a very strange one. Convinced that her son is in love with Atalanta, she retorts:

> Look you, I speak not as one light of wit,
> But as a queen speaks, being heart-vexed; for oft
> I hear my brothers wrangling in mid hall,
> And am not moved; and my son chiding them,
> And these things nowise move me, but I know
> Foolish and wise men must be to the end,
> And feed myself with patience; but this most,
> This moves me, that for wise men as for fools
> Love is one thing, an evil thing, and turns
> Choice words and wisdom into fire and air.
> And in the end shall no joy come, but grief,
> Sharp words and soul's division and fresh tears
> Flower-wise upon the old root of tears brought forth,

Fruit-wise upon the old flower of tears sprung up,
Pitiful sighs, and much regrafted pain.
These things are in my presage.

Althaea is a married woman, so her objection cannot be to conjugal love, as such. It is the state of being enamoured which she sees as dangerous, because of the strong tides of emotion it involves. She concludes her speech:

And now, before these gather for the hunt,
I will go arm my son and bring him forth,
Lest love or some man's anger work him harm.

In her following conversation with her son, however, she begins to formulate a precise objection against Atalanta:

Praise be with men abroad; chaste lives with us,
Home-keeping days and household reverences.
. . .
Love thou the law and cleave to things ordained.
. . .
. . . what god applauds new things?
. . .
Child, if a man serve law through all his life
And with his whole heart worship, him all gods
Praise; . . .
. . .
So shall he prosper; not through laws torn up,
Violated rule and a new face of things.
A woman armed makes war upon herself,
Unwomanlike, and treads down use and wont
And the sweet common honour that she hath,
Love, and the cry of children . . .

Here speaks the archetypal conservatism of the traditional, domesticated woman: against the new Cythna-like woman of Shelley's conception, who rides about with men and takes part with them in war and affairs of state. Here speaks classicist against romanticist, and it is remarkable that Swinburne, whose temperament inclined so extremely to the romantic, could produce the note with accents of such authenticity, unless he had a model in some older woman near him. As his mother does not seem to have taken this line, it may not be too imaginative to suggest that his model might be Lady Mary Gordon, his aunt and hostess, and even to see in her criticism of Atalanta some tension in relation with her daughter, the younger Mary, who rode about the Isle of Wight with Swinburne. It is not impossible that the younger Mary Gordon may have seemed 'pure iron'. Evidence for this will transpire later.

Meleager answers the older woman by reminding her of the adventures which he experienced when, with his comrades, he sailed in search of the golden fleece, and the description is that of Swinburne's own experience of the sea:

> . . . we heard
> Clefts hoarse with wind, and saw through narrowing reefs
> The lightning of the intolerable wave
> Flash, and the white wet flame of breakers burn
> Far under a kindling south-wind, as a lamp
> Burns and bends all its blowing flame one way;
> Wild heights untravelled of the wind, and vales
> Cloven seaward by their violent streams, and white
> With bitter flowers and bright salt scurf of brine;
> Heard sweep their sharp swift gales, and bowing birdwise
> Shriek with birds' voices, and with furious feet
> Tread loose the long skirts of a storm; and saw
> The whole white Euxine clash together and fall
> Full-mouthed and thunderous from a thousand throats;

In this magnificent description one may recognize both his boyhood climb up Culver Cliff, where the sea-birds screamed about his head, and the beach at Tynemouth, where the sea foamed through a thousand mouths and nostrils, here become a thousand throats.

With all this experience behind him, Meleager is able to assure his mother that he never saw one like Atalanta:

> . . . but there
> Seeing many a wonder and fearful things to men
> I saw not one thing like this one seen here,
> Most fair and fearful, feminine, a god,
> Faultless; whom I that love not, being unlike,
> Fear, and give honour, and choose from all the gods.

Despite further pleading from his mother that he should remember the time when he was a baby and:

> The small one thing that lying drew down my life
> To lie with thee and feed thee;

Meleager, the fire-brand, goes out to ride, with the maiden Atalanta, to the hunt.

Atalanta speaks, for the first time, and utters a prayer to Artemis:

> Sun, and clear light among green hills, and day
> Late risen and long sought after, and you just gods
> Whose hands divide anguish and recompense,
> But first the sun's white sister, a maid in heaven,
> On earth of all maids worshipped – hail, and hear,
> And witness with me if not without sign sent,
> Not without rule and reverence, I a maid
> Hallowed, and huntress holy as whom I serve,
> Here in your sight and eyeshot of these men
> Stand, girt as they toward hunting, and my shafts
> Drawn;

It was Artemis who had sent the boar, but Artemis was a virgin goddess (in what seems to have been the Greek sense, of a woman never having vowed obedience to a man, rather than what we mean by virgin), and therefore might look with favour on a mortal virgin, untamed and fearless. Atalanta is therefore the best person to address the goddess and to ask her to bless the hunt and let them kill the boar which the goddess herself had sent. The goddess might hear her prayers where she would not hear those of any other.

Thus it is that Atalanta prays:

> . . . Artemis I bid be favourable
> And make this day all golden, hers and ours,
> Gracious and good and white to the unblamed end.

In awe of her, as though she were incarnate with the goddess she invokes and represents, Meleager says:

> For thy name's sake and awe toward thy chaste head,
> O holiest Atalanta, no man dares

Praise thee, though fairer than whom all men praise,
. . .
Pure, and a light lit at the hands of gods.

But Meleager's uncles, who are also of the hunt, like his mother resent
Atalanta, and murmur in a denigrating manner. To take the edge off
their resentment at her presence among them, and at her freedom from
domestic women's duties, she says:

But if toward any of you I am overbold
That take thus much upon me, let him think
How I, for all my forest holiness,
Fame, and this armed and iron maidenhood,
Pay thus much also; I shall have no man's love
For ever, and no face of children born
Or feeding lips upon me or fastening eyes
For ever . . .

She is not simply unwed; she is dedicated; and in her dedication there is
loneliness, which she foresees and accepts. Was there in this, already, a
touch of Swinburne's own foreknowledge that the muse would be his
only bride?

The King bids Atalanta be in good heart and the men be at peace with
her, as they will hunt together to bring down the boar:

O flower of Tegea, maiden, fleetest foot
And holiest head of women, have good cheer,
Of thy good words: but ye, depart with her
In peace and reverence, each with blameless eye
Following his fate; exalt your hands and hearts,
Strike, cease not, arrow on arrow and wound on wound,
And go with gods and with the gods return.

The chorus now breaks again into speech, obscurely foreseeing
trouble; trouble doomed of the gods, who are castigated for their cruel
caprice:

Who hath given man speech? or who hath set therein
A thorn for peril and a snare for sin?
. . .
And circled pain about with pleasure,
    And girdled pleasure about with pain;
. . .

Who makes desire, and slays desire with shame;
  Who shakes the heaven as ashes in his hand;
Who, seeing the light and shadow for the same,
  Bids day waste night as fire devours a brand,
Smites without sword, and scourges without rod;
  The supreme evil, God.

These were the lines which Christina Rossetti was later, in her copy, to cover by pasting over them a thick strip of paper,[1] as also, presumably, over the tremendous climax:

Because thou art cruel and men are piteous,
  And our hands labour and thine hand scattereth;
Lo, with hearts rent and knees made tremulous,
  Lo, with ephemeral lips and casual breath,
  At least we witness of thee ere we die
That these things are not otherwise, but thus;
  That each man in his heart sigheth, and saith,
  That all men even as I,
All we are against thee, against thee, O God most high.

This tremendous comminatory passage, though expressing what many, particularly Shelley in his *Prometheus Unbound* and Byron in his *Cain*, have felt about the operations of an apparently irresponsible and uncaring Deity, seems un-Greek, and out of key with the narrative, unless as the foreshadowing of tragedy to come.

The hunters then ride off:

Through woods and waste lands cleft by stormy streams,
Past yew-trees and the heavy hair of pines,
And where the dew is thickest under oaks,
This way and that . . .

in search of the boar. At last they sight 'The blind bulk of the immeasurable beast'. One of Meleager's uncles draws his bow, but his arrow misses, merely rousing the boar. The men all stand, afraid to close nearer to him. Atalanta alone goes firmly forward and, taking a cool aim, shoots the first arrow which scores a hit. After that they all shoot, and it is Meleager's missile which effects the kill. The carcass is then flayed, and Meleager gives the head and hide to Atalanta.

[1] Packer, *Christina Rossetti,* p. 353.

SWINBURNE

The uncles are incensed that she should be given the spoil, when the destruction of the boar was the work of all of them. This was ungracious, for it was probably only for her sake that Artemis let the beast be slain. Meleager, immeasurably indignant at their meanness of spirit, kills both of them.

Althaea, when she is told this by a messenger, to avenge her brothers takes from its place of safety the charred brand she has preserved since Meleager's birth, and commits it to the fire. Watching it consume, she says:

> Meleager, a fire enkindled at mine hands
> And of my hands extinguished; this is he.
> . . .
> I did this and I say this and I die.

That her brothers should be dearer to a mother than her child seems psychologically unusual, but it is in accordance with the Greek myth; Swinburne did not invent it.

Having acted, Althaea realizes how she has bereaved herself, and her mother's nature reasserts itself:

> I am kindled with the flames that fade in him,
> I am swollen with subsiding of his veins,
> I am flooded with his ebbing; my lit eyes
> Flame with the falling fire that leaves his lids
> Bloodless; my cheek is luminous with blood
> Because his face is ashen. Yet, O child,
> Son, first-born, fairest – O sweet mouth, sweet eyes,
> That drew my life out through my suckling breast,
> That shone and clove mine heart through–O soft knees
> Clinging, O tender treadings of soft feet,
> Cheeks warm with little kissings–O child, child,
> What have we made of each other?

Meleager, feeling his life ebbing from him, begs Atalanta not to let his name perish, and, as he is about to die, to kiss him and to lie upon him:

> And stretch thyself upon me and touch hands
> With hands and lips with lips . . .

Atalanta, presumably after doing as he has asked, says:

> Hail thou: but I with heavy face and feet
> Turn homeward and am gone out of thine eyes.

It is customary to regard *Atalanta in Calydon* as a work expressing an extreme fatalism, wherein the humans are no more than pawns of gods, doomed. Yet, except for the magical *rapport* between Meleager and the brand, there is nothing which happens to the characters which was not in their power to avert. Althaea did not have to be so insanely jealous of her son's joining the hunt with Atalanta, the uncles so grudging, Meleager so hot-headed as to murder them, nor Althaea to avenge them by murdering her son. Though it seems so stark, the tragedy is of the characters' own making.

The Triumph of Time

ONLY once in his life did Swinburne make an overture to a woman, and it is the maddening nub of Swinburne studies that her identity is a matter of deduction.

His first biographer, Edmund Gosse, publishing in 1917, equated her, on the authority of his recollection of a conversation with Swinburne in 1876, with 'a young kinswoman' of a Dr. and Mrs. John Simon whom Swinburne would have known through Burne-Jones. Three light but charming stanzas entitled *To Boo* were produced from among Swinburne's papers, after his death, by the too well known T. J. Wise, and 'Boo' was the pet-name of this girl, Jane Faulkner, niece and adopted daughter of the Dr. Simon in question. All subsequent writers on Swinburne: Chew, Nicolson, Hughes and Shanks, following Gosse and Lafourcade, took it for granted that this was the girl to whom Swinburne declared himself. The composition of *The Triumph of Time*, which tells of the rejection of this unique affection, was then ascribed to 1862, when he knew her, until the American scholar, Mr. John Mayfield, made a thorough investigation. The most startling of the facts Mr. Mayfield uncovered was that in 1862 Jane Faulkner would have been only ten years old.[1]

Gosse was somewhat given to reliance upon his recollection of conversations without the special checking which oral testimony requires, particularly when, as in this case, forty years had elapsed between the hearing and the setting down. Doubtless Swinburne at some time mentioned this child to him, and in his mind he confused what he heard with the great tragedy of Swinburne's life.

To whom, then, did Swinburne write the desolated lines beginning:

> Before our lives divide for ever,
>> While time is with us and hands are free,
> (Time, swift to fasten and swift to sever
>> Hand from hand, as we stand by the sea)
> I will say no word that a man might say

[1] *Swinburne's Boo*, 1954, p. 7.

Whose whole life's love goes down in a day;
For this could never have been; and never,
   Though the gods and the years relent, shall be.

Is it worth a tear, is it worth an hour,
   To think of things that are well outworn:
Of fruitless husk and fugitive flower,
   The dream foregone and the deed forborne?
Though joy be done with and grief be vain,
Time shall not sever us wholly in twain;
Earth is not spoiled by a single shower;
   But the rain has ruined the ungrown corn.

It will grow not again, this fruit of my heart,
   Smitten with sunbeams, ruined with rain.
The singing seasons divide and depart,
   Winter and summer depart in twain.
It will grow not again, it is ruined at root,
The bloodlike blossom, the dull red fruit;
Though the heart yet sickens, the lips yet smart,
   With sullen savour of poisonous pain.

Rhythm and music so knit each stanza into a whole, and one is so pulled onward by the forward motion of the poem, that it is easy to pass over the significance of individual lines. Yet there are several over which it is worth while to pause, for their autobiographical content. The poet's 'whole life goes down in a day'; such a phrase surely evokes not a sudden infatuation for a girl whom he knew only for a short period, but the ruin of a relationship which had been meaningful to him through his whole life, the shattering of 'a dream', which he had tried to bring into the world of reality.

It is generally assumed that Swinburne had proposed marriage to the person to whom he wrote this poem, but nowhere in the poem do we find regret for a domestic future which might have been, but only for 'the deed forborne', in other words a single act of sex, which seems an unusual thing to ask of an unmarried girl who had been a companion to him all his life, unless there were some reason why they could not marry. Perhaps it was the case, as he says, that 'this could never have been'. The only unmarried girl with whom he is known to have been friends was his cousin, Mary Gordon, and if *The Triumph of Time* was written of something which happened in the Isle of Wight, the natural assumption would be that it must be she. They were cousins, but at first sight there would appear to be no impediment to their marriage. When, however, one looks into it, a different situation emerges. Not only were their mothers sisters, both daughters of the Earl of Ashburnham, but their fathers were first cousins, being the sons of two brothers, who were, in their turn, first cousins to the Countess of Ashburnham. Mary and Algernon had common blood by so many streams that it may well have been thought these two should not marry, particularly as Algernon's twitching, and his epileptiform fit if the family knew of it, may in itself have been taken as a warning against the danger of inbreeding. Their parents, or Mary's parents, may have represented to them that to bring into the world children still further inbred would be irresponsible; though that being the case, it seems cruel, or at least thoughtless, to have brought them up so much together. It was a family like that which Swinburne had depicted in *Love's Cross Currents*, in which cousins revolved around cousins as though no outside persons existed, and the danger had not been seen until the eleventh hour.

We have not yet proved that the setting of the drama is Northcourt; but one thing is certain: it did not take place in London, as it would have to have done had its focus been the 'Boo' Swinburne knew through Burne-Jones. Not only do Swinburne and the girl with whom he must have no closer link stand hand in hand 'by the sea', the coastal and country setting is further described and developed in verses which come later:

I have put my days and my dreams out of mind,
. . .
But clear are these things; the grass and the sand,
Where, sure as the eyes reach, ever at hand,
With lips wide open and face burnt blind,
   The strong sea-daisies feast on the sun.

The low downs lean to the sea; the stream,
   One loose thin pulseless tremulous vein,
Rapid and vivid and dumb as a dream,
   Works downward, sick of the sun and the rain;
No wind is rough with the rank rare flowers;
. . .

There are many sea-coasts; Swinburne often described the rock and
shingle beaches of Northumberland, but this was a coast with a sandy
beach, down to which swept low, grassy downs, and between them a
stream. 'Rank rare flowers' are curious, because rare, if it means rarified,
is the contrary of rank or coarse. Perhaps 'rare' is put in only for alliteration, thoughtlessly. Or, just conceivably, it could mean rare in the sense
of a seldom found species.

He tells us more about the nature of his passion:

> There will no man do for your sake, I think,
>   What I would have done for the least word said.
> I had wrung life dry for your lips to drink,
>   Broken it up for your daily bread:
> Body for body and blood for blood,
> As the flow of the full sea risen to flood
> That yearns and trembles before it sink,
>   I had given, and laid down for you, glad and dead.
>
> Yea, hope at highest and all her fruit,
>   And time at fullest and all his dower,
> I had given you surely, and life to boot,
>   Were we once made one for a single hour.
> But now, you are twain, you are cloven apart,
> Flesh of his flesh, but heart of my heart;
> And deep in one is the bitter root,
>   And sweet for one is the lifelong flower.

It may be that when this was written Swinburne had just been told it
had been arranged for Mary to marry Colonel Leith, and that she had
agreed. Because it was a violation of the special relationship which
existed between them, he says passionately.

> Yea, I know this well; were you once sealed mine,
>   Mine in the blood's beat, mine in the breath,
> Mixed into me as honey in wine,
>   Not time, that sayeth and gainsayeth,
> Nor all strong things had severed us then;
> Not wrath of gods, nor wisdom of men,
>   . . .

He reproaches her:

You have chosen and clung to the chance they sent you,
   Life sweet as perfume and pure as prayer,
But will it not one day in heaven repent you?
   Will they solace you wholly, the days that were?
Will you lift up your eyes between sadness and bliss,
Meet mine, and see where the great love is,
And tremble and turn and be changed?

He thinks of what might have been:

But you, had you chosen, had you stretched hand,
   Had you seen good such a thing were done,
I too might have stood with the souls that stand
   In the sun's sight, clothed with the light of the sun.

Beaten by the situation, he seeks relief in the sea:

I will go back to the great sweet mother,
   Mother and lover of men, the sea.
I will go down to her, I and none other,
   Close with her, kiss her and mix her with me;
Cling to her, strive with her, hold her fast;
O fair white mother, in days long past
Born without sister, born without brother,
   Set free my soul as thy soul is free.

O fair green-girdled mother of mine,
   Sea, that art clothed with the sun and the rain,
Thy sweet hard kisses are strong like wine,
   Thy large embraces are keen like pain.
Save me and hide me with all thy waves,
Find me one grave of thy thousand graves,
Those pure cold populous graves of thine
   Wrought without hand in a world without stain.

Was this sea, in which he plunges to extinguish his fever that which
lapped the Isle of Wight, and near to Northcourt?

There are other, lesser, poems which may be taken with *The Triumph
of Time*. One is *A Leave-Taking*, which obviously treats the same theme,
his rejected love and refuge in the sea:

Let us rise up and part; she will not know.
Let us go seaward as the great winds go,

Full of blown sand and foam; what help is here?
There is no help: for all these things are so,
And all the world is bitter as a tear.

There is another poem, which, though it was composed earlier and printed in the *Spectator* of 1862, and has nothing of tragedy, I take with these poems of parting because it mentions his love and has the same setting: it is *The Sundew*:

A little marsh-plant, yellow green,
And pricked at lip with tender red.
Tread close, and either way you tread
Some faint black water jets between
Lest you should bruise the curious head ...

Wind blows and bleaches the strong grass,
Blown all one way to shelter it
From trample of strayed kine, with feet
Felt heavier than the moorhen was,
Strayed up past patches of wild wheat.

You call it sundew: here it grows,
. . .
O red-lipped mouth of marsh-flower,
I have a secret halved with thee.
The name that is love's name to me
Thou knowest, and the face of her
Who is my festival to see.

This, then, was a plant that they had seen together, either on holidays at Capheaton or during their walks and rides in the Isle of Wight. I consulted a number of works on flowers and herbs in the hope of discovering that it might have, in addition to its usual name of *Sundew*, some popular name which contained the name 'Mary', or some homophonic syllables. This I was unable to trace, but what I did find was more remarkable. The plant, which is carnivorous, and covered on the leaves with coarse, bristly red hairs, is rare in England, one of the few places where it is to be found being the Isle of Wight.[1]

[1] *Green Medicine* by Mrs. C. F. Leyel (Faber), p. 122.

12

Landor: Howell: Aimless Days

SWINBURNE had intended resuming residence at Cheyne Walk when he returned disconsolate, from the Isle of Wight to London, but he found now that Rossetti did not wish him to come back. A manuscript note found after his death attached to *A Record of Friendship* reads:[1]

> It was not without surprise that after a separation of many months spent by me in the country I received from my friend a letter, couched in language as affectionate and cordial as had been the terms in which we parted when an impelling domestic affliction had summoned me from London, but intimating with all possible apology that he wished to have the house at Chelsea to himself; . . .

Nevertheless, it seems that Swinburne went back, if only briefly, for a letter dated February 22, which being about his essay on Blake seems to be of 1864, bears the address 16 Cheyne Walk.

After that, he went for a holiday to Italy. On March 31, that is just before his twenty-seventh birthday, he wrote from Florence to Milnes, or, as he had recently become, Lord Houghton. They had travelled together as far as Paris, and Swinburne's letter was chiefly to say that he had made the acquaintance in Florence of Walter Savage Landor, with whom Milnes had been friends since before Swinburne's birth. Swinburne had written to and received an invitation to call upon the elder poet,[2] who was in his ninetieth year:

> . . . . and found him as alert, brilliant and altogether delicious as I suppose others may have found him twenty years since. I cannot thank you enough for procuring me this great pleasure and exquisite satisfaction – I am seriously more obliged for this than for anything that could have been done for me. . . . I should like to throw up all other things . . . and devote myself to playing valet to him for the rest of his days. I should black his boots if he wore any – moi. He has given me the great shock of adoration which one feels at thirteen toward great men . . . Not that I am disloyal to Tennyson, into whose church we were all in my time born and

[1] Lafourcade, *La Jeunesse*, Vol. I, p. 219.
[2] Lang, Vol. I, pp. 96–98.

baptised as far back as we can remember at all; but he is not a
Greek nor a heathen; and I imagine does not want to be; . . .

Gosse does not give his source for the story that Swinburne went
down on both knees to Landor, and it may be an exaggeration.

On his return to London we find him writing first from Bedford
Street, near the British Museum, and then from his Aunt Julia's in
Mount Street, in each case to his old friend John Nichol, from whom he
received a letter two days after his return from Italy. Nichol was coming
to London for three days, and they met again. In June Swinburne wrote
that since their meeting he had read the whole of Browning's new book;
he admired the power of *Caliban* and *Sludge*, but: 'In all the rest of the
book I see much that is clever and nothing that is good—much that is
ingenious and nothing that is right.'[1] When one recalls how great had
been his early hero-worship of Browning, one realizes that here was a
big change of attitude.

Though he had moved from Cheyne Walk, he still called there without formality, and met at Rossetti's a slightly sinister character, George
Augustus Howell, who had, in 1864, just returned to London after five
years in Portugal. It was said that he had fled there because he was
suspected of complicity in the Orsini conspiracy. He had been born in
Oporto, on March 10, 1840,[2] the son of an English businessman and a
Portuguese woman, and had been brought up in Portugal. He made
many fanciful claims, and was notoriously light-fingered where rare
porcelain, books and paintings were concerned, being a collector; but
Rossetti, though not under any illusions as to his character, found him
amusing. He composed a limerick:[3]

> There's a Portuguese person named Howell
> Who lays on his lies with a trowel;
> When I goggle my eyes
> And start with surprise
> It's at monstrous big lies told by Howell.

This person entered to some extent into Swinburne's life, and was not
amongst the most helpful influences he encountered.

About this time a young Cornish artist, Henry Treffry Dunn, came
to live at Cheyne Walk as art assistant to Rossetti. Before long, he was

[1] Lang, Vol. 1, p. 100.
[2] Angeli, *Pre-Raphaelite Twilight*, p. 28.
[3] Angeli, *Rossetti*, p. 131.

unofficial keeper of the accounts, which brought him into rivalry with
Fanny, who felt that he was impinging on her side of things. With
Treffry Dunn, Swinburne seems to have got on well, a common bond
being perhaps that they both resented the presence of Fanny: rather un-
fairly, for it is difficult to see what Rossetti would have done without 'the
good elephant' to look after his creature comforts.

Treffry Dunn wrote in his memoirs:[1]

Swinburne was a frequent visitor at Cheyne Walk, and I
remember well his calling one evening when Rossetti was absent
on some china-collecting expedition. It had been a very sultry day,
and with the advancing twilight, heavy thunder-clouds were
rolling up. The door opened and Swinburne entered. He appeared
in an abstracted state, and for a few minutes sat silent.

Soon, something I had said anent his last poem set his thoughts
loose. Like the storm that had just broken, so he began in low
tones to utter lines of poetry. As the storm increased, he got more
and more excited and carried away by the impulse of his thoughts,
bursting into a torrent of splendid verse that seemed like some
grand air with the distant peals of thunder as an intermittent accompaniment. And still the storm waxed more violent, and the vivid
flashes of lightning became more frequent. But Swinburne seemed
unconscious of it all, and whilst he paced up and down the room,
pouring out bursts of passionate declamation, faint electric sparks
played round the wavy masses of his luxuriant hair.

I lay on the sofa in a corner of the studio and listened in wonder
and with a curious awe, for it appeared to me as though the very
figures in the pictures that were on the easels standing about the
room were conscious of and sympathized with the poet and his
outpurings. The 'Proserpine' gazed out more mournfully. . . .

On the other side looked out through her frame the 'Blessed
Damosel', and . . . 'Cassandra', away in the farthermost part of the
studio, peered through the gloom, as though joining with the others
in watching the poet as he impetuously strode up and down the
room, each flash of lightning revealing him as one inspired, his
wealth of hair giving forth a scintillation of tiny electric sparks
which formed, as it were, a faint halo round his head. Amidst the
rattle of thunder he still continued to pour out his thoughts, his
voice now sinking low and sad, now waxing louder as the storm
listed.

[1] Quoted by his great-nephew, Pedrick, *Life with Rossetti*, pp. 102–3 and 97.

How long his ecstasy would have lasted I know not. I was
wondering, when the sounds of a latchkey and the closing of the
hall door were heard. In another minute Rossetti entered the
studio, boisterously shaking off the raindrops from his Inverness
cape, and with a 'Hullo! old fellow!' welcomed Swinburne. Divest-
ing himself of his cape, he lit the gas, sat down with his friend, and
the night began anew. Their conversation, upon many things,
went on hour after hour, until the dawn began to appear.

Apart from this most evocative recapturing of the atmosphere of
things past, Treffry Dunn gives us an occasional more casual glimpse:[1]

> Smoking was indulged in by most of Rossetti's friends, although
> he, to his frequent regret, could never venture to touch either
> pipe, cigar, or cigarette. William Michael Rossetti, however, made
> up for his brother's inability on this score. Swinburne was also a
> non-smoker. I do not think I ever saw him attempt even a cigarette.
> Howell was never without one; from morn till night he smoked,
> and the amount of cigarette ends he threw away in a day might well
> have made a good ounce weight of tobacco.

Swinburne did not smoke, but he drank. His inebriation became, in
later days, so legendary that Gosse, when he came to write his biography,
was surprised to find that neither Lord Bryce nor Lord Sheffield who
knew him at Oxford could recollect his ever having been the worse for
liquor during his time there. Lord Redesdale told Gosse he believed it
was Richard Burton—whom Swinburne had met in 1861 at Milnes'
house—who had introduced him to brandy; but it seemed to be only
from 1864 or 65 that the habit of excessive drinking so seized Swinburne
as to cause all his friends distress and alarm.

In other words, he drank immoderately only from the time of his
return from the Isle of Wight with the knowledge that his cousin, Mary
Gordon, would not be his. He plunged into alcohol to kill the misery.

In some ways, it was unfortunate for Swinburne that his father made
him so generous an allowance. It is true that a creative writer needs
leisure if he is to produce any volume of work; yet if in the days of his
grief he had had to go to an office at regular hours the discipline might
have been helpful to him. As it was, there was nothing for him between
poetry and debauchery. He had filled in some time by making the pil-
grimage to see Landor before he died, but having done that and come
home, his days were aimless; which is the worst condition for fighting a
disappointment in love.

[1] Ibid, p. 97.

13

Dolores

IT is not possible to determine exactly when Swinburne composed *Dolores*, but it was probably in this period. When (later) William Michael Rossetti suggested that, for a special edition, *Dolores* should be bracketed with *The Garden of Proserpine* and *Hesperia*, Swinburne replied:[1] '. . . I should not like to bracket "Dolores" and the two following as you propose. I ought (if I did) to couple with them in front harness "The Triumph of Time", etc., as they express that state of feeling the reaction from which is expressed in "Dolores."'

In other words, *The Triumph of Time*, which tells of his rejection by his cousin Mary, should be placed first, and the other poems, which tell of his consequent desolation and of the bitter and angry turbulence of his feelings following that rejection, should be placed after it. This suggests that Mary Gordon is 'Dolores':[2]

> Cold eyelids that hide like a jewel
> > Hard eyes that grow soft for an hour;
> The heavy white limbs, and the cruel
> > Red mouth like a venomous flower;
> When these are gone with their glories.
> > What shall rest of thee then, what remain,
> O mystic and sombre Dolores,
> > Our Lady of Pain?

It may not be too fanciful to see in the 'red mouth like a venomous flower' a similitude to the 'red-lipped mouth' of the carnivorous plant by which, rather ominously, they had walked or sat and perhaps made love in the Isle of Wight.

Of course, Swinburne exaggerates in this poem the wickedness of his 'Lady of Pain'; but he had done this before when, in the try-out for *Love's Cross Currents*, he had endowed Reginald with the sister, Helen, who gloated as she watched the life of a man being beaten out upon the rocks. There he had been developing to monstrous proportions, under the influence of de Sade, what was presumably but a slight trait of

[1] Lang, Vol. I, p.197.

114

sadism in her character. De Sade, the coast at Tynemouth and Mary had together inspired that fragment; he had set his cousin, in his imagination, upon such a rock as he could see, and developed the situation as de Sade might have done, had he thought of anybody being murdered by the sea. In a similar way, he had drawn her as Mary Stuart, when he had made her stretch out her neck, her eyes shining, to watch the beheading of Chastelard.

In the same way, Swinburne builds up his poem upon Mary's bad characteristics rather than her good ones, and exaggerates them when he says:

> Seven sorrows the priests gave their Virgin;
>   But thy sins, which are seventy times seven,
> Seven ages would fail thee to purge in,
>   And then they would haunt thee in heaven;

Reproach to her for having become engaged to someone with whom she will not have a life of the same passion may be seen in lines reminiscent of *The Triumph of Time*:

> Bite hard, lest remembrance come after
>   And press with new lips where you pressed.
> For my heart too springs up at the pressure,
>   Mine eyelids too moisten and burn; . . .

> In yesterday's reach and tomorrow's
>   Out of sight though they lie of today,
> There have been and there yet shall be sorrows
>   That smite not and bite not in play.
> The life and the love thou despisest,
>   These hurt us indeed, and in vain,
> O wise among women, and wisest,
>   Our Lady of Pain.

It is the following lines, however, which represent the beginning of an embroidery. Mary was an unmarried girl and probably: except for whatever embraces she may have given Swinburne, without sexual experience.

> Who gave thee thy wisdom? What stories
>   That stung thee, what visions that smote?
> Wert thou pure and a maiden, Dolores,
>   When desire took thee first by the throat?

Even in his undergraduate days, in the fragment *Laugh and Lie Down*, he had built her up as the courtesan Imperia; so now, again, he develops her character into that of a great courtesan, and in so doing produces one of his most famous lines:

> We shift and bedeck and bedrape us,
>   Thou art noble and nude and antique;

It is always possible that they had seen each other nude, if they bathed without costumes, as might have been the case when they were children. One should remember that in the *Kirklowes* fragment Helen watches Reginald, aged fourteen already, swimming in a pool apparently naked. It may have been thought, naïvely, that the brother and sister familiarity in which they had been brought up would preclude the possibility of desire.

One famous couplet, however, seems simply to play upon the themes and sub-titles of *Justine* and *Juliette*, and shows how strong was still the influence of de Sade:

> Could you hurt me, sweet lips, though I hurt you?
>   Men touch them, and change in a trice
> The lilies and languors of virtue
>   For the raptures and roses of vice;

Though one knows from the regret in *The Triumph of Time* that his union with Mary was never 'once sealed' by a complete act of sex: one wonders how far their embraces may not have gone, when one comes to the lines:

> Ah beautiful passionate body
>   That never has ached with a heart!
> On thy mouth though the kisses are bloody,
>   Though they sting till it shudder and smart . . .

Again:

> As our kisses relax and redouble,
>   From the lips and the foam and the fangs . . .

He builds her up and, in the same way that, in his first play, he had made Rosamund claim identity with Helen of Troy as the archtype of the eternal seductress, so now he sees 'Dolores', his 'Lady of Pain', as one of the women of ancient Rome who sat in the Colosseum to watch men torn to pieces by wild beasts or fighting each other to the death:

> There the gladiator, pale for thy pleasure,
> Drew bitter and perilous breath;

This, though it may seem melodramatic, is probably very shrewd psychological observation. Finally, going further back, he compares her to the goddess Cybele, whose rites were celebrated on Dindymus' hill, to Astarte and to Ashtaroth. Only one comparison he fails to make, and, Swinburne's erudition being so great, it is extraordinary he overlooked it; and that is with the Brauronian Artemis, for whose worship boys were whipped.

14

Faustine

WITH this picture of 'Dolores' in one's mind, can one doubt that *Faustine*, the greatest of Swinburne's diabolic poems: prefixed with the words used by the gladiators to salute the empress before combat began, though composed earlier, was equally a tribute to his cousin?

FAUSTINE

Ave Faustine Imperatrix, Morituri te salutant

> Lean back, and get some minutes' peace;
>   Let your head lean
> Back to the shoulder with its fleece
>   Of locks, Faustine.
>
> The shapely silver shoulder stoops,
>   Weighed over clean
> With state of splendid hair that droops
>   Each side, Faustine.
>
> Let me go over your good gifts
>   That crown you queen;
> A queen whose kingdom ebbs and shifts
>   Each week, Faustine.
>
> Bright heavy brows well gathered up:
>   White gloss and sheen;
> Carved lips that make my lips a cup
>   To drink, Faustine,
>
> Wine and rank poison, milk and blood,
>   Being mixed therein
> Since first the devil threw dice with God
>   For you, Faustine.
>
> Your naked new-born soul, their stake,
>   Stood blind between;

God said 'Let him that wins her take
    And keep Faustine.'

But this time Satan throve, no doubt;
    Long since, I ween,
God's part in you was battered out;
    Long since, Faustine.

The die rang sideways as it fell,
    Rang cracked and thin,
Like a man's laughter heard in hell
    Far down, Faustine.

A shadow of laughter like a sigh,
    Dead sorrow's kin;
So rang, thrown down, the devil's die
    That won Faustine.

A suckling of his breed you were,
    One hard to wean;
But God, who lost you, left you fair,
    We see, Faustine.

You have the face that suits a woman
    For her soul's screen—
The sort of beauty that's called human
    In hell, Faustine.

You could do all things but be good
    Or chaste of mien;
And that you would not if you could,
    We know, Faustine.

Even he who cast seven devils out
    Of Magdalen
Could hardly do as much, I doubt,
    For you, Faustine.

Did Satan make you to spite God?
    Or did God mean
To scourge with scorpions for a rod
    Our sins, Faustine?

I know what queen at first you were,
    As though I had seen
Red gold and black imperious hair
    Twice crown Faustine.

As if your fed sarcophagus
    Spared flesh and skin,
You came back face to face with us,
    The same Faustine.

She loved the games men played with death,
    Where death must win;
As though the slain man's blood and breath
    Revived Faustine.

Nets caught the pike, pikes tore the net;
    Lithe limbs and lean
From drained out pores dripped thick red sweat
    To soothe Faustine.

She drank the steaming drift and dust
    Blown off the scene;
Blood could not ease the bitter lust
    That galled Faustine.

All round the foul fat furrows reeked,
    Where blood sank in;
The circus splashed and seethed and shrieked
    All round Faustine . . .

It must be said that the poem has a wonderful, never faltering firmness of texture, and the feat of making the second line in every verse rhyme with Faustine, though a tour de force, hardly ever forced or awkward. The lines fall with a weight, and the poem has a certain carved quality, which could be compared to the effect of sculpture.

The poem first appeared in the *Spectator*, in May 1862, and according to Whistler's *Journal* was composed in a train, when a small party of friends which included Rossetti and Meredith made a joint expedition to Hampton Court:[1] '. . . between Waterloo and Hampton Court each wrote a poem. Swinburne's poem was *Faustine*. He wanted to know how many rhymes he could find to the name.' But it was more than a joke, or an exercise in virtuosity. Swinburne had seen his model plain.

[1] Lafourcade, *La Jeunesse*, Vol. I, p. 261 n.

But his cousin had inspired not only the Satanic poems. The romantic lyric, *Madonna Mia*, relates evidently to Northcourt:

> Under green apple-boughs
> That never a storm will rouse,
> My lady hath her house
>   Between two bowers;
> In either of the twain
> Red roses full of rain; . . .

One remembers the wet flowers in *Rosamund*, and recognizes a recurrent symbol of ill-presaged love.

Rococo again tells of the parting:

> We twain once well in sunder,
>   What will the mad gods do
> For hate with me, . . .

while the lines:

> Say March may wed September,
> And time divorce regret;

refer plainly to the fact that Colonel Leith, his cousin's fiancé, was twenty-one years older than she was.

In *The Garden of Proserpine* she becomes, as it were, the essence of the poppies which give sleep. And in *Hesperia* the two ideas, of Proserpine and Dolores, are gathered up together in the lines:

> Was it myrtle or poppy thy garland was woven with,
>   O my Dolores?
>   . . .
> . . . Our Lady of Pain
>   . . .
>   Our Lady of Sleep.

But *Hesperia*, as the title implies, is Venus when the planet is in the west, and is written, obviously, on or in memory of a coast from which one could look westward to see Venus becoming visible over the sea as the sun sets behind its rim:

Out of the golden remote wild west where the sea without shore is,
    Full of the sunset, and sad, if at all, with the fullness of joy,
As a wind sets in with the autumn that blows from the region of stories,
    Blows with a perfume of songs and of memories beloved from a boy,

Blows from the capes of the past oversea to the bays of the present,
Filled as with shadow of sound with the pulse of invisible feet,
Far out to the shallows and straits of the future, by rough ways or
    pleasant,
Is it thither the wind's wings beat? is it hither to me, O my sweet?
For thee, in the stream of the deep tide-wind blowing in with the water,
Thee I beheld as a bird borne in with the wind from the west,
Straight from the sunset, across white waves whence rose as a daughter
Venus thy mother, . . .

In other words he is standing, in recollection, upon a western seaboard,
and so can see Venus over the sea in the evening, as would be the case
if he went down to the sea from Northcourt, at any beach between St.
Catherine's Point and the Needles, though not from the side of the
island on which was his parents' home. The planet becomes his human
love, in one of the few passages in which she is represented as, at precious
moments, kind:

Thine eyes that are quiet, thine hands that are tender, thy lips that are
    loving,
Comfort and cool me as dew . . .

And one wonders how it could have been overlooked that it was in
the Isle of Wight his one love affair had its setting when one comes to
the lines:

By the sands where sorrow has trodden, the salt pools bitter and sterile,
By the thundering reef and the low sea-wall and the channel of years,
Our wild steeds press on the night, strain hard through pleasure and
    peril,
Labour and listen and pant not or pause for the peril that nears;
And the sound of them trampling the way cleaves night as an arrow
    assunder,
And slow by the sand-hill and swift by the down with its glimpse of
    grass,
Sudden and steady the music, as eight hoofs trample and thunder,
    . . .

'Eight hoofs' are not the kind of detail a poet puts in at random, for
atmosphere. They are the hoofs of Swinburne's and Mary's horses as
they rode all over the island.

The volume of Swinburne's writing at this time altogether exceeded that of his publications. His brief connection with the *Spectator* had come to an end, and he had had no book published since the ill-fated *Rosamund and The Queen Mother*, of which no copy had sold. Rossetti, however, was trying to help him, and had, in despite of Ruskin's unfavourable opinion, sent *Chastelard* to his own publisher, Macmillan, in March 1864, with a letter saying:[1]

> My dear Macmillan,
> I have been wishing to write to you respecting the poems of my friend Mr. Swinburne, of which you have I think already heard something both from me and others – They are still unpublished, their author being more apt to write new ones than to think of the old. I hardly know how to give you an adequate idea of what not I alone, but many excellent judges who have seen them, think of their astonishing beauty. They inspire a certainty that Swinburne, who is still very young, is destined to take in his own generation the acknowledged place which Tennyson holds among *his* contemporaries.

He thought, he continued, that the tragedy of *Chastelard* was the best adapted to come first before the public. (Swinburne, if he had written the most important part of *Atalanta* at Northcourt, was still putting his final touches to the manuscript.)

Macmillan kept the manuscript between two and three months and then returned it with a letter to Rossetti, saying:[1]

> ... I certainly thought it a work of genius, but some parts of it were *queer*–very.

He did not make an offer for *Chastelard*, but asked if he might see 'the minor poems'. Rossetti went through Swinburne's poems and made a choice of those which seemed to him least liable to incur a charge of queerness or impropriety, and sent them to Macmillan; but they were returned, again with a negative decision. All Rossetti could do was write to Swinburne on September 15 assuring him the manuscripts at least were safe:

> My dear Swinburne,
> Mac has spoken. Don't swear more than you can help. I have your M.S.S. safe again....[1]

[1] Packer, *The Rosetti-Macmillan Letters*, pp. 21–31.

Swinburne had stayed in London, perhaps in the hope of news, until at least the first week in August, as one can tell from his correspondence, but by the time he received this disappointing news he was with the painter J. W. Inchbold, in Tintagel, Cornwall.

His first letter from there, dated September 2, is to his cousin Mary, and the extract she has vouchsafed to posterity begins:[1]

> I could have wished for your company yesterday night when we took out horses, borrowed from a neighbouring farmer and rode through the dusk and the dark to the adjacent city of Boscastle.

What follows is a good description of Boscastle, and of Tintagel itself, with its great headland and isthmus dividing two bays, and its virtual lack of beach, even at low water; but the letter, and those that follow it, tell us little of his relationship with his cousin, except that, despite the passion of the parting, he could still include in his letters to her reference to ordinary or day-to-day things.

It is, however, his letter of October 2, 1864 to Mary, which, in its incidental remarks, reveals that he must, by this time, have written at least the early parts of *Lesbia Brandon*.

[1] Leith, p. 21.

15

Lesbia Brandon

THE novel was not published in Swinburne's lifetime. The manuscript, which is in the British Museum,[1] has always appeared in places clearly defective.

Nor is it known what title Swinburne intended to give it. Gosse, in his biography of Swinburne, referred to it as *Lesbia Brandon*, and this is the name under which it has come to be known. Yet Lesbia Brandon is not the chief character, and a remark made by Swinburne in one of his letters shows that it was Margaret Wariston whom he considered 'the heroine'.[2]

The first chapter consists entirely of a description of two faces, a woman's and a boy's, so alike as to be differentiated only by their age and sex. It is the woman's face which Swinburne describes first. She had golden eyes:[3]

> ... The eyelashes and eyebrows were of a golden brown, long and full; their really soft shade of colour seemed dark on a skin of white rose-leaves, between a double golden flame of eyes and hair. Her nose was straight and fine, somewhat long, and the division of the nostrils below a thought too curved and deep, but their shell exquisite in cutting and colour; the point where it rose from the forehead was hardly hollow at all, and a dimmer golden down was perceptible between the brows; which took a deep and rich curve toward the temples. The cheeks were perfect in form, pale but capable of soft heat and the flush of a growing flower; the face reddened rarely and faintly and all at once, never with a vivid

[1] British Museum: MSS. Ashley, 5264.   [2] Lang, Vol. IV, p. 40.
[3] In supplying references for my quotations from *Lesbia Brandon*, I shall give two sets. First, I shall give the numbers in red ink on the leaves of the manuscript, not because I believe this numbering by Wise always to represent the order in which the leaves should be read, but because it denotes that in which they have in fact, rightly or wrongly, been bound. Secondly, for convenience of those who have not access to the manuscripts, I shall give a second series of references, to the pages of the edition of the novel published in 1952 by Randolph Hughes. For the above quotation, the references are:
Wise: ff. 1–2.
Hughes: pp. 1–2.

partial blush, but as if the skin were suddenly inlaid with the petals of a young rose from the lowest ripples of the springing hair to the fresh firm chin, round and clear as a fruit, planted as with tender care above a long large throat, deeply white and delicately full.

The golden eyes can be discounted, as having a literary origin in Balzac's novel *La Fille aux Yeux d'Or*, a novel about a Lesbian. That he had this in memory emerges when he describes Margaret's shoulders as 'exquisitely attached'; the phrase reads oddly in English, but Balzac's heroine had a *'pied bien attaché'*.

This borrowing apart, the description is obviously so particularized that one feels he must have had a real model for it. Perhaps his association with painters had taught him to observe with such care all the details of the structure of a face; and we are the gainers, for we can recognize in this portrait details which, in the *Kirklowes* fragment, belonged to Reginald's sister Helen; the perfect form of the cheeks and the large, long neck. It might also be remarked that eyebrows going right across, or with down, however soft, between them, are usually considered a sign of bad temper, and that a chin as round as a fruit is the indication of a very wilful nature.

The manuscript, as bound by Wise and presented to the British Museum, has always broken off in the middle of the description of the brother and sister, so that it appeared that the end of the first chapter and the beginning of what has always been considered the second were missing. Presumably, they were missing when, after Swinburne's death, Wise acquired the manuscript from Watts-Dunton. Recently, however, Mr. John Mayfield, making a purchase in a New York bookshop, found between the pages two leaves of manuscript in a hand which, as a collector, he immediately recognized to be Swinburne's. Study of the words convinced him that the leaves were those missing from *Lesbia Brandon*. Mr. Mayfield presented the leaves to the library of the University of Syracuse (New York), where he is curator of rare books and manuscripts and to which he had donated his own Swinburne collection, on condition that the authorities at Syracuse then presented them to the British Museum. The leaves were formally handed by the Chancellor of Syracuse to the British Ambassador in Washington and have now arrived. The Trustees of the British Museum accept them as genuine and have bound them into the manuscript of *Lesbia Brandon*, between folios 3 and 4, giving them the folio numbers 3* and 3**. I applied for and obtained permission to see them, and was told that I was the first person to do so.

3* continues and finishes the description of the brother and sister, and consists of but a single paragraph, saying that 'She was larger for a girl than he was for a boy, but Herbert was light and slight for his stature . . .'

Folio 3** begins, 'A little after the marriage her father died,' and goes on to speak of the boy's feeling of desolation following their bereavement. The description of his grief fills the leaf. He had the strangest sense of unreality, and even of dissociation from the child he had been until that time. 'He held up one hand and watched it, wondering if this ever were real. Something more bitter than fear had fallen upon him.'

Swinburne's own father was alive when he wrote *Lesbia Brandon*, and reading this description a young boy's shock at a bereavement, I wondered whether the lines did not tell us how he had felt when Sir John Swinburne, his adored grandfather, died.

The opening sentence, beginning, 'A little after the marriage' leaves me with some doubt as to whether there is not still something missing, since in the first chapter nothing was said about the sister's marrying; nevertheless, it is possible that Swinburne intended to fill something about this in later, and never did so, for the finding of the two leaves together suggests that they belong together, and the end of 3**, 'fear unmistakable and unavoidable grief laid hold of him again as it were by' seems to link on very naturally to the first words on folio 4, which are, 'the senses and the flesh'.

If Herbert and his father are modelled on Swinburne and his grandfather, can one doubt that in the description of Herbert's sister one has once more that of Mary Gordon?

Here, as in the *Kirklowes* fragment, she is the young hero's brother. The latter is again modelled on Swinburne himself, but his name, this time, is Herbert Seyton, and there is a great difference in their ages. He is twelve, she a married woman, Lady Wariston, the mother already of children. Perhaps it was his cousin's impending marriage which had caused him to look ahead and to imagine her as she might become. Herbert, or, as he is usually called, Bertie, is, as was Redgie, the victim of continual flogging, but this time, as their parents are dead and he lives with his married sister and her family, it is his tutor, Denham, who flogs him.

The biggest difference the author has made is that the sister no longer gloats over this. True, Margaret never intercedes for Bertie:[1] '. . . she gave him all condolence but no intercession'. Nevertheless, her character has been so much softened that one could not, from reading *Lesbia Brandon* alone, dream how ghoulish was her suppressed predecessor.

The place names in the book are fictitious, but the scene is obviously Northumberland, and it is probable that Ensdon, the Wariston family's home, is Capheaton, moved for a thin disguise a little nearer to the sea:[2]

> . . . Rains and sea-winds had worn it and the crumbling sandstone here and there had fallen away in flakes, being soft and unmanageable stuff. The whole place had a stately recluse beauty; fields and woods divided the park from the sea-downs; behind it were terraces, old elaborate flower-beds and the necessary fishponds devised by Catholic artifice for pious purposes in Lent and retained by Protestant conservatism for picturesque purposes all the year round: framed in low flowering bushes and ranged at equal lengths with turfed walks passing into the under-wood and dropping down the terraces. A green moist place, lying wide and low, divided from the inland moors by a windy wall of bare broken crag . . .

Swinburne is not thought of primarily as one gifted with outstanding powers of description, yet houses and places are, like faces, observed in his prose with a reverence for detail and considerable ability to evoke atmosphere. He describes his own days at his grandfather's house when he continues:[3] '. . . the boy fell upon the Ensdon library shelves with miscellaneous voracity, reading books desirable and otherwise, swallowing a nameless quantity of English and French verse and fiction'. Passages from the ensuing pages, describing the Northumbrian countryside over which he ran wild, have been quoted earlier in the present work. One can add the description of the sea-weeds left in the rock-pools by the retreating tide:[4] ' . . . the sharp and fine sea-mosses, fruitful of grey blossom, fervent with blue and golden bloom, with soft spear-heads and blades brighter than fire; the lovely heavy motion of the stronger rock-rooted weeds, with all their weight afloat in the languid water, splendid and supine; . . .' These were the weeds which had gone into the description of those encountered by Sir John Franklin in *The Discovery of the North West Passage.*

[1] Wise: f. 17. Hughes: p. 17.　　[2] Wise: f. 6. Hughes: p. 7.
[3] Wise: f. 6. Hughes: pp. 7-8.　　[4] Wise: ff. 8. Hughes: p. 9.

One understands better the nature of the idleness with which his father (in *Love's Cross Currents*) reproached him when one reads:[1]

> Being by nature idle and excitable he made himself infinite small diversions. . . . among the reefs he ran riot, skirting with light quick feet the edge of the running ripple, laughing with love when the fleeter foam caught them up, skimming the mobile fringe that murmured and fluttered and fell . . . At other times he would set his face seaward and feed his eyes for hours on the fruitless floating fields of wan green water, fairer than all spring meadows and summer gardens, till the soul of the sea entered him . . . he went as before a steady gale over sands and rocks, blown and driven by the wind of his own delight, crying out to the sea between whiles . . .

It is the sort of idleness which is often a characteristic of deeper minds, potentially creative, because in it are absorbed and stored so many minute impressions and larger atmospheres, while it allows the unself-conscious development of contemplation; it is the idleness particularly needful to a poet. When Margaret Wariston's first child arrives, the author comments:[2] 'the mother was not by nature a specially maternal woman'. This one can well believe, if the model was indeed his cousin Mary. The boy, however, is interested in the baby:

> its helpless and hopeless defects of size and weight, its curious piteous mask of features, its look of vegetable rather than animal life, its quaint motions and soft red overflow of irregular outlines touched and melted him in a singular way: he grew visibly fond of the red and ridiculous lump, and it put out impossible arms and fatuous fingers when he came in sight. Towards all beasts and babies he had always a physical tenderness; a quality purely of the nerves, not incompatible with cruelty nor grounded on any moral emotion or convinction. It was pleasant to him to press the warm senseless flesh with lips or fingers, and bring into the wide monotonous eyes and upon the loose dull mouth a look and a light of recognition and liking . . .

This passage is particularly revealing and significant for the understanding of a twist Swinburne's nature was to take in very much later life.

The description of this first baby is given in a flash-back, for by the time the story opens, Margaret has borne four children and Bertie is rising twelve and ripening for Eton. The year is 1848. It will be noticed

[1] Wise: 6–9 Hughes: pp. 8–9.   [2] Wise: f. 10. Hughes: p. 11.

that Swinburne has made Bertie almost his own age. It is to prepare him
for Eton that Denham is brought in, the tutor who administers the
birchings that Margaret never tries to prevent. The boy accepts this in-
difference as proper:[1] '. . . it had grown into a point of honour with him
to take what fate sent him at his tutor's hands with a rebellious reticence,
and bear anything in reason rather than expose himself to an intercession
which he could not but imagine contemptuous; and thus every flogging
became a duel without seconds between the man and the boy'.

In the sea, Bertie is able to forget the punishment:

> . . . he panted and shouted with pleasure among breakers where he
> could not stand two minutes; the blow of a roller that beat him off
> his feet made him laugh and cry out in ecstasy: he rioted in the roar-
> ing water like a young sea-beast, sprang at the throat of waves that
> threw him flat, pressed up against their soft fierce bosoms and
> fought for their sharp embraces; grappled with them as lover
> with lover, flung himself upon them with limbs that yielded
> deliciously, till the scourging of the surf made him red from the
> shoulders to the knees, and sent him on shore whipped by the sea
> into a single blush of the whole skin, breathless and untired.*

Sometimes Denham comes with him into the waves, as his father
apparently did, and in the sea their duel is forgotten in sportive comrade-
ship. These lighter-hearted moments between them are, however, marred
by one episode.

If, at the beginning, the reader felt distressed by the accounts of repeated floggings endured by the boy, and especially by some cancelled
phrases in the manuscript concerning 'the tutor's growing appetite' and
'relish for his work',[2] one begins to understand the situation differently
when one reads that, the tutor having forbidden bathing one day when
the sea was particularly rough, the boy slips into the waves, fully knowing (obviously) what the penalty will be. In more cancelled lines one
reads:[3] 'The sting of every cut was doubled or trebled; and he was not
released till blood had been drawn from his wet skin, soaked as it was in
salt at every pore: and came home at once red and white, drenched and
dry. Nothing in his life had ever hurt him so much as these.' One understands now that the boy courts the floggings, and through them reaches

[1] Wise: f. 17. Hughes: p. 17.
*Hughes has *untried* for *untired*. My inspection of the manuscript leaves me in no
doubt that the word Swinburne wrote is *untired*; and it makes better sense.
[2] Wise: f. 17. Hughes: p. 503.   [3] Wise: f. 20. Hughes: p. 506.

a state of exaltation. They represent the high point of his emotional life, the crest of his defiance, the peak of his heroism; he seeks and will seek repetition of the crisis.

The book is not, however, a simple recapitulation of the author's childhood; though there is much of that in it, there is also a plot. Denham, the tutor, suffers from a suppressed passion for Margaret, who does not notice him; this is given as his reason for taking it out upon the boy.

A month later, the sea being again so rough that bathing is forbidden, Bertie and a friend of his own age, Walter Lunsford, go down to the beach and Bertie bathes. He has come out and is dressing when they notice that a rowing-boat, too near the rocky shore for safety and manned by a boy, vanishes for a moment in a trough, to rise with the next wave empty. Herbert immediately begins to undress again, in order to go to the rescue. Lunsford tries to stop him, but, in a passage of magnificent description:[1]

> . . . . being naked and wet, his lithe body twisted and slipped out of Walter's hands. He went straight at the next wave, laughing; sprang into it with shut eyes and was hurled back with the thunder in his ears, with limbs and face lashed by lighter shingle driven straight through the yellow water. The sea was thick and solid with sand and flying pebbles, and waifs of weed fastened round the boy's throat and hampered his legs. Feeling the shingle under him, he rose reeling on his feet in the sudden shallow, breathed deep and made for the next breaker. A few short sharp strokes brought him close and the recoiling water sucked him into the curve of the sea. Loose foam fluttered along the edge of it, but he got over before the crash, swimming lightly across the heaving half-broken ridge of wrinkled water. Then, half in half upon the following wave, he saw something struggle and labour. The groundswell had forced him some yards to the left already. In the instant after the last breaker fell through and hurled itself inshore with all its foam and weed, the sharp side of the reef showed naked, baring its black shark-toothed edge. . . . He could not swim any further in the heavy refluent sea that shifted and seethed; keeping half afloat in front of the breaker, he was drawn out again towards it by the fierce rapid reflux, lifted into it and with it as it came in gathering up all the strength and stream of the sea and repelling the reluctant ebb of the spent wave. To swim with it was easy, and for a breath of time he kept high on the broad grey back of the wave about to break; then with one furious stroke which seemed to drain his breast

[1] Wise: ff. 28–29. Hughes: pp. 26–27.

of breath he reached and caught at the head of the figure. At the same minute he felt a hand clutch at his side and slip off, and the wave as it went over and flew into foam with the thunder and hiss and impulse of a cataract hurled both at once, blind and deaf and breathless and fearless, far up on the shingle.

The account is very circumstantial, and one wonders whether it was not based on an incident in Swinburne's own life, of which he never told. In the book, Bertie binds to silence both Lunsford and the boy – one of the boys from the village – whom he has rescued. It is difficult to understand why he feels so excessively embarrassed at the prospect of being thanked.

When he gets home, of course, he receives the usual birching; but later in the day the boy's father (the boy told after all) comes up to the house to express his gratitude for his son's life having been saved. Lady Wariston sends a servant to fetch Bertie. For a moment she presses him to her, then, after presenting him to the fisherman at the door to be thanked formally, takes him off Denham's hands for the rest of the day:[1]

> She made herself pleasant beyond words to the boy all the rest of that day . . . She played and sang to him as he stood by her, to his infinite enjoyment. Voice and memory were alike faultless; . . . Old words passed between them and old things revived; there was nothing yet of bitter or black in the memory of either. In the past time towards which they had turned back, their thoughts and lives had not been more clean and frank and sweet.

This is the first indication that there was to come a time when their relations ceased to have this innocent quality. The 'past time' to which they turned back in memory was that of their childhood, in their parents' home, and when one learns that this was called Kirklowes one realizes how closely this novel, though the names of the young hero and other characters have been changed, is connected with the *Kirklowes* fragment and *Love's Cross Currents*.

One character has come over from *Love's Cross Currents* with the name still the same: that is Lady Midhurst. Only this time it does not appear that she is the boy's grandmother; indeed, it is never specified what relation she is. Perhaps she is just a friend of Lord and Lady Wariston, or an in-law. But her character is unchanged; and the schoolboy hero is still her favourite.

[1] Wise: f. 45. Hughes: pp. 39–40.

Introduced with Lady Midhurst, and said to be the same age, is a Mr. Linley, whose early life in France and connection with French political affairs seems to have been exactly that of Swinburne's grandfather, the late Sir John Swinburne. He is the uncle of Lord Wariston. Lady Midhurst and this Mr. Linley, having been invited to a house party at the Wariston's, travel up together on the same train and share a cab to Ensdon. Other guests include a Lord Charles Brandon. Lord Wariston had been out when the fisherman called, and returning only just before dinner learns from Margaret of Bertie's heroism, which he details to his guests, much to the boy's confusion. They all sit down to dinner at which the conversation takes a rather unpleasant turn, the fact that Bertie is about to go to Eton causing everybody to think of flogging; the men are inspired to recall their own boyhoods, in which they were horsed and flogged, and from the teasing remarks addressed to Bertie, they seem to relish the thought of the punishments which lie before him.

One is tempted to think that Swinburne, obsessed with flogging, grafts it on to every scene he writes. In this supposition one may do him, at least in part, an injustice. He knew very well the kind of people he was writing about. Most of the characters have a model in some individual of his personal acquaintance. The circle and its way of living and talking is that of his own family. The dialogue sounds very natural; the phrases are such as could have been caught on the wing. The author doubtless picks out particularly those veins of conversation which fascinated him; nevertheless, part of the interest of Swinburne's novels is that they present a picture of the intimate life of a section of the English upper classes in the Victorian era by one who knew it from the inside, and was part of it.

In the course of the dinner the name of Lord Brandon's daughter Lesbia is mentioned. She is a 'good horsewoman', says her father, promising Bertie a mount should he come to stay with them:[1]

> 'But Miss Brandon writes, doesn't she—verses?'
> 'Ah, you know that? It doesn't spoil her riding: do you care for verse?'
> 'Awfully,' said Herbert; adding with a judicious reserve, 'when it's good.'
> 'Lesbia could do your verses for you when you go to Eton; she can manage elegiacs; never could myself and was always getting swished for mine some fifty years ago . . .'

[1] Wise: f. 60. Hughes: pp. 52–53.

Margaret had earlier mentioned Lesbia Brandon to Bertie as someone whom he could very suitably marry when he grew up, so Bertie is naturally interested to hear about her character and gifts. The peculiar name, Margaret had explained to him, was Irish. Girls used, in fact, sometimes to be christened with the name, by parents who cannot have connected it with the Lesbian poetess. That Swinburne means us to do so, however, becomes evident from the way in which, from now on, he develops the clues to her psychological make-up.

The question arises as to where Swinburne obtained his model for Lesbia. He had read much of Lesbians in the pages of de Sade, Latouche, Balzac, Baudelaire and other French writers, but it does not seem that he ever knew a Lesbian woman. The girl whose main passion is horse-riding, but who toys at writing and at Greek, suggests once again his cousin, Mary Gordon. Though Margaret in part derives from her, he has taken horse-riding away from Margaret, because in this book he has made her older and endowed her with the husband, children and domestic responsibilities which Mary Gordon did not yet have; it is the interests and occupations of Mary at her present age which he has isolated and given to Lesbia. He obviously did not suppose her engagement to Colonel Leith to proceed from passion, and since she had decided against himself it may have passed through his mind, in partial explanation of her behaviour, that there was in her a vein of suppressed masculinity, such as he had read about. Neither would this thesis seem impossibly wide of the mark. She had written one story which was published, at her family's expense, in 1859, that is to say before anything of Swinburne's, entitled *Mark Dennis, or the Engine Driver*.

This, as its title suggests, is mainly about trains and engine driving, and the clergyman who wrote a preface taking it at its face value as a morality against fast driving missed the point that, to a young and eager person, the whole excitement of trains is that they are fast, rushing, furiously roaring things, belching fire and smoke: fiery, noisy dragons. The juvenile author, as Blake said of Milton, was of the Devil's part without knowing it. To wish to be an engine driver is a boy's rather than a girl's ambition. Mary must have learned a good deal about locomotives and signalling to write that story, and her enjoyment of horse-riding may have been part of her passion for power and speed. In the course of a long life she was to write sixteen books, including two of verse (each of which contains more than one poem addressed to different horses of her acquaintance); the majority of the rest are novels or stories, and in

LESBIA BRANDON

more than one of them the protagonist is a young boy. She identified herself with boys, or at any rate with boys' occupations.

But Lesbia is not on the scene yet. She is being spoken of, but the guests are still gathered at Ensdon. Dinner is now over, and the men have joined the ladies in the drawing-room. Bertie gets pinned down by Mr. Linley, who has gloatingly teasing things to say about flogging. Almost in tears with fury and humiliation, he escapes at last. One of the young men, seeing what has happened, says to him quietly:[1] 'Was he chaffing you about getting swished? What a damned shame... Old chaps will, they like to see a small boy wriggle. I say, how he made you smoke; I thought you were going to blub, twice. Those sort of fellows know nothing else about boys, you see, and they think it's the sort of thing to say;...' The ghastly evening over at last, Bertie goes up to bed, but is so tired that he falls asleep while undressing. Margaret, true to a promise given him earlier, to sing to him before he slept, comes to him in his room, and wakes him with a kiss on the lips. She sings him a beautiful Border ballad (of Swinburne's own composition). The fire in the grate has sunk while she was singing, and when she stops he slips to his knees:[2]

> Her perfume thrilled and stung him; he bent down and kissed her feet, reached up and kissed her throat.
> 'You smell of flowers in a hot sun,' he said, kissing her feet again with violent lips that felt the sweet-scented flesh pressing them back through its soft covering. She laughed and winced under the heat of his hard kiss. . . .
> 'I say, let your hair go,' said Herbert, pressing his arms under hers; she loosened the fastenings, and it rushed downwards, a tempest and torrent of sudden tresses, heavy and tawny and riotous and radiant over shoulders and arms and bosom . . .
> His whole spirit was moved with the passionate motion of his senses; he clung to her for a minute, and rose up throbbing from head to foot with violent love. . . .
> He fell asleep with her kisses burnt into his mind, and the ineffaceable brand of love upon his thoughts: and dreamed passionately of his passion...

Up to this point in the story, none of the leaves on which the manuscript is written bear a watermark later than 1864, which is the date of 12 out of the 40 used so far; the rest are 1863, except for one which bears

[1] Wise: f. 77. Hughes: pp. 67–68.   [2] Wise: ff. 91–92. Hughes: pp. 80–81.

135

an 1859 watermark but text which follows on from that on the '63 leaves. The novel was not only unpublished in Swinburne's lifetime; Swinburne made no fair copy of it. It is written on paper of different sizes, ranging from foolscap to small sheets, and of different colours; some of it is on white and some on different kinds of blue paper. Most of the leaves bear writing on the recto only. Some of it is in black ink and some of it in red. Only some of the chapters are numbered, in a hand which may be Swinburne's. Except for the first three chapters, which bear consecutive numbering, where foliation occurs it is from the beginning of the chapter or run of leaves numbered, not from the beginning of the book. As there is no table of contents, it is therefore exceedingly difficult to know in what order the chapters should follow one another. T. J. Wise arranged the leaves in the order he saw fitting, bound them in leather and, with an arrogant disregard for the sanctity of original documents, numbered the leaves in red ink in the order that he had bound them. That this is in several places a false order has already been shown by the late Mr. Randolph Hughes, who has in his edition of the book placed or rather reproduced certain of the chapters, as well as leaves within the chapters, in a different order, while discounting certain leaves as not belonging to the book at all. I accept these discards as bearing only such relation to *Lesbia Brandon* as the *Kirklowes* fragment does to *Love's Cross Currents*. Nevertheless the text, even as Hughes has printed it, though more satisfactory than the Wise arrangement, leaves incongruities of matter which no ingenuity of rearrangement can resolve, and I would go further than he has done in rejecting from the text of the story as originally conceived leaves bearing a watermark later than 1864.

Of course, a watermark only shows a date prior to which the text on the leaf cannot have been written. Nevertheless, one knows that the early part of *Lesbia Brandon*, the part concerned with Bertie's floggings, must in fact have been composed early enough for Mary Gordon to understand what Swinburne meant when, on October 2, 1864, he wrote to her from Tintagel, describing a bathe he had just taken:

> . . . I just ran . . . into the water and up and down over some awfully sharp and shell encrusted rocks which cut my feet to fragments, had twice to plunge again into the sea, which was filling all the coves and swinging and swelling heavily between the rocks; once fell flat in it, and got so thrashed and licked that I might have been —— in ——'s clutches, . . .[1]

[1] Leith, pp. 24–25.

The names Mary Leith has suppressed in her editing of the letter are certainly Bertie (or Herbert) and Denham. She has put a footnote to the dashes: 'Characters in a story.' Rather than to edit in this way, it would have been less trouble to print the text with the names in it. Why should she have suppressed them? Probably because she did not wish to appear as having read a manuscript rumoured to be unpublishable because of its impropriety.

When had she read it? As it seems unlikely that Swinburne would have posted for her inspection the untidy leaves, with their innumerable deletions and alterations, it is probable that she saw the manuscript as it was being written, concurrently with *Atalanta*, during the autumn and winter of 1863 and the early weeks of 1864, when he was staying at her home in the Isle of Wight. She was during this time writing her second novel, or rather long short-story, *The Children of the Chapel*, with which, as she acknowledged, he had helped her. Set in Elizabethan times, it is about children who were practically kidnapped to sing in the Queen's chapel. There is a great deal about beating in it, and some of the little verses inserted in the text, which must be by Swinburne, are in the exact vein of his *Flogging Block* poems. That she should have accepted them for inclusion in her manuscript, and considered it publishable—she did publish it—seems to show, at the very least, a passively morbid interest in the subject, which gives some substance to the suspicion that she like Helen 'fed with a soft sensual relish on the sight or conceit of physical pain'. There are touches, in this sense, which I should judge are veritably her own, not his. (Perhaps it was not so much cruelty as a short of fearful curiosity, which appears in the questions she makes one of her characters ask.)

Though Mary had clearly read the flogging scenes in *Lesbia Brandon*, which occur mainly in the early part, it is possible and indeed highly probable she did not read of the introduction of Lesbia or the dénouement with Margaret. As she was the model for both, Swinburne would not want her to see what he had done with her. But he would, I submit, have driven straight on until he came to the end, as he originally conceived it, before the year was out.

A curious thing I have discovered is that if one mentally discards all the leaves bearing watermarks later than 1864, certain problems are at least simplified.

Passing over a leaf bearing an 1866 watermark, we come next, then, to another September evening and another house-party, six years after

the first one. The year is now 1854, and this time Miss Brandon is one
of the guests, with her father. Bertie is now eighteen. He is cast for a
feminine role in the charades which are to form the evening's diversion,
and the dress rehearsal in the afternoon goes on for so long that the
participants are still in their fancy clothes when the Brandons arrive. So
it happens that Lesbia Brandon sees Herbert for the first time dressed as
a girl:[1]

> Miss Brandon was dark and delicately shaped; not tall, but erect
> and supple; she had thick and heavy hair growing low on the
> forehead, so brown that it seemed black in the shadow; her eyes
> were sombre and mobile, full of fervour and of dreams, answering
> in colour to the hair, as did also the brows and eyelashes. Her
> cheeks had the profound pallor of the complexions at once dark
> and colourless; but the skin was pure and tender, the outline clear
> and soft: she was warm and wan as a hot day without a sun. She
> had a fine and close mouth, with small bright lips, not variable in
> expression; her throat and shoulders were fresh and round. A
> certain power and a certain trouble were perceptible in the face,
> but traceable to no single feature . . .

Lafourcade has suggested that Lesbia is modelled in part on Christina
Rossetti. In so far as concerns her horse-riding side, this seems to me
false; the model was one whom Lafourcade did not suspect, Mary
Gordon, who also wrote poetry, if not at the level of Christina's. But
it is possible that for the face he used Christina; having used Mary's
face for Margaret, he needed a second model and may have chosen
Christina as being the only beautiful and interesting-looking woman
whom he knew who was, mysteriously, without a male companion.
I accept the thesis of Mrs. Mosk Packer's biography of Christina,
that the reason the poetess remained single was that she loved William
Bell Scott, who was married; but Swinburne, knowing nothing of
the inner drama, would have seen only her reserve and a certain re-
moteness in her manner towards the men in whose company he saw
her.

For a joke, the players in the charade present Bertie to Lesbia as
Margaret's sister, Helen; and Lesbia is not for some time undeceived.

There follows (if one skips a chapter on paper with an 1866 watermark) a chapter headed *On the Downs*. It is on paper which bears no
watermark but may well belong to the original draft. On the downs are

[1] Wise: f. 99. Hughes: p. 89.

Bertie and Lesbia. Bertie is now twenty-four, and obviously in love with her. She says:[1]

> ... 'If I could love or marry, I am sure I could love and marry you ... But I can't. I don't know why, at least I don't wholly know. I am made as I am, and God knows why – I suppose. You quite deserve that I should be fair to you, and truthful. I never felt for anyone what I feel for you now, and shall while I live. I do really in a way, so to speak, love you. And you can see in my way of telling you this that I can never by any chance love you other-wise or love you more ... but there must be no more lovemaking. I am not marriageable ...'

She adds words that sound conventional, but have the echo of what seems to have been Mary Gordon's thesis:[2] 'I don't know if you would like it or not, but I should like to feel thoroughly that we were not less than brother and sister. . . .' Swinburne first wrote, but crossed out: 'were brother and sister'.

Passing over several chapters of later watermark one comes next, straight, to the crucial and most mysterious chapter of the book.

On a leaf embossed in the top left-hand corner *Gubbins Newport*, suggesting that the paper was purchased in the Isle of Wight, this begins:[3] 'He stood away from her and spoke softly, with head bent and fallen face. . . .' Who 'he' is, is not explained. Neither can his identity be determined by reference to the chapters of later watermark interpolated between this and those preceeding. He speaks to her:[4]

> ... 'This ought to end. It is a great misery. Let us keep something like honour. We cannot go away together. You have broken my life between you; you two. I want to die sane. Do you think I can live? seriously. Look at me then. Ah! don't cry. It's not to set her free; nor to spare you. I know it will hurt you ...'

One realizes that they have just had sexual intercourse, and that he is threatening, or promising, to commit suicide. One realizes, also, that the woman is Margaret. They cling to each other again, and she says:[5]

> 'I will die instead. My love, my beloved; because you love me. Oh, I cannot have you killed; for I never was good to you. I have

---

[1] Wise: ff. 105–6. Hughes: pp. 99–100.   [2] Wise: f. 107. Hughes: p. 100.
[3] Wise: f. 159. Hughes: p. 129.   [4] Wise: f. 159. Hughes: p. 129.
[5] Wise: ff. 149 and 151 (Wise leaves out of order). Hughes: p. 130.

only harmed you and hurt you. You made me feel my life pleasant
for a year . . . She has no eyes and no heart or soul. Oh, I cannot let
you go now. . . . I cannot lose you; cannot.'
'Yes, he said, 'and our honour? what shall we get for that?
Darling, you know nothing in the world stays after it. And it will
go. We have not strength.'

She says, now, that there is no reason for either of them to commit
suicide:[1]

'. . . We will settle to see each other sometimes: no harm shall
come of it. And you will be good to her: ah, but she will not let
you; nor deserve it. . . . We shall live and grow old–I shall be
soonest old you know, by so much–and keep alive each by
knowing that the other lives . . .'

She falters, realizing how impossible for them would be this way of
living, which would be without 'honour' if they both lived:[2] 'No, we
we must save something. There is only that to hold by. Keep my honour
for me; and yours. . . .'

If one has already read *Chastelard*, one remembers Mary telling
her lover that he must die for their honour's sake. Yet the passion
here is more credible, more natural. Margaret is almost beside
herself:[3]

. . . Her voice with its broken words was more piteous than a hurt
child's. What she said was hard to make out for the thin harsh
undernote of incoherent and sobbing sound. She called him all
the most tender names, gave him all the most loving looks that
could live upon her drowning eyelids and strangling voice. 'Not
the face, darling; ah, not your face . . . You are too young . . .'

One realizes she means he should not shoot himself through the face,
because it would spoil his beauty. They clasp once more; and he goes.
Margaret, in a frenzy, flings herself about the room, beats her face into
the cushions, crams her mouth with her own hair and bites it. At last,
she washes, in cold water, does her hair, and goes downstairs to find
her children. To pass the intolerable time she sings to them, French
ballads and ballads of the Border. After what seems an interminable
period, she hears steps and voices in the hall; her husband enters, white
faced:[4]

[1] Wise: f. 151. Hughes: pp. 120–1.   [2] Wise: f. 151. Hughes: p. 131.
[3] Wise: f. 148. Hughes: p. 131.   [4] Wise: f. 182. Hughes: p. 156.

'An accident,' he said, speaking low and fast: 'His gun went off in getting through a hedge.'

'Lodged where?' said Lady Wariston, as she passed between him and the children.

'In the heart: killed on the spot.' Then she passed him, and going into the passage saw her dead lover carried in; made a few more steps towards the bearers, then reeled and fell with a great short cry.

This is nothing more that does not bear evidence of having been written at a later date, and in my belief this is Swinburne's original end to the book. I presume that the lover is Bertie. Previous critics have presumed it to be Denham. Objections to its being Denham are that (even if one takes into consideration additions on later paper) Margaret is never shown as taking any interest in the tutor, and that there is no second woman in Denham's life. The woman who 'has no eyes and no heart' and who 'will not let' him be good to her is surely Lesbia; Margaret thinks of her because it had always been supposed she and Bertie would marry until she made her unmarriageability plain. An even more serious objection to its being Denham is that Denham is past thirty; one does not know Margaret's age, but as women married young in those days and had children in rapid succession, the fact that she has borne four does not necessarily make her old enough to refer to him as much younger than herself. Moreover, it has nowhere been suggested that Denham's face possessed any beauty of feature such that, so as not to mar it even in death, the bullet must lodge elsewhere.

Bertie is, of course, Margaret's brother; but from the very beginning it was the situation between these two that was built up. We were told first of the early innocence, when there was 'nothing yet of bitter or black in the memory of either', and their lives and thoughts had not been 'more clean and frank'. Then there was the scene in which she came into his room and they embraced in a manner which was very sensuously described; and now this.

The over-riding consideration, for me, is that it is totally unnatural to write a whole chapter, of this climactic order, without once mentioning by name the heroine's lover, unless, as in the case of his being her brother, his identification would immeasurably shock readers. Swinburne's mind ran on incest, not solely because of his reading. His cousin Mary was so closely related to him that it must have seemed natural, as well as conventional, to say, when refusing him, that theirs could only be a brother and sister relationship. I submit that in *Lesbia Brandon* he took this theme and developed it to a savage conclusion and wish-fulfilment. Consideration of later-written parts of the book, and of what I believe to have been alternative endings, I shall reserve until a later chapter.

16

Circus Road: Reincarnation: Rumours

MARY CHARLOTTE JULIA GORDON was married to Robert William Disney Leith, Colonel, 106th Light Infantry, in the parish of Shorwell, Isle of Wight, on June 14, 1865.[1] There is no reference to this event in any letter of Swinburne's which has survived.

Colonel Leith now took his bride to live in his home in Aberdeenshire. Swinburne's connection with the Isle of Wight ended when his father gave up East Dene and bought Holmwood, a house in Oxfordshire. A letter from Swinburne to Lady Trevelyan, written on March 15, 1865, says he believes his family to be moving into their new home during the next month. In February or March, at his father's expense, he had had *Atalanta* printed and published by the firm of Moxon and Co. The contrast with the failure of his first book, *Rosamund and the Queen Mother*, could not have been more marked. This time the reviews were so many and so laudatory that the small edition sold out, and a reprint was put in hand. At the age of twenty-eight, he found himself suddenly established as a poet. Following up his success he sent Moxon *Chastelard*, and that was put in hand also.

This should have been a period of joy for Swinburne; but there is not much jubilation in his letters. In fact, there are not many letters bearing dates within this crucial period, and those that there are show his mind beginning to run again on flagellation. Writing to Lord Houghton, who had said he found *Chastelard* obscure, he starts:[2] 'Please, Sir, don't hit very hard this time – I haven't been swished yet this half...' This might be all very well for an amusing opening, but throughout the whole of a fairly long letter he keeps up the pretence of being a boy and the imagery of the school punishment is maintained.

> let down my breeches, pull up my shirt, and kneel down (for the hundredth time) on the flogging block ...

Finally he signs the letter with the pseudonym he had used in the poem written as his part of the covenant:

> Your affectionate though much-flogged pupil, Frank

[1] Copy of Marriage Certificate obtained by author from Somerset House.
[2] Lang, Vol. I, p. 121.

143

The next letter, written in May or June, and therefore just about the time of his cousin Mary's wedding, is to Howell and reveals that Howell is now also party to the covenant to produce flagellant literature:[1]

> P.P.S. (*private*) I want you to compose for me a little dialogue (imaginary) between schoolmaster and boy—from the first summons 'Now Arthur (or Frank or Harry) what does *this* mean. . . .' —to the last *cut* and painful buttoning up . . . I want to see how like real life you will make it. Write me this—and you shall have more of my verses—a fair bargain.

To Lord Houghton he writes again in July, from a new address, 22a Dorset Square,[2]

> I may hope to be a good boy again, after such a 'jolly good swishing' as Rodin alone can and dare administer. The Rugby purists (I am told) tax Eton generally with Maenadism during June and July, so perhaps some old school habits return upon us unawares—to be fitly expiated by old school punishment.

Behind these phrases may lie a story, for which they serve as a half-shield.

When Gosse published his biography of Swinburne he omitted from it all reference to drink or peculiarities. There is, however, in the British Museum, 'Reserved from Public Use', a *Confidential Paper on Swinburne's moral irregularities* by Gosse. Together with it are letters to Gosse from Max Beerbohm, A. E. Housman, William Michael Rossetti and others, to whom he had circulated the paper privately. These letters are in themselves interesting. Max Beerbohm wrote:

> . . . how definitely dreary and ghastly and disgusting the whole thing becomes. Why should anyone in posterity *know* that Swinburne did these things? Without your statement, no doubt there would be rumours, but rumours, even if they are believed, have much less effect on the mind than the authoritative and established fact. . . . Why not let the lovers of his poetry hereafter be immune from *definite* knowledge . . .

A. E. Housman, on the other hand, replied to Gosse, thanking him for the paper, which, he said, unabashed: 'I have read with a great deal of pleasure.' William Michael Rossetti though not scandalous minded, wrote:

[1] Lang, Vol. I, p. 123.   [2] Lang, Vol. I, p. 124.

'I think this ought to be in print and in the great libraries, I do really. There is nothing very awful about it.'

The *Confidential Paper*, which only a handful of people have been privileged to see in the original, starts off by explaining the difficulties under which Gosse had written his biography. The opposition of Swinburne's sister, and more particularly of his cousin. Mrs. Disney Leith, had made it impossible for him to treat all aspects of Swinburne's life; and yet, since the book had been published, he had been criticized by friends for his omissions. He was therefore setting all that he knew down in this paper. In the following paragraphs, he deals with Swinburne's drunkenness. Then he comes to the flagellation.

While Swinburne was living 'near Dorset Square', he came to know a man named Savile Clarke. One evening when Swinburne was visiting Savile Clarke at the latter's lodging house, Savile Clarke took him down into the basement and introduced to him a boy, who, though only half educated, read poetry. The boy's name was John Thomson, and later through Swinburne Rossetti also met him. John Thomson had an interest, perhaps a share, in a house in St. John's Wood, where, in luxuriously furnished rooms, two fair-haired and rouged ladies whipped gentlemen who came to them for this service. A third, elder lady, very respectable in appearance, welcomed the guests and took their money. John Thomson introduced Swinburne to this house, and he became a regular client.[1]

This is the sum of the precise information on this head, posthumously bequeathed to the world by Sir Edmund Gosse. Professor Lang to whom it was first made available, has been able to gather a little more by reference to George R. Sims' *My Life: Sixty Years' Recollections of Bohemian London*, in which there is mention of John Thomson; it being there stated that his mother kept a lodging house in Bloomsbury, in which Savile Clarke lodged. John Thomson, however, did not live in his mother's lodging house; 'He lived in one of the side roads of St. John's Wood, then playfully referred to as "The Grove of the Evangelist", and the house in which he lived was sumptuously furnished.'[2] This sounds as though he lived in the same house as the flagellant ladies, and pimped for them. Professor Lang checked from the Post Office Directory of 1876 that John Thomson lived at 7 Circus Road, St. John's Wood.[3] This was probably the address of the brothel.

[1] British Museum, Ashley MSS. 5753, ff. 27–28.
[2] Lang, Vol. I, pp. 314–15 n. [3] Lang, Vol. VI, p. 245 n.

I was able to obtain a check on Gosse's *Confidential Paper* by reference to the *Index Librorum Prohibitorum* of Pisanus Fraxi. There is in the British Museum *Private Case* a copy of the latter in which Fraxi has inserted handwritten leaves between the printed pages. Opposite p. xlvi of the *Introduction* (Vol. 1), there is a bunch of such interleaved sheets, being a statement, dated 1875, from a Mr. Hankey, of 2 Rue Lafitte, Paris, for Mr. Ashbee (Pisanus Fraxi) concerning flagellation brothels recently or actually existing in London, for use in the work Fraxi was compiling. Because it contained a reference to an establishment still extant, Fraxi did not commit the matter to print but preserved it in this manner, in his private copy. According to Hankey, there was a Mrs. Colletti who ran a place first in Tansworth Court Gardens, afterwards in Portland Place and finally in Bedford Street (Russell Square), where she died; and there was a Mrs. Potter, who 'ran a good business for a few years near Tottenham Court Road' until imprisoned. Hankey adds, 'The birch at most of these places was provided by a Mrs. Potter living at Walworth.' One may reflect that to keep all these places going there must have been considerable numbers of men who shared Swinburne's perversion.

'The only establishment I know of now is in Regent's Park,' continues Hankey. At this one, he says, are two very young girls, who pretend to be schoolmasters and 'whip fearfully severely'. They would belabour clients across the knee, like children, which some clients liked, or in another position (the handwriting is poor, and I cannot read, though it is easy to guess, the alternative posture). The premises can hardly have been 'in' Regent's Park literally, and the reference is probably to the house in Circus Road, St. John's Wood (near Regent's Park), which was Swinburne's resort.

Gosse gives no indication of the date at which Swinburne began to patronize this place, but his (Gosse's) reference to Dorset Square provides a clue. It had been some time early in the summer of 1865 that Swinburne took chambers in 22a Dorset Street, and his letter to Lord Houghton containing the phrase 'old school habits return upon us unawares', written on a Tuesday in July, is the earliest of his preserved letters sent from that address. Swinburne was to keep these chambers for the next three years, so that the introduction to the house in St. John's Wood could have been at any time during this period.

In any case, it seems clear that the recourse to prostitutional flagellation followed closely upon his cousin's marriage. He made one great stretch in the direction of normality when he tried to persuade Mary to marry him. Perhaps had she accepted him, he would never have committed himself to this form of perversion; as it was, in the listlessness that must have followed upon the final death of all he had to strive for in Mary's direction, the shades of Eton reclaimed him and he found release from his tensions in the re-enactment, in a strange drawing-room, of the ancient drama of the flogging-block and a re-creation of the only excitement he had completely known.

On the brighter side, he was able, on August 10, to send Victor Hugo an advance copy of *Chastelard*, bearing the dedication to the French poet which the latter had gracefully accepted when Swinburne asked him some time previously. He was also in correspondence, about his essay on William Blake and other matters, with Seymour Kirkup, who had known Blake personally. Apart from making his dislike of Christian dogma plain, Swinburne left few clues as to what he believed concerning the eternal mysteries of life and death. One of these few occurs in a letter which he wrote to Kirkup on August 11, 1865, in reply to one he had received:[1]

> I was much struck by the passage in your last letter to me, where you speak of the Theory of Transmigration. Whether or not it be affirmed or denied by spirits I know that it has always appeared to me a very probable article of faith.

Blake, for all his absorption in Neoplatonism, Thomas Taylor, Jacob Behmen, and the latter's English translator and commentator William Law, did not come out in a direct manner upon the subject of reincarnation, though veiled references to the doctrine can be discerned in his work here and there. Blake apart, however, Swinburne did not lack, in the pages of his favourite authors, pointers in this direction.

Victor Hugo was explicitly interested in the idea. His verse assumes the truth of the doctrine, as for example in the beautiful poem, *Le Revenant* (*Les Contemplations I*, No. XXIII); in this, a mother who has greatly loved her first child mourns its death. Her husband, trying to restore her happiness, tells her they can have another. She becomes pregnant once more, but the idea of accepting a substitute or replacement is repugnant to her, and when she is delivered of her second baby she at first tries to put it from her. Then suddenly, as though she heard it speak with her first child's voice, she realizes that it is her first child, who has come back to her.

[1] Lang, Vol. I, p. 128.

Balzac, in his novel *Seraphita*, presents a doctrine of both previous and successive existences and, as we know from a letter cited earlier, that Swinburne had read this book at an early age.

Shelley worked his own way towards the doctrine of reincarnation, with a seriousness which shows above all in his letters; and Shelley was Swinburne's favourite English poet.

At the end of the year, Swinburne realized suddenly that his private life had become the subject of rumour. On December 4 we find him writing:[1]

> My dear Lady Trevelyan,
>
> I know not how to thank you sufficiently for the kindness of your letter. I cannot express the horror and astonishment, the unutterable indignation and loathing, with which I have been struck on hearing that any one could be vile enough to tax me, I do not say with doing but with saying anything of the kind to which you refer. The one suggestion is not falser than the other. I am literally amazed and horrorstruck at the infamous wickedness of people who invent in malice or repeat in levity such horrors.
>
> ... I can only imagine 1) that the very quietness of my way of living as compared with that of other men of my age exposes me, given up as I always am to comparative solitude, to work at my own art, and never seen in *fast* (hardly in *slow*) life – to spitefulness and vicious stupidity, 2) that as you say I must have talked very foolishly to make such infamies possible. All I can ever recollect saying which *could* be perverted was (for instance) that 'the Greeks did not seem to me worse than the moderns because of [sic] things considered innocent at one time by one country were not considered so by others'. Far more than this I have heard said by men of the world of the highest character ... I do remember saying, 'if people read the classics, not to speak of the moderns very often, they must see that many qualities called virtues and vices depend on time, climate and temperament'. The remark may have been false or foolish but who could have imagined it (until he had proof) capable of being twisted into an avowal that I approved vice and disapproved virtue?

This seems disingenuous. Swinburne was saturated in de Sade, and such was his enjoyment of the works of 'le divin Marquis' that he could still hardly write a letter to Lord Houghton in which there was not a reference either to *Justine* or *Juliette*. I do not imagine that Swinburne considered

[1] Lang, Vol. I, p. 137.

cruelty preferable to kindness, but as his letters show, he certainly found
the sexual licence of de Sade's characters vastly entertaining, in all their
variety.

His letter to Lady Trevelyan ends with a postscript:

> I do not ask you who spoke to you against me as having *heard*
> me say things I never did say. If you thought it right to tell me as a
> warning I know you would.

She did not tell him, but it was William Bell Scott who, some days
previously, had written to Lady Trevelyan saying:[1]

> ... I do think you could do A.S. very much benefit by seriously
> writing him. The remark you make on his behaviour at Walling-
> ton I believe I quite understand, he suffers under a dislike to ladies
> of late—his knowledge of himself and of them increasing upon him.
> His success too is certainly not improving him, as one might easily
> suppose with so boundless a vanity.

One is at liberty to suspect some degree of malice here, perhaps occasioned by envy of the literary success of Swinburne to which Bell Scott
refers. Had his feeling towards Swinburne been purely friendly, he
would either have kept his thoughts to himself, or, if he thought him to
be running into real danger, warned him himself. This he could have
done the more easily as they were both at this time in London. That he
concealed his hand and relayed a message of this kind through Lady
Trevelyan makes a bad impression.

Lady Trevelyan must have written to tell Bell Scott of the reply she
had received from Swinburne, for we find Bell Scott writing to Lady
Trevelyan again on December 10:[2]

> What you say of A.S. is only to a certain extent gratifying.
> You know he has been warned in all sorts of ways by Gabriel and
> myself and has scouted the warnings, and now his collapse into
> deprecation and denial is only, I fear, through cowardice. He is a
> craven when it comes to the point. Your threatening him with a
> demi monde was an admirable hit.

On the same day that Bell Scott wrote this, Swinburne was writing to
Lady Trevelyan that he believed many rumours against him all derived
from:[3]

[1] Lang, Vol. I, p. 135.   [2] Lang, Vol. I, p. 142n.   [3] Lang, Vol. I, p. 140.

one infamous source. When it is found out, we may hope to suppress it once for all. Meantime, upon the double suspicion, I have refused to meet in public a person whom I conceive to be possibly mixed up in the matter.

A further letter from Bell Scott to Lady Trevelyan says:[1]

Did you see A.S. and give him good advice? He was to come out here on Sunday evening by appointment with Simeon Solomon,—I hope he has not jumped to the belief that I was your informant—

I shall defer consideration of the question whether Swinburne was, in fact, partly homosexual to a later chapter, where Simeon Solomon, comes more into the story.

[1] Lang, Vol. I, p. 143n.

17

Poems and Ballads

Poems and Ballads, Swinburne's first collection of his lyrics, appeared in July 1866. Lady Trevelyan had written to him, in touching terms:[1]

> Now do, if it is only for the sake of living down evil reports, do be wise in which of your lyrics you publish. Do let it be a book that can be really loved and read and learned by heart, and become part and parcel of the English language, and be on every one's breakfast table without being received under protest by timid people. There are no doubt people who would be glad to be able to say that it is not fit to be read. It is not worth while for the sake of two or three poems to risk the widest circulation of the whole.

One understands her feelings, but one understands, also, why Swinburne did not want, for the sake of the family breakfast-table, to sacrifice some of his powerful poems. In his reply, he tactfully skated round the issue by saying that all his friends gave him different advice as to which ones he should omit, and if he took out all to which anyone had objected there would be not a line of his work left.

Lady Trevelyan had for some years had much illness and on May 13, 1866, died prematurely at the age of only forty-nine or fifty. Gosse has said that Swinburne could never afterwards speak her name without emotion. It is believed that before she died she held in her hands the proofs of *Poems and Ballads*.

Publication was delayed because, apparently, there were so many printer's errors as to make several sets of proofs necessary. Also, it seems that Swinburne put in some new poems, including *Felise*.[2] This is a poem which, if in fact it was composed at this date, is very difficult to fit into the story of his life. It has all the character of a poem addressed to Mary:

> What shall be said between us here
> Among the downs, between the trees,
> In fields that knew our feet last year,
> In sight of quiet sands and seas,
> This year, Felise? . . .

[1] Lang, Vol. I, pp. 139–40 n.   [2] Lafourcade, p. 134.

My snake with bright bland eyes, my snake
  Grown tame and glad to be caressed,
With lips athirst for mine to slake
  Their tender fever! who had guessed
  You loved me best!

I had died for this last year, to know
  You loved me. Who shall turn on fate?
I care not if love come or go
  Now, though your love seek mine for mate.
  It is too late.

The dust of many strange desires
  Lies deep between us; . . .

The opening suggests that he had been back to the Isle of Wight, which seems from all points of view unlikely. It may have been a poetic device. One does not know where Mary and her husband were at this moment. Had he and Mary met again? Was this poem merely a wish-fufilment, or had Mary, bored after a year with the Colonel, tried to turn back to her cousin?

The 'dust of many strange desires' lying now between them seems eloquent of what had in fact happened. His life had been cleft by her. One part of him was dead. Since all that part of him that was invested in her had been stricken, he had found other pleasures. He concludes:

Live and let live, as I will do,
  Love and let love, and so will I,
But, sweet, for me no more with you:
  Not while I live, not though I die.
  Goodnight, goodbye.

The volume contained, of course, *The Triumph of Time*, and *Hesperia*. It also contained *Dolores, Faustine, Laus Veneris, Hermaphroditus, Fragoletta*, a Sapphic and savage piece called *Anactoria*, and the grand but anti-Christian *Hymn to Proserpine*, which contains the lines:[1]

Though these that were Gods are dead, and thou
  being dead art a God,
Though before thee the throned Cytherean be fallen,
  and hidden her head,
Yet thy kingdom shall pass, Galilean, thy dead shall
  go down to thee dead.

Of the maiden thy mother men sing as a goddess
    with grace clad around;
Thou art throned where another was king; where
    another was queen she is crowned.
Yea, once we had sight of another: . . .

The publishers were extremely nervous, not entirely without reason, since they had, some years previously, been prosecuted for issuing a reprint of Shelley's atheistic poem *Queen Mab*. Because of this nervousness, they had insisted on the prior issue of a limited edition, as a test, of *Laus Veneris*. The story of the knight who found the ancient and immortal goddess Venus, deprived of her temples in a Christian age, sleeping among the bushes above the Rhine, had been made widely known by Wagner's opera; Swinburne's treatment of the legend, however, contained dangerous lines:

Lo, she was thus when her clear limbs enticed
All lips that now grow sad with kissing Christ,

When the poem appeared as a small separate pamphlet, little notice was taken, but when it reappeared, in the company of so many other startling poems, in the more sizeable *Poems and Ballads*, the reaction was immediate. On August 4, the *Saturday Review*, in a long and deprecating notice of the book, referred to the author as 'the libidinous laureate of a pack of satyres'. On the same date hostile reviews appeared also in the *London Review* and *The Athenaeum*. As a counterbalance to the attack, he received a friendly letter from Lord Lytton, who had earlier written to Swinburne to express his admiration for *Atalanta*. Swinburne replied:

Dear Lord Lytton,
    Your letter was doubly acceptable to me, coming as it did on the same day with the abusive reviews of my book which appeared on Saturday. While I have the approval of those from whom alone praise can give pleasure, I can dispense with the favour of journalists.

During the next week events moved to a climax. Word became current that a worse review yet was to appear in *The Times* and that the publisher as well as the author would be held up to execration. According to the memoirs of a certain Sir William Hardman, the article was actually set up in type when a 'private hint was given to Moxon, in order that he

[1] Lang, Vol. I, p. 170.

might, if so inclined, disconnect himself from the bawdry'.[1] Rossetti, calling at Moxon's, found Payne, now the general manager, in a state of panic and only too anxious to dissociate himself from the publication. Rossetti reported to Swinburne. Swinburne wrote to Lord Lytton:[2]

> Dear Lord Lytton,
>   ... if Lord Houghton had not gone off to Vichy, I should certainly take counsel with him. As it is, I am compelled to decide without further help. I have no relation with Messrs. Moxon except of a strictly business character, and considering that the head of their firm has broken his agreement by refusing to continue the sale of my poems, without even speaking to me on the matter, I cannot but desire, first of all, to have no further dealings with any one so untrustworthy. The book is mine. I agreed with him to issue an edition of 1000 copies, he undertaking to print, publish, and sell them, and if the edition sold off, I was to have two-thirds of the profits. He does not now deny the contract which he refuses to fulfil; he simply said to a friend who called on him as my representative [Rossetti] that on hearing there was to be an article in *The Times* attacking my book as improper, he could not continue the sale.

In fact, the article in *The Times* never appeared. Lytton replied to Swinburne by inviting him to come and stay for a few days at his home to talk things over. While he was there, Swinburne received a letter from another publisher, John Camden Hotten, offering to take over and continue the sale. To Howell, Swinburne wrote from Knebworth:[3]

> ... I've just had a note from Hotten which I must answer at once. Lord Lytton advises my reissuing the Poems at once with him, and breaking off wholly with Payne. He says either Hotten should buy the surplus copies of the edition, in his own interest which would be impaired if Payne sold it as waste paper. Or–I must buy them up under a friend's name *as* waste paper, if he so designs to sell them. Or–Payne must be compelled to destroy them instead.– This is his advice as a man of business. Will you tell Hotten this and let him act on it.

Howell was obviously a connection of Hotten's, and it was probably on his prompting that Hotten had addressed himself to Swinburne. Howell may have been in some ways a rascal, but his intervention at this

---

[1] *The Hardman Papers, a further selection, 1865–1868*, ed. by S. M. Ellis, p. 192.
[2] Lang, Vol. I, p. 172.   [3] Lang, Vol. I, p. 175–6.

moment was providential, even if—as is very possible—he was getting a rake-off as agent. Swinburne's letter continues:

> Please too find out what H. proposes about my Blake, which is nearly all in type. If he offers to buy it up I shall not allow Payne to publish it or anything more of mine. Please ask also about the *remainders* and next edition of Chastelard – Atalanta – and the Q. Mother. Lytton thinks H.'s offer very fair . . .

Swinburne subsequently transferred his interests wholly to Hotten, and within a short time all his books reappeared under the latter's imprint.

18

A Song of Italy : Songs Before Sunrise

MAZZINI, the Italian patriot, had been an early hero of Swinburne's and the subject of one of the latter's Oxford poems. He had sent him a copy of *Atalanta*. Gosse has a curious story, apparently communicated to him by Lord Carlisle, about a meeting, to which Carlisle was party, at the house of a man named George Howard. Also present were Dr. Jowett, the Master of Balliol, and Mazzini, who was brought by the German exile Karl Blind, to discuss 'what could be done *with* and *for* Algernon'.[1] It was apparently felt that the latter's gifts and energy ought to be channelled into something other than the rather peculiar erotica which caused his friends distress. Mazzini was shown Swinburne's *Ode on the Insurrection in Candia*, and, touched by it, volunteered to try to harness Swinburne's talents to the cause of Italian liberty.

He wrote to Swinburne, in March 1867, thanking him—after a delay of two years—for the copy of *Atalanta* and praising the *Ode*. Then he went on: 'Give us a series of "Lyrics for the Crusade". Have not our praise, but our blessing. You *can* if you choose.'[2]

In point of fact Swinburne had, by this time, already written his long poem *Song of Italy*, which he finished in February 1867. Mazzini would have been even more touched had he read this, in which the Spirit of Freedom thus addresses the prostrate Italia:

> My lesser jewels sewn on skirt and hem,
>   I have no need of them
> Obscured and flawed by sloth or craft or power;
>   But thou, that wast my flower,
> The blossom bound between my brows . . .

and she is bidden rise:

> With girdles of green freedom, and with red
>   Roses, and white snow . . .

Green, red and white being the colours of the Italian flag. The theme is continued in the verses which follow, in which Swinburne apostrophizes

[1] Gosse, p. 166.   [2] Lafourcade, p. 149.

Mazzini and then celebrates Garibaldi's liberation of Sicily and Southern Italy.

> Praise him, O gracious might of dews and rains
>   That feed the purple plains,
> O sacred sunbeams bright as bare steel drawn,
>   O cloud and fire and dawn;
> Red hills of flame, white Alps, green Apennines,
>   Banners of blowing pines,
> Standards of stormy snows, flags of light leaves,
>   Three wherewith Freedom weaves
> One ensign that once woven and once unfurled
>   Makes day of all a world, . . .

The first meeting between Swinburne and Mazzini took place on March 30, 1867, at the house of Karl Blind, to whom Swinburne had been introduced by Thomas Purnell. To meet Mazzini, he missed an occasion of seeing George Powell, a Welshman who had written to him after the publication of *Atalanta*, and who had become to some extent a friend. Writing to Powell the next day, Swinburne confessed frankly that he had disappointed him in order to be introduced to Mazzini, 'my beloved chief'.[1] To his mother, he wrote:[2]

> I must . . . tell you what has happened to me. All last evening and late into the night I was with Mazzini. . . . The minute he came into the room, which was full of people, he walked straight up to me (who was standing in my place and feeling as if I trembled all over) and said 'I know *you*', and I did as I always thought I should and really meant not to do if I could help–went down on my knees and kissed his hand.

He not only knelt, he produced from his pocket, and read to him, while still at his feet, the whole of *A Song of Italy*. It was, of course, still in manuscript, and it was the first time that the poem had been heard. Mazzini is said to have been quite overwhelmed, though whether with emotion or exhaustion is not recorded. There are over seven hundred lines.

The poems Swinburne wrote in response to Mazzini's exhortation were *Songs Before Sunrise*. To William Michael Rossetti he wrote, on October 9, from his parents' new home at Holmwood:[3] 'After all, in spite of jokes and perversities–malgré ce cher Marquis et ces foutus

---

[1] Leith, pp. 91–92.   [2] Lang, Vol. I, p. 236.   [3] Lang, Vol. I, p. 195.

journaux—it is nice to have something to love and to believe in as I do in Italy. It was only Gabriel and his followers in art (l'art pour l'art) who for a time frightened me from speaking out . . .'

Before a Crucifix opens with a beautiful description of the Italian peasant women:

> Here, down between the dusty trees,
>   At this lank edge of haggard wood,
> Women with labour-loosened knees,
>   With gaunt backs bowed by servitude,
> Stop, shift their loads, and pray, and fare
> Forth with souls easier for the prayer.

Surveying the figure on the cross, the poet reflects that the clergy and dogma have so come between those, like himself, now living and the man who was crucified that it is no longer possible to know what he was really like. The attitude is not one of crude atheism; what is presented is rather an agnostic's query as to the value of the fruits of sacrifice.

> O hidden face of man, whereover
>   The years have woven a viewless veil,
> If thou wast verily man's lover,
>   What did thy love or blood avail?

In *Tenebrae*, a vision of the destiny of the spirit of man, which he conceives as a metaphysical entity, a flower in which the individuals are the petals, Christ is a hero figure. It is the voice of prophesy which is speaking to the poet:

> 'Seeing each life given is a leaf
>   Of the manifold multiform flower,
> And the least among these, and the chief,
> As an ear in the red-ripe sheaf
>   Stored for the harvesting hour.

> 'O spirit of man, most holy,
>   The measure of things and the root,
> In our summers and winters a lowly
> Seed, putting forth of them slowly
>   Thy supreme blossom and fruit;

'In thy sacred and perfect year,
   The souls that were parcel of thee
In the labour and life of us here
Shall be rays of thy sovereign sphere,
   Springs of thy motion shall be. . . .

'There, whosoever had light,
   And, having, for men's sake gave;
All that warred against night;
All that were found in the fight
   Swift to be slain and to save;

'Undisbranched of the storms that disroot us,
   Of the lures that enthrall unenticed;
The names that exalt and transmute us;
The blood-bright splendour of Brutus,
   The snow-bright splendour of Christ.'

One cannot help being impressed by the firmness of the verse, recalling in its austerity the carved quality of *Faustine*, though dedicated now to a more noble cause.

English sentiment has always favoured the cause of Italian liberty, but, inevitably, many of the poems in this volume, relating as they do to relatively minor episodes in the long struggle for independence, have lost interest for today. Swinburne himself was obviously aware of this danger, and tried to balance the necessary topicality of the volume with some poems dedicated to the more permanent concerns of the human spirit. In the humanistically entitled *Hymn of Man*, paradoxically, he expresses his real and positive philosophical belief, which proves to be in a pantheistic monism:

. . . the God that ye make you is grievous, and
   gives not aid,
Because it is but for your sake that the God of your
   making is made.
Thou and I and he are not gods made men for a
   span,
But God, if a God there be, is the substance of men
   which is man.
Our lives are as pulses or pores of his manifold body
   and breath;

As waves of his sea on the shores where birth is the
    beacon of death.
We men, the multiform features of man, whatsoever
    we be,
Recreate him of whom we are creatures, and all we
    only are he.
Not each man of all men is God, but God is the fruit
    of the whole;
Indivisible spirit and blood, indiscernible body from
    soul.

Obviously, there is a debt here to Blake, but so had Blake his debt to
Neo-Platonism and to Plato. It is, in parenthesis, curious that Swinburne
never seems to have tackled Plato direct.

In *Hertha* he voices the same philosophy, but speaks from the point
of view of the universal being behind the dual forces of spirit and matter:

> I am that which began;
>   Out of me the years roll;
> Out of me God and man;
>   I am equal and whole;
> God changes, and man, and the form of them bodily;
>   I am the soul. . . .

> A creed is a rod,
>   And a crown is of night;
> But this thing is God,
>   To be man with thy might,
> To grow straight in the strength of thy spirit, and
>   live out thy life as the light. . . .

> For truth only is living,
>   Truth only is whole,
> And the love of his giving
>   Man's polestar and pole;
> Man, pulse of my centre, and fruit of my body, and
>   seed of my soul.

> One birth of my bosom;
>   One beam of mine eye;
> One topmost blossom
>   That scales the sky;

> Man, equal and one with me, man that is made of
>   me, man that is I.

Here perhaps one feels more the debt to the humanistic mysticism of
Whitman, and indeed the volume contains the famous ode *To Walt
Whitman in America*. In it Swinburne calls to the American poet to send
a song for the Campaign, from the new world:

> Sweet-smelling of pine-leaves and grasses,
>   And blown as a tree through and through
> With the winds of the keen mountain-passes,
>   And tender as sun-smitten dew;
> Sharp-tongued as the winter that shakes
> The wastes of your limitless lakes,
>   Wide-eyed as the sea-line's blue.

With such exalted poems as these, one may say that the volume contains
much of his best work. Also, it has in it nothing that is morbid or disagreeable. Lady Trevelyan, had she lived to see it, would have appreciated *Songs Before Sunrise* more than *Poems and Ballads*.

Mazzini, in evoking the lyrics, had done more for English poetry than
for Swinburne himself. One might have thought that the sustained
elevation of so much of the writing betokened a buoyant mood, but in
fact, according to Gosse's *Confidential Paper*, Swinburne was still at this
time frequenting the house in St. John's Wood. To reach it from Dorset
Square, he would walk through Regent's Park, and, sometimes arriving
too early for his appointment, would take a seat and write down verses
which had been forming in his head while he walked. Some of the *Songs
Before Sunrise*, says Gosse, were composed on these occasions.

Whatever the accuracy of this story, it is clear that Swinburne was
now in correspondence about flagellation not only with Lord Houghton
and with Howell, but with Powell too. On August 13, 1867, he wrote
to Powell:[1]

> A thousand thanks for your gift which is trebly valuable for
> interest and external belongings and as the seal of friendship. I
> long to thank you in person and to enjoy the sight and touch of the
> birch that has been used. I don't think I ever more dreaded the
> entrance of the swishing room than I now desire a sight of it. To
> assist unseen at the holy ceremony some after twelve I would give

---

[1] Lang, Vol. I, pp. 259–60.

any of my poems. The locket is exquisite, worthy of the relic . . .
What fun it would be to enact (I did once with another fellow—)
the whole process, exchanging the parts of active and passive in
turn.

Swinburne's songs for Italy are often compared with Victor Hugo's
Les Chatiments, sometimes to their disadvantage, on the grounds that
Hugo had an experience of involvement in political rebellion which
Swinburne lacked. Yet just because Hugo was a political exile from his
native country, his poems about the cause have a bitterness, not untinged
by self-pity, which is absent from Swinburne's fresh and inspiring
hymns.

19

Adah Menken

To refer again to the *Confidential Paper* of Gosse, it appears Rossetti was concerned that Swinburne, though nearly thirty years of age, had never had a sexual connection with a woman, and, hoping to break him of his visits to the whipping ladies in St. John's Wood, took advantage of the visit to London in December 1867 of the actress Adah Menken. He gave her £10, then a considerable sum of money, to seduce Swinburne.

Born in Louisiana on June 15, 1835, aged thirty-two and five times married, she was considered a natural charmer and indeed a photograph of her in tights shows a shapely and good-looking young woman. Her most famous exploit was to ride a horse on to the stage in a version of Byron's *Mazeppa*, but she was not without cultivation and had studied sculpture in Ohio, written an article in *The Israelite* about Baron Rothschild's admission to Parliament, and a poem called *Infelicia*.

The go-between introduced for this purpose by Rossetti, was, oddly, John Thomson, the same who had introduced Swinburne to the whipping ladies in St. John's Wood. That Rossetti should have employed him shows that he knew enough about John Thomson to have been Gosse's source not only for the story about Adah Menken but for the story about St. John's Wood. John Thomson apparently took Swinburne to the theatre to see Adah Menken play, and told him of her great admiration for his poetry, and that she wrote poetry herself. She, having been previously briefed by Rossetti in Chelsea, then paid Swinburne a visit, and, upon her own insistence, stayed the night.

What, however, happened? Swinburne, years afterwards, talking to Gosse, said that in the morning she sat on the edge of the bed swinging her legs and reading him her own poetry; an anecdote which might suggest they had become lovers. Rossetti, however, told Gosse that Adah Menken, after having for some time been a frequent visitor to Swinburne's rooms, gave the £10 back to him, saying she had not been able to bring Swinburne 'up to scratch'. Explaining her failure, she said to Rossetti, 'I can't make him understand that *biting's* no use!'[1]

[1] British Museum: MSS. Ashley 5753, f. 30.

There is a letter from Swinburne to the journalist Thomas Purnell dated December 9 (1867), in which he says:[1]

> ... If you see Dolores before I do, tell her with my love that I would not show myself sick and disfigured in her eyes. I was spilt last week out of a hansom, and my nose and forehead cut to rags—was seedy for four days, and hideous.

Dolores was a name by which Adah Menken had earlier been known, and Swinburne wrote into her album the lines:[2]

DOLORIDA

Combien de temps, dis la belle,
Dis, veux-tu m'être fidèle?—
Pour une nuit, pour un jour,
  Mon amour.

L'Amour nous flatte et nous touche
Du doigt, de l'oeil, de la bouche,
Pour un jour, pour une nuit,
  Et s'enfuit.

This has made some writers think that Adah Menken was the original *Dolores* of *Poems and Ballads*, but that volume appeared in July 1866, whereas Adah Menken did not make this visit to England until October 1867. The probability is that, knowing he had written a poem called *Dolores*, she made the most, to him, of having earlier borne that name.

It may have been while under the influence of drink that Swinburne was 'spilt from a hansom cab'. Gosse relates such an incident, though he puts it at a later date.

If the intimacy between Swinburne and Adah Menken stopped short of that for which Rossetti had given her money, Swinburne nevertheless made the most of it. Writing to Lord Houghton on December 24, he said:[3]

> ... I also enjoy (certainly) not less the bonds of a somewhat

---

[1] Lang, Vol. I, p. 276.

[2] *Adah Menken, a fragment of autobiography.* This misleadingly entitled pamphlet is neither by Adah Menken nor, as stated on the flyleaf, 'by' Swinburne. It contains these lines and extracts from some letters of Swinburne, but the matter is put together and introduced by someone who signs himself X.Y.Z.

[3] Lang, Vol. I, p. 281.

riotous concubinage. I don't know many *husbands* who could exact or expect from a *wife* such indulgences as are hourly laid at my feet.

To his Welsh friend, Powell, he wrote on January 26, 1868:[1]

> I am ashamed to have left your last note so long unanswered—but I have been so worried of late with influenza, love-making, and other unwholesome things—... that I have 'left undone all I should have done'. I must send you in a day or two a photograph of my present possessor—known to Britannia as Miss Menken, to me as Dolores (her real Christian name)—and myself taken together. We both came out very well. Of course it's *private.*

Whatever the insufficiencies of the liaison, one has the impression that Swinburne was pushing the news of it to his friends because it counteracted the rumours of his homosexuality. He had, however, gone too far in his distribution of the photographs; through some agency unknown, suddenly, prints of them appeared on sale in the windows of several shops. To Powell he wrote again on April 17:[2]

> ... only today have I been able to get one copy of either photograph. There has been a *damned* row about it; paper after paper has flung pellets of dirt at me, assuming or asserting the falsehood that its publicaton and sale all over London were things authorised or permitted or even forseen by the sitters: whereas of course it was a private affair, to be known (or shewn) to friends only.

At the End of May, Adah Menken returned to France, and the affair was at an end. On July 22, we find Swinburne writing to his old friend John Nichol:[3]

> ... I am none the worse for a fainting fit brought on by the damnable unventilated air of the Museum ... I went early to the Brit. Mus. to look up certain references—met a man I know, about to leave—and agreed to wait till he could return at 1 or 1.30, when we were to go and lunch together—began to feel giddy and faint in an hour or so (no wonder, you would say, if you had breathed the atmosphere that day) but thought I would hold out and keep my promise, and consequently after some twenty minutes' struggle fainted right out, and in falling cut my forehead slightly.

[1] Lang, Vol. I, p. 286.   [2] Lang, Vol. I, p. 295.
[3] Lang, Vol. I, pp. 302–3.

It was as he was being carried out that the late Sir Edmund Gosse, his future biographer, first saw Swinburne, and this is the famous 'fit' in the British Museum to which Gosse refers. The newspapers next day carried accounts of the accident which alarmed his friends, and Jowett sent Swinburne a kindly letter of advice written on the hypothesis that the cause was intemperance. Whether it was epilepsy or inebriation can never now be known. Certainly, Swinburne had had an epileptiform fit in Whistler's studio, but he was by this time drinking heavily; the question is complicated because epileptics, of all people, should avoid alcohol, as it increases their liability to fits. It remains, however, a fact that the atmosphere of the British Museum Reading Room, under the dome, is somewhat oppressive, and even healthy people sometimes feel unwell in it.

On July 13, three days after the mishap, Rossetti and his brother, William Michael, having read of the mishap in the papers, called together to see Swinburne, and found him in excellent spirits, though with pieces of sticking plaster on his forehead.[1]

On August 10, in Paris, Adah Menken suddenly died, aged only just thirty-three. Swinburne wrote to Powell, on August 26, briefly but not without feeling:[2]

> ... I am sure you were sorry on my account to hear of the death of my poor dear Menken—it was a great shock to me and a real grief—I was ill for some days. She was most loveable as a friend as well as a mistress.

One still feels that there is a significance in his insistence upon the word mistress.

[1] *Rossetti Papers*, pp. 318–19.   [2] Lang, Vol. I, p. 307

20

'The Last of Lesbia Brandon'

IT was over five years since Swinburne had met Sir Richard Burton, the explorer, at Milnes house, but they had kept contact. Luke Ionides recalled having seen Burton carrying Swinburne down some stairs:[1] '... after putting him down on the pavement he called a hansom. Swinburne could not find the step and complained "hansoms were getting higher and higher each year".'

This sounds like another episode in which Swinburne was the worse for drink. However that may be, on January 11, 1867, he had written to Burton:[2] '... I have in hand a scheme of mixed verse and prose—a sort of étude à la Balzac—*plus* the poetry—which I flatter myself will be more offensive and objectionable to Britannia than anything I have yet done.' This was *Lesbia Brandon*, on which he was working again. He now introduced into the story a character called Mariani, an Italian patriot modelled upon Mazzini, whom Bertie meets in London, and with whom he has long talks about the Italian struggle for independence. Three of the leaves carrying these conversations bear 1866 watermarks; but Swinburne did not meet Mazzini until 1866, so that one would have known without the evidence of the watermarks that these sections could not have been composed earlier.

There is also a chapter written in, concerning a demi-mondaine whom Bertie meets in London, named Leonora Harley. It is written on three leaves, each of which bears an 1866 watermark. The description of her opens:[3]

> There was afloat in London about this time a lady of aspiring build, handsome beyond the average and stupid below the elect of her profession. She had a superb and seductive beauty, some kindness of nature, and no mind whatever. Tall, white-faced, long limbed, with melancholy eyes that meant nothing and suggested anything, she had made her way in good time. Her trick of mournful and thoughtful manner, assumed where other women let fall their grave or gay assumptions, was an implement

---

[1] *Transatlantic Review*, March 1924, p. 24 and Lang, Vol. I, p. 223 n.
[2] Lang, Vol. I, p. 224.　　[3] *Lesbia Brandon*, Wise: f. 132. Hughes: p. 103.

which stood her in good stead: her sad eyes and drawn lips forged money in mints where swifter and brighter faces had failed. She was a shining light in what her patron, Mr. Linley, called the demi-monde. 'Above the street, below the boudoir,' ... Coarse or fine, she never said a good thing. She had not even the harlot's talent of discernment. A preacher might have yawned under the infliction of her talk.

... Her hands were exquisite, soft and keen at once, made to caress and to repel. Her small rounded feet could curl up and strike out. ... Nothing in her was not pleasant; nothing was durable. She was full of life, and suggestive of change. She was active, and vital, and stupid ... a woman too stupid for vice or virtue ...

This, surely, is Swinburne's not very kind picture of Adah Menken. Hughes, in his commentary,[1] takes Lafourcade to task for suggesting the portrait owes something to Adah Menken, and asserts that it must be Fanny Cornforth, Adah Menken being too cultivated a woman to be described as stupid. Against Hughes's argument, it must be pointed out that Swinburne could have put Fanny Cornforth into the novel when he first wrote it, in 1864, when she would have been fresher in his memory. It was Adah Menken who would have been fresh in his mind when writing on paper bearing an 1866 watermark. Certainly, Adah Menken had some cultivation, and Swinburne himself had written to Hotten to ask him to print her poem *Infelicia*; he may nevertheless have found her literary pretensions, and her expression of her ideas, boring rather than interesting. Five husbands plus as many liaisons by the age of thirty-two betokens some flightiness, and since she took Rossetti's £10 to sleep with Swinburne she clearly was venal, though to give it back was disarmingly honest. If the passage seems unkind, one must remember that it may have been composed before her death, and without premonition that it was imminent. Fanny Cornforth did not interest Swinburne sufficiently for him to have written of her at all.

With this woman Bertie does, in a later chapter, on paper which bears no watermarked date, have at least some sort of an affair: he[2] 'felt the attraction of the woman, and was drawn to her without knowing it; she caught him round the head and kissed his hair'. After some verbal sparring, she:[3]

[1] *Lesbia Brandon,* pp. 356–59.
[2] *Lesbia Brandon,* Wise: f. 138. Hughes: p. 116.
[3] Wise: f. 139. Hughes: p. 117.

again kissed his wet lips after they had touched the leavings of her draught; and again repelled him. A face unlike her's rose between her eyes and his; with close melancholy lips, full of meaning and of passion; with sombre and luminous eyes, with deep thick eyelids and heavy lashes that seemed as though sodden and satiate with old and past tears; with large bright brows, and chin and neck too sensitive and expressive to be flexible as these before him.

The face that rises between him and the harlot is meant to be that of Margaret or else of Lesbia Brandon; but can one doubt that it was th face of Mary Gordon, and the memory of her, that rose between Swinburne and Adah Menken? Surely one has here Swinburne's real expression of his feelings about his pathetic and (though he did not know it) engineered affair with Adah Menken.

These new chapters concerning the Italian patriot and the demimondaine have been inserted between the scenes at Ensdon while Bertie was still a child, and the dénouement, but have little, indeed no effect on the plot. Something has, however, been inserted which has a big effect. Following the scene in which Margaret comes in to Bertie's room, on a leaf watermarked 1866, we read:[1] 'Margaret . . . made less of him than before . . . She told him he was not half a boy and was more than kind or gracious to young Lunsford.' These are the lines cited by Hughes when taking Lafourcade to task for assuming that the lover of Margaret was Denham. The watermark reveals the leaf to be a late addition, not a link in the plot as originally conceived. The previous chapter had ended in such a way that the reader felt that the relationship between Bertie and Margaret was becoming sexual; the introduction of these lines concerning Lunsford is surely to distract the reader from the developing theme of incest, and to make him uncertain. This is an interpolation put in to mask the story. Whatever he said to Burton about flattering himself that the novel would be offensive and objectionable, he was at this time thinking of getting it published, and to that end, making the theme unclear.

There is also a chapter, for which nothing in the story has prepared one, in which Mr. Linley makes the most extraordinary revelations to Denham, that he is the son of Lesbia's mother by Margaret's father, and that, being illegitimate, he was brought up by Mr. Linley and his wife, who was Denham's mother's sister. This seems very forced, as there was no previous hint of Denham's being under the protection of Linley, or

[1] Wise: f. 93. Hughes: p. 83.

of his being related to anyone in the story. His becoming Margaret's half sister would make a relationship between them incestuous though not to the same extent as if the lover were Bertie. This chapter extends over leaves of which seven are watermarked 1865.

The most dramatic additions, however, are of two chapters which come after the dénouement between Margaret and her lover which culminates in his suicide. One of these is marked by Swinburne at the top *For penultimate chapter*. This chapter is written upon two leaves, the second of which bears an 1866 watermark, and the text refers both to the demi-mondaine and to the Italian patriot. One would know from the matter, if one did not from the watermark, that it was written after Swinburne's acquaintance with Mazzini and with Adah Menken; but in it he makes the Italian patriot die. Mazzini did not, in fact, die until 1872; Swinburne may have been anticipating the event, or this chapter may have been written at this much later date. It refers to Bertie as still alive, and says that what the future has in store for him is still unknown. It is because Bertie is still alive at the end of the story that it has never struck earlier biographers that he could have been Margaret's lover, who committed suicide. But, this ending being written at any rate as late as 1866, forms part of Swinburne's attempt to disguise the fact that, as originally conceived, it was Bertie with whom Margaret fell in love.

Hughes has put this chapter at the end, because, to his mind, the tidying up of the fates of the minor characters, and of Bertie himself, suggests that Swinburne changed his mind about its being the penultimate, and turned it into the ultimate chapter. I cannot accept Hughes's contention that the words *For penultimate chapter* mean merely notes for this. The style is too literary for that of notes.

For once, there is something to be said for the arrangement of Wise, who keeps the 'penultimate chapter' as the penultimate, and puts after it the chapter which deals with the last meeting of Lesbia and Bertie, which bears on the first sheet the words, 'His old friend's death had hurt him for a time . . .'[1] Bertie's old friend, surely, is the Italian patriot, who died in the penultimate chapter. Hughes, of course, takes it to be Denham, since he takes Denham to be Margaret's lover, or Lunsford, if the lover was meant to be Lunsford. But 'old friend' seems an impossible description of Denham, who did nothing for Bertie but beat him, and I have shown above that the single phrase connecting Lunsford with Margaret is of late interpolation.

[1] Wise: f. 185. Hughes: p. 157.

The rest of this chapter describes the meeting of Bertie and Lesbia, at the latter's bedside. She has taken fatal doses of eau-de-Cologne and opium, and has called him only to say good-bye. The chapter ends:[1] 'And that was the last of Lesbia Brandon, poetess and pagan.' This, in the Wise binding, is the last sentence of the book, and justifies, poetically, the title given to it by Wise, *Lesbia Brandon*. However, it should be noticed that at one moment Lesbia says to Bertie, 'I wish I were dying in Italy. Your friend never will.'[2] This would seem to justify the refusal of Hughes to consider the Italian patriot as the 'old friend' who had died already, though I find his alternative suppositions unacceptable.

After prolonged juggling with the pieces of this literary jig-saw, I have come to the conclusion that there is no way in which they can be arranged so that they all fit into place.

Swinburne wrote alternative beginnings to his fiction. There is the *Kirklowes* fragment, which seems to be a discarded beginning to the story of Reginald Harewood, which later became *Love's Cross Currents*. He also wrote alternative middle sections, such as the sheets bound into *Lesbia Brandon* by Wise but rightly discarded from it in Hughes's edition, in which there is no Lady Wariston but a Lady Waristoun, and Margaret is not this Lady Waristoun but Margaret Lunsford, and Bertie's surname is not Seyton but Winwood. These are obviously discarded tries for something that was not continued in the terms envisaged when they were written. I submit that he also wrote alternative endings, or rather, that he wrote three chapters, each of which was, when he wrote it, intended to be the last chapter of the novel known as *Lesbia Brandon*: the first grand dénouement, in which Bertie became Margaret's lover and committed suicide; the second grand dénouement in which Lesbia committed suicide, with Bertie at her bedside; and the 'penultimate chapter' which, as Hughes pointed out, came to take on the character of a possible last chapter.

Both Wise and Hughes wished to make of Lesbia Brandon an organic whole. Wise wanted to present within his expensive blue Morocco binding a complete, unpublished novel by Swinburne. Hughes wished, after making an investigation of the text for which he must be respected, to present to the public a complete novel by Swinburne published for the first time in his edition.

In fact, there is not a completed text of this work. It is a very rich collection of fragments.

[1] Wise: f. 195. Hughes: p. 166.   [2] Wise: f. 187. Hughes: p. 159.

21

Interludes in Etrétat and Vichy

SWINBURNE, during the summer of 1868, was pining for the sea. After his fainting fit in the British Museum he wrote to Nichol, on July 22, of his doctor's advice that:[1] 'I should be the better for tonics and sea-bathing (I should think so as to the latter – I am dying for it – there is no lust or appetite comparable) . . .

On July 28 he wrote to Powell, who had rented a villa in Etrétat:[2]

> My 'accident' was merely a fainting fit brought on by heat and bad ventilation – I was out next day – the cut on my forehead is nearly healed. I too am suffering from diarrhoea . . . Oh shan't I be glad to accept your invitation! 1) to see you and cheer and be cheered if ill or worried 2) to satiate my craving (ultra Sapphic and plusquam Sadic) lust after the sea. I must go by Boulogne . . . My life has been enlivened of late by a fair friend who keeps a maison de supplices à la Rodin –

In other words a flagellation brothel. Humphrey Hare, in his book on Swinburne, quotes the phrase 'maison de supplices à la Rodin' between inverted commas, and then adds, as if on some other authority, 'in the Euston Road'.[3] Hare never gives his sources, and the list of such establishments given by Fraxi does not include an address in the Euston Road. Certainly the Euston Road, at one end, is near Regent's Park, but Fraxi's Regent's Park address is probably the house in Circus Road, which, according to Gosse's *Confidential Paper*, was the one patronized by Swinburne until he quarrelled with the ladies about their fees. Hare may be mistaken about the Euston Road, or Swinburne may have found there a new address, the existence of which escaped Fraxi's informant.

One would think that continual whipping must have contributed to the weakness of his condition. As for the diarrhoea, to which he often refers in his letters, I have seen this referred to as his 'alcholic dysentery', but I consulted a medical man[4] on the point, and am informed that the term is misleading in that it implies an infection, from infected food or water; what Swinburne might have had, as a consequence of his drink-

[1] Lang, Vol. I, p. 303.   [2] Lang, Vol. I, p. 305.
[3] Hare, p. 151.   [4] Dr. H. Gordon Smith, M.D.

ing, was an inflammation of the bowel, causing the diarrhoea of which he complained. Swinburne, himself, never admits any connection between his drinking and his condition.

In September 1868 Swinburne joined Powell in Etrétat. Here, off the coast of Normandy, he was able to indulge his craving for swimming in the sea, but one day, getting caught in a current, he was almost drowned. He was carried out to sea for a considerable distance, two miles as he says, but was rescued by some fishermen who pulled him aboard their boat. By a curious coincidence, the episode was witnessed by one of the great writers of France. Guy de Maupassant, then only eighteen and spending the summer at Etrétat, heard some seamen shout that a man was drowning, and, seeing them launching a boat, jumped into it in the hope that he might be able to help pull the luckless swimmer aboard. A boat already out reached the swimmer first, but because de Maupassant had gone to the rescue he received an invitation to lunch with Swinburne and Powell the next day, at Powell's chalet.

De Maupassant is the only person to have given us a description of Powell. He says he was short and fat; also that he did translations from Icelandic. Both he and his guest were regarded by the local people as eccentric, which was not surprising, seeing that parts of skeletons and a hand, said to be that of a parricide were placed as if negligently on the tables, while an uncaged and very active monkey was somewhat hostile to the young French visitor. Nevertheless, he found his hosts fascinating:[1]

> Pendant tout le déjeuner on parla d'art, de littérature et d'humanité; et les opinions de ces deux amis jetaient sur les choses une espèce de lueur troublante, macabre, car ils avaient une manière de voir et de comprendre qui me les montrait comme deux visionnaires malades, ivres de poesie perverse et magique.

Later, de Maupassant used the episode in one of his stories, *L'Anglais d'Etrétat*.

Returned to England, Swinburne went to stay with his parents in Oxfordshire.

On January 12, 1869, there is an interesting entry in the *Rossetti Papers*:[2] 'Swinburne is excessively enthusiastic about the Mahabharata

[1] De Maupassant, 'Notes sur Swinburne', in *Poemes et Ballads de A. C. Swinburne*, p. viii.
[2] Lafourcade, p. 176.

which he has been looking at in a French translation under the auspices of Bendyshe.' The *Mahabharata* is the great Hindu epic of which the *Bhagavad Gita* forms part. It is refreshing to find Swinburne reading anything so elevating. The doctrine is one of 'Action without attachment to the fruit of action', right action being, in itself, its own reward.

Swinburne, though he had begun the *Songs Before Sunrise* immediately upon Mazzini's prompting, had been working slowly, and it would seem not impossible that the sublimity of the passages in *Hertha* and the *Hymn of Man*, neither of which was composed until after this date, owes something not merely to the normally accepted sources, Blake and Whitman, but to this direct acquaintance with one of the great religious and mystical scriptures of the world. (Whitman, of course, had read the *Bhagavad Gita*, which may have been Swinburne's reason for deciding to do so.)

This was not an eventful period in Swinburne's life. In the summer of 1869 he visited Vichy with Burton, and they took the cure. In North Africa, today, bottled Vichy Water is regarded as remedial for dysentery, or enteritis, and it is possible that Burton knew of a reputation which it may have had even then, and may have led Swinburne to Vichy with his unacknowledged condition in mind. At any rate, Vichy benefited him. On July 29, 1869, Swinburne wrote to Powell:[1] 'The place suits me splendidly for health–I have been here five days, and am better than I have been for five months.' On August 10, he was able to write to his sister Alice that he and Burton had climbed to the top of the Puy de Dôme. To do this, he must have been considerably restored, for, apart from being practically shadeless, the ascent is steep.

[1] Lang, Vol. II, p. 19.

22

Simeon Solomon

SOON after his return to England, probably in the late September of
1869, Swinburne received the following letter from the young painter
Simeon Solomon:[1]

> My dear Swinburne,
>   I am so sorry I missed you the other morning when you called.
> I very much desired to see you and say how pleased I was to hear
> from Powell that you had been so well when you were away and
> that you had enjoyed your travels so well . . . Have you heard
> that Campbell is going to publish a popular 'Justine'? We are
> coming to a sense of what is right. Send me a little letter.
>   With love,
>   Ever yours,
>   S. Solomon

This was not the first letter Swinburne had received from Solomon.
Seven years earlier, he had received a letter very much more revealing:[2]

> My dear Swinburne,
>   Really I feel so divided between flattered vanity and anger that
> I hardly know what to say to you; the first is in a great degree on
> account of your telling me that my letter was interesting, (I
> feared it was horribly dull,) and anger that you should fill a
> letter and spend so much time on me about a subject which, [sic]
> I regarded with the deepest and most unqualified horror not
> unmixed with feelings of deep commiseration!!!! I assure you that
> I wept at the recital of the boyish agonies you depicted in your last,
> I was doubled up with grief at the idea of so many tender posteriors
> quivering under the pitiless strokes of the rod.
>   My friend who has excited so much sympathy and interest in
> your breast, is called William Eden Nesfield . . . he is a fat, jolly
> hearty fellow, genuinely good natured, very fond of smoking, and
> I deeply grieve to say of women; although doubtless bearing the
> marks of the many Etonian rods I mentioned, feels no more the
> *real* merit and meaning of that instrument of delight than my pen
> does; I should unhesitatingly pronounce him to be not at all of a

[1] British Museum: MSS. Ashley 1755.   [2] Ibid.

sensual temperament in your and my conception of the term; the way in which the subject was brought up was as follows. I had bought a week or two before I saw him a penny paper of no merit whatever, called Peter Spy, exceedingly coarse, silly, and unsatisfactory but the week I bought it there happened to be a picture on the first page, which, though not in a first-rate style of art, was sufficiently inviting to purchase for the mean sum of a penny. The subject treated was entitled 'The disgraceful act of Flagellation from the earliest ages to the present time,' . . . I showed it to Nesfield, and naturally the subject of rods turned up, whereupon he gave up the account of his flagellation that I described in my last; it will be by no means difficult for you to meet him. . . . I showed the paper of which I have been speaking to Moore and when he read it he asked me with open mouth and eyes what it meant; he was entirely ignorant of the whole subject, and I sighed to think how I was in his happy, innocent condition before I knew a certain poet whom I will forbear to mention. . . . I began yesterday evening here, pour m'amuser, the autobiography of a man of irregular affections. I will give you a few extracts. . . .

'I will at once candidly unbosom to my readers, my affections are divided between the boy and the birch; I think it is neither necessary or important here to say which has the greater portion of my swelling heart, perhaps the division has been equal for, although I have always felt an inexpressible and thrilling pleasure in the company and *confidence* of handsome boys, these without that instrument of flagellant delights have not completely satisfied. There has been a sensible void: I have yearned for something more . . .' 'On the other hand, the rod, radient (*sic*) and blooming as it is with flowers of Love has never yielded me the true joy when separated from the blushing bottom which Providence has destined to receive its strokes.' . . .

Extracted from an MS. autobiography of

A —— Z ——

Being completely ashamed of myself and having I should imagine tired you sufficiently I shall, my dear Swinburne, bid you good-bye, on my return I will make you many drawings.

I remain,

Yours sincerely,

Simeon Solomon

In the bottom left-hand corner, Solomon has drawn a medallion representing, as he explains in a caption, *The Queen presenting rods to the*

Schoolmasters of the United Kingdom. Within the circle of the medallion, beneath the drawing, is written: MDCCCLXIII. This surely establishes the year in which the letter was written as 1863. Being written small, it must have escaped the eye of the person (perhaps the British Museum authority) who has pencilled in the top right-hand corner of the first leaf of the letter: *?1869.* The later date was presumably suggested because Solomon's other letters to Swinburne, preserved at the Museum can from their internal references be ascribed to the year 1869 and onwards. Solomon never dated his letters, in the ordinary sense, but for an artist to mis-date a drawing would surely be unheard of, and this drawing, being on the letter, surely dates it.

The letter is on black bordered paper, and it occurred to me that a recent death in Solomon's family, if a death could be traced, should support the date in the medallion. A note by Professor Lang, in his edition of Swinburne's letters, refers the reader to Bernard Falk's memoir, *Five Years Dead,*[1] for details concerning Solomon and his family. I obtained this work, and read there that Simeon Solomon's brother, Abraham, died on the day he was elected an A.R.A. I thereupon wrote to the Royal Academy, asking for the date of this double event. The reply I received was that Abraham Solomon was never elected an A.R.A. At an election on July 30, 1861, he received one vote; and he died, not on this date, but on December 19, 1862.[2]

This constituted supporting evidence for the date inscribed in the medallion; for, his brother having died in December 1862, it would be natural that Simeon Solomon should be using black edged notepaper during the early part of 1863. It must have been during the early part of the year that the letter was written, for by the middle of the summer Swinburne had left Rossetti's (where according to Falk he and Solomon chased each other naked round the studio) and gone to the Isle of Wight. It is obvious that the letter was written to Swinburne while he was in town, as Solomon refers to the ease with which he could see Nesfield, who has rooms in Argyll Street, near Solomon's own.

One can say then that the relationship between Solomon and Swinburne had made some headway while Swinburne was still at Rossetti's in the early part of 1863. The remaining letters from Solomon to Swinburne in the British Museum must have been written from

[1] Lang, Vol. II, p. 31, n. and Falk, pp. 311–31.
[2] Letter to the author from Sidney C. Hutchinson, Librarian of the Royal Academy of Arts, dated October 12, 1966.

1869–72. I found thirteen, in all, not ten, as according to Professor Lang; but nine are in one folder, and the others scattered in different files.

Four years younger than Swinburne, Simeon Solomon was born on October 9, 1840, at 3 Sandys Street, Bishopsgate. On his birth certificate, a copy of which I drew from Somerset House, his father's occupation is given as Embosser. In 1858, when he was only eighteen, Simeon exhibited his first picture at the Royal Academy, entitled in the catalogue number 1066 'And the Lord said, Take now thy son, thine only son Isaac and offer him there for a burnt offering upon one of the mountains I will tell thee of'; in fact, he exhibited regularly at the Royal Academy every year from 1858 to 1872.[1]

Simeon Solomon was a draughtsman and painter of great delicacy; he was also, as the letter above quoted shows, a homosexual. The quotation marks in the last paragraph, and the pretence that the text enclosed within them is an extract from the autobiography of some third person, is a disguise for his own predilections; a veil meant to be pierced. Had Swinburne not been homosexually inclined, he would have taken fright at this letter, and eschewed the acquaintance; but one notices that Solomon assumes Swinburne's homosexuality when he says that Nesfield, a man fond of women, was 'not at all of a sensual temperament in your and my conception of the term'.

One can take as mere joking his pretence of having been horrified by Swinburne's letter describing whipped and quivering posteriors, and of having himself been 'innocent' until he met Swinburne. The final paragraph proves his own prior experience. Swinburne himself was given to joking of this kind in his letters to Milnes and others, wherein he occasionally pretends a mock horror of some subject obviously exciting to himself and his correspondent. To assume, as does Falk, that Swinburne corrupted Solomon is unfair to Swinburne, in the same way that Lafourcade, in blaming Milnes for the corruption of Swinburne, is unfair to Milnes. In each case, the younger man was pressing.

Reading Solomon's and Swinburne's letters, the conviction was borne in on me that their sexual perversion, and that of their friends, was related to the floggings they had received at school, and that they were not therefore wholly responsible for their peculiarity. It may, in my view, be pertinent to ask whether there is not a direct connection between sodomy and punishment on the buttocks. It seems obvious that the concentration

[1] Sidney S. Hutchinson, Librarian of the Royal Academy of Arts.

of sensation here, by the use of the birch or rod, produced in this area a new erogenous zone. In some cases, the perversion may have begun before they came to school, with smacking across their mother's or nannie's knee. This is suggested by the frequency with which a woman did the beating in a brothel, and Fraxi's information that some of the clients of the house near Regent's Park liked to be belaboured across the harlot's knee 'like children'.

Gosse, even in his *Confidential Paper*, avoids mention of Swinburne's homosexuality. Indeed, he seems to be contradicting public suspicion when he assures the reader that when he has known of the irregularities set forth in this paper (the drunkenness and the flagellation), he knows the worst, and makes that his pretext for writing upon the subject. What he fails to perceive is that the obsession with flagellation, involving always and only one area, was in itself sodomite in character.

Gosse's view (which I cannot share) is simply that Swinburne had very little sexual impulse. He writes, 'I believe the generative instinct was very feebly developed in Swinburne'. [1] This would seem to suggest impotence, especially as Gosse follows the hint with the story of Adah Menken's failure to seduce the poet. After dealing with the episode of Adah Menken, Gosse asserts, 'This was the first and only liaison in Swinburne's life.'

Failure to consummate it does not prove impotence, since it is plain from Swinburne's portrait of her as Leonora Harley that she was repulsive to him. Even more hopeless had been Rossetti's earlier enterprise in making Swinburne hold a kissing pose with Fanny Cornforth, by whom he was revolted. Ironically, the only woman (apart from his cousin Mary) for whom Swinburne ever felt a romantic emotion was Rossetti's wife, Lizzy. Could Rossetti have been subtly aware of that?

This seems the moment at which to remark that there exists a letter from Rossetti, dated October 26, 1869, which begins:[2]

> My dear Swinburne
> I want to tell you some thing lest you should hear it first from any one else. It is that I have recovered my old book of poems. Friends had long hinted such a possibility to me, but it was only just lately I made up my mind to it. I hope you will think none the worse of my feeling for the memory of one for whom I know you had a true regard.

[1] British Museum: Ashley MSS. 5753, f. 23.
[2] British Museum: Ashley A. 3870, f. 26.

This disposes of the story, to be found in some books, that Swinburne was present at the opening of Lizzie's grave, or urged him to or was party to it. It was Howell who was present at the opening of the grave, and who lifted the poems from it, Rossetti waiting in Howell's house for the result of the operation, undertaken at Howell's prompting. Swinburne knew nothing about it until the news was broken to him in the letter from Rossetti quoted above.

In February 1871, there is a series of three letters from Swinburne's parents to Rossetti.[1] In the first, it is Lady Swinburne who writes to him on February 9:

> My dear Sir
> We are in great trouble & anxiety about Algernon his father received a letter this morning telling him that Algernon was again in the state in which he has four times been obliged to go & insist upon his coming home. ...

By 'home' she means their new home, at Holmwood, near Henley, Oxfordshire. The following day, February 10, it was Admiral Swinburne, who was writing to Rossetti:

> My dear Sir
> I beg to acknowledge the receipt of your letter of the 9th instt. We are much obliged to you for your kind attention in writing. That which you mention respecting my Son's present state is a relief to us, and I hope that the letter you have addressed to him may induce him to come home, where he is free from the temptations which he seems to be quite incapable of resisting. The letter we enclosed to you last night was to urge his doing so at once.
> The last letter received from him was dated the 22nd ulto and informed us that he was staying with a friend, 'Mr. Thomson', but was without address: this and your friendship for him must plead my excuse for having troubled you so much.
> > Believe me to be
> > > my dear Sir   Very truly yours,
> > > > > > > > C. H. Swinburne

On the next day again, February 11, it was Lady Swinburne who was once more writing to Rossetti:

> My dear Sir
> ... Your letter to him brought one from him to his father, which reached us last evening after our post was gone—he again

[1] Lang, Vol. II, p. 136.

tells us that he is staying with a friend, a Mr. Thomson, but still he abstains from giving any address. . . . We do most earnestly wish that he would not take lodgings in Town at all events for the present—and we urged him when he was here to have everything he wanted in the way of furniture and books sent down here. I fear his having his books would not keep him here—it is impossible but a mind like his should require the society of persons with minds and pursuits similar to his own, unless he could make up his mind to remain here as a means of conquering his fearful propensity—. . .

By 'his fearful propensity' she may only mean drink. Yet it is a strong phrase, and evokes the suspicion that something else lurked at the back of her mind. A letter which she wrote many years later, and which I shall quote later in the story, shows that she did in fact regard Algernon as sexually abnormal.

If one rejects the notion that Swinburne was partially homosexual, one has to suppose that a man exceedingly interested in sex lived his whole life without any form of sexual expression, which is highly un-likely.

It is unfortunate that we have only Solomon's letters to Swinburne; not Swinburne's letters to Solomon. The fact that these have vanished may be significant. Mr. John Mayfield, the American Swinburne collec-tor, has given me his reasons for believing that they are extant, in the hands of a private person, whose attitude makes it unlikely that they will come on the market or be made available for inspection.

That Simeon Solomon's letters to Swinburne have been preserved is something for which to be thankful. The two quoted above form part of a collection of nine preserved in one folding-case at the British Museum. At the bottom of the folding-case I was startled to find a letter in a different hand, which read:[1]

My dear Wise

The enclosed letters from Simeon Solomon contain direct reference to his notorious vices, and an implication that A.C.S. was quite aware of their nature. I therefore suggest to you that they should be destroyed at once, if you agree. I have kept another note of S.S. which is quite innocuous and has an interesting feature.

Ever yours,
Edmund Gosse

[1] British Museum: MSS. Ashley 1755.

It should not, however, be thought that all Solomon's letters to Swinburne are concerned with personal obsessions. He speaks of Swinburne's and his own work. The two were linked when he drew three heads representing his idea of Lady Midhurst, Lesbia Brandon and Bertie on a sheet (watermarked 1812) which has been, by Wise, bound into the manuscript of *Lesbia Brandon*. Oddly enough, Solomon has omitted to draw Margaret; his Lesbia is straight-nosed as a Greek, his Bertie a tousle-headed notion of Swinburne as a boy, and his Lady Midhurst is sub-titled in his hand 'Aged 30', which is very much less than her age in the book.

None of Simeon Solomon's letters are dated. One that appears to have been sent in November 1869 contains curious passages:[1]

> My dear Swinburne
> ... Did I tell you that I saw Powell when he was here and that he carried off a little picture of mine that I painted in Rome? I have had it photographed and I write a line under it from 'Hermaphroditus' 'Love turned himself and would not enter in.' ... I had a shocking dream the other night. I dreamed that a cat and a sheep had connection and the hideous offspring appeared a few minutes after the event, it was a little black creature with long nails of wire which fastened into me, and as I pulled them out they became alive like worms, wasn't that shocking?

The nightmare shows that something in his own life was frightening him.

In the close of the next, perhaps sent in late February 1870, there is a use of the word 'swell' in what, today, we think of as the American slang sense:[2]

> I did not see Powell at all in town which I extremely regretted. Please do not consider this a letter at all, it is simply an acknowledgement of your swell literary presents to me. Do come to town soon and solace your affectionate friend,
>
> S. Solomon

Swinburne was at this time staying at his parents' home in Oxfordshire.

Another letter from Solomon, thought to have been sent at the beginning of May 1870, reveals that Swinburne's to him were sometimes indiscreet:[3]

[1] British Museum: MSS. Ashley 1755.
[2] Ibid.   [3] Ibid.

My dear Swinburne

I am happy to say that your letter reached me and was not lost on its way and opened and read by the authorities of the P.O. Alas! what would have been the consequences? We dare not, indeed, surmise.

This may have been intended as a warning to Swinburne that he should be more careful what he put on paper.

Solomon cherished the desire to become, like Rossetti, a poet as well as a painter, and as a beginning produced a curious piece of poetic prose entitled *A Vision of Love Revealed in Sleep*. It is a dialogue between the poet, his soul and the spirit of Love, rather nebulous in its terms, but ending in an encounter with a six-winged seraphim, who touches him upon his forehead and his lips so that he receives understanding. While obviously based upon Isaiah VI, 6, this passage has an affinity with Pushkin's poem *The Prophet*, in that it is the poet himself who is so touched. Reading it, I have wondered whether Solomon, being a Jew, whose ancestry perhaps had continental roots, could have been familiar with the work of the Russian poet. *A Vision of Love Revealed in Sleep* appeared, illustrated with some of Solomon's own drawings, in 1871.

There is a run of his letters to Swinburne which refer to this. Early in May, he writes:[1]

> I want to ask you a favour, which I hope you will at once refuse or comply with, as you think proper. I want to know if you will write a little article about my book in connection with my pictures, etc. I remember your saying that if I ever published it you would say something about it. I should so much like you to do so, and I will do anything for you (des supplices, des supplices). I am sending a copy to the 'Dark Blue' and if you comply I will at once let the magazine know. I am sure it would do me good. . . .

He concludes by saying he has now read all Swinburne's Songs Before – and he sketches, instead of writing, a rising sun.

A few days later, he was writing:[2]

> Many thanks for your kindness. I have just sent a letter to the editor of the Dark Blue telling him of your offer and suggesting that it might be in the June number and as I know how swiftly you write, I think that would be possible, would it not? it is today only the 15th. (I hope I have done nothing in bad taste

[1] British Museum: MSS. Ashley 1755.
[2] Ibid.

in thus writing to the D.B. (O Monsieur) but if I don't look after myself no one will do it for me. I cannot tell you what pleasure it will give me to see something by you on me (that sounds rather improper) and in print.

Your letter is delightful and I could* tell you much for on Friday I was taken by Hurt's counsel to the trial. . . .

There ensues a longish paragraph concerned with the trial of some transvestites charged with conspiracy to commit or to incite others to the commission of immorality. Simeon Solomon was apparently a witness for the defence, and after the morning's hearing, finding them in a near-by restaurant at lunch with their solicitors, he sat down with them. The said persons were in fact acquitted.

A further letter, which has not been published before, for which reason I give it in full reads:[1]

My dear Swinburne

I have just received your letter and think all you say is quite right and certainly very pleasing and flattering to me. You may be sure that the longer and fuller what you write will be the more advantage it will give me; I have just written to Freund giving him the substance of your letter (not the whole of it) and I said that if your MSS. did not arrive in time for insertion—I thought he might put a little critical advice of the 'vision' at the end of the number as he thought of doing because I said that you would probably speak of my pictures and drawings and use the booklet only as a sort of accompaniment, I hope I did right?—but I should think he would not put a notice in at all as he would think that you would more than exhaust the subject may I mention a few of my things that I should like you to think of? I painted the Antinous Dionysious [sic] 6 years ago. There was nothing improper about it then I did 'Habet' and that picture you wrote a poem about 'Erotion'. You know all my sketches I think 'Love and Lust' 'Sleep and Charity' then my Dudley Gallery things 'Bacchus' 'Greek Bishop'

*This line reads in Lang:
Your letter is [*word illegible*] and I could not tell you much . . .
Simeon Solomon's writing is often difficult, but the 'illegible' word is certainly *delightful*, and the word *not* does not appear in Solomon's text. Moreover, he had a lot to tell, as appears from the details ensuing, which would however be tedious to quote.
[1] British Museum: MSS. Ashley A 4273, f. 210. This letter is missed out in Lang, possibly because it is preserved at the Museum in a different file from those of Solomon's which Professor Lang has printed.

['] Heliogabolus' 'Sacramentum Amoris' 'Youthful Eastern Saint' 'A Song' ['] group of girls and youths' ['] one girl singing' 'Summer Twilight ['] ['] Young Rabbi'—then I had an oil picture of the 'Bride and friend of the Bridegroom' and lastly 'The Evening Hymn to the Lovers' one of my best things for color I think. Now I have 'Mystery of Faith' just waiting (?) the post (?) and the drawings 'Singing of Love' 'Love's Sleep ['] Memory Dreams Pleasures Lust and Death, but your memory is so tremendous that you always seem to retain everything you have once seen or heard.

I will not bore you any more by correspondence on this subject. I think it is arranged now and I cannot do better than leave it in your hands and make no more suggestions. You never have anything in the Fortnightly now, how is this? I miss your contributions greatly.

I have a model waiting so I must send this off at once; I will soon write again, and if I can an amusing letter, but I suppose you will be soon in Town.

Affecly yr's
· S. Solomon

Swinburne sent his review to Solomon, for his approval, before he sent it to the magazine. Solomon replied with another letter which has not appeared before:[1]

My dear Swinburne

10,000,000 thanks for your great kindness—it is really too good of you to have occupied so much of your time for so unworthy an object but the result is splendid—I have told Freund that he must not omit any part of it for it is so complete and finished that it must be delayed till the July number if it be too long for this; I am sure you will agree in this, for you would not desire or even permit your work to be clipped. I have only one fault to find and that is that you much overrate my capacity; I [*sic*] my sentiment is a gift, no credit to me, but my work, alas! is below your estimate of it, however it seems so ungrateful to comment even upon what you have done that I will desist—this is merely a grateful acknowledgement of what you have sent—I will write again and tell you more of Cecil who is without exception one of the naughtiest boys I ever knew; could you guess what he did the other day? but no, I will not create fresh prejudices against him—

Ever yours affly
S. Solomon

[1] British Museum: MSS. Ashley 5752, ff. 181–82.

It is not necessary to assume from the references to 'Cecil' that Solomon was consorting with juveniles. One remembers Swinburne's pretence of being a schoolboy, whom Houghton whipped; this pretence of being still a schoolboy seems to be in the vein of flagellant literature, and Cecil was very probably an adult fellow flagellant.

There must be a letter which has escaped collection, but the next we find is, in view of the one above quoted, rather surprising:[1]

> My dear Swinburne
> I received your letter of yesterday and I am very sorry to find from its tone that what I said in mine must have been very awkwardly and ungraciously done—it is very difficult for me to know what to say to you but I am quite sure that whatever I may say will not imply a want of gratitude for and acknowledgement of your kindness in writing the article in the 'Dark Blue'. And you must promise to forgive me if I speak the whole truth about it. When you sent me the M.S. and I read it, I saw and appreciated the full beauty of the paper and the great honour that had been done me by the most brilliant of our writers, but I saw that there were certain parts which I could have desired to be omitted but I dared not ask you to eliminate or even to modify them, for I thought it would have been a liberty, and, as a beggar who had had so large a boon conferred upon him, I felt it would have been unjustifiable: when the article appeared in print one or two very intimate friends said 'eloquent and beautiful as it is, I think it will do you harm'. You know, of course, my dear Algernon, that, by many, my designs and pictures executed during the last 3 or 4 years have been looked upon with suspicion, and, as I have been a false friend to myself, I have not sought to remove the impression, but I have gone on following my own sweet will; in pecuniary and some other ways I have had to suffer for it, and shall probably have to suffer still. I really hardly know how to say more, but I wish to make you feel that what I said in my last letter and what I repeat in this arises from no want of gratitude for the honor you did me and the kindness you showed me and I hope you will send me a letter absolving me from such an imputation in your mind.
>   Ever affectly yr's
>   S.S.

Solomon means that his reputation has suffered from his association with Swinburne, but if he had felt that this was bringing him into

[1] British Museum: MSS. Ashley 1755.

suspicion it was perhaps unwise of him to have suggested that their names be linked in print. Moreover, he seems to have forgotten that after seeing the text, sent him for his approval, he had specifically urged that nothing should be omitted. Perhaps he did not fully appreciate, until the article was in print and his friends pointed it out, the sinister impression that might be created by such a phrase in it as 'There is a mixture of utmost delicacy with a fine cruelty in some of those faces of fair feminine youth'.

Swinburne must have sent an amiable reply, for we next find Solomon writing:[1]

> My dear Algernon
> I was so pleased and relieved by your last letter and the kind manner in which you so completely exonerated me from the charge of ingratitude and ungraciousness; I saw by it that you entirely understood what I meant although it was awkwardly conveyed; I cannot at this moment call to mind the precise passages which I felt I should have liked modified but if it be worth while I will try to do so when I see you which I hope will be soon; I think, disagreeable as it is for me to have to do so, that in much of my (slighter) work I have given grounds for the kind of remarks that have been made. I intend now to go in for a different kind of work and cultivate that element that was more prominent some years ago, I mean the dramatic (on the intellectual side) and the effective (on the artistic side.) . . .

There are no more letters from Simeon Solomon for some time; the next, which from its subject matter (which relates to his suggestion that Swinburne should offer his memorial verses to Théophile Gautier to Sidney Colvin to publish in a magazine) must have been written in November 1872 reads:[2]

> Dear Swinburne
> If you send a letter to the Savile Club, Savile Row, it will reach S.C. as he is there nearly every day:–he will be delighted to receive your offering and of course will do all you want with regard to forwarding it to its right destination.
> I am very sorry that you have been suffering so much, but this weather will account for every thing; here it rains almost unceasingly. I went to Eton last week for a couple of days, but the weather was dreadful; have you heard that Johnson has left and

[1] British Museum: Ashley 1755.   [2] Ibid.

changed his name to Cory, it is creating a sensation at Eton. I suppose you will [be] in Town about Christmas.

Believe me
Yrs ever
S. Solomon

The Johnson who had changed his name to Cory was an assistant master at Eton, who had left after the attention of the authorities had been drawn to a letter written by himself to one of the boys which had homosexual overtones (and for other reasons).

I found in the British Museum one further letter from Simeon Solomon which has escaped publication:[1]

My dear Algernon

I enclose a letter from Colvin the contents of which, as he says, will no doubt interest you—I thought I should have heard from you and have almost felt that you must have had some (I hope, slight) cause of annoyance with me, but I trust that is not the case. I was heartily glad when I called at your rooms and found you had left London, for I must frankly say that I think *that* the only course for you as regards health and comfort, but I also hope that you will be and remain well in your new rooms which I consider charming—George Powell has been at great pains to do your behests—his quest of the Tragedy of Arden was worthy of a knight of the round table, but success, as I daresay you will know by this time, has crowned his efforts—he is very unselfish and only happy when he is doing some service for others.

I remain
always truly yours
S. Solomon

I have had many enquiries after you. I spent the evening with two friends of mine a little time since, the Misses Forbes who told me they had met some members of your family at a house in Scotland and expressed a great wish to see you.

Not long after this, probably early in 1873, Simeon Solomon was arrested on a homosexual charge, and sentenced to a short term of imprisonment.

[1] British Museum: MSS. Ashley A 1754, f. 155.

23

Swinburne and Rossetti

ALTHOUGH Swinburne had not been a party to the opening of Lizzie's grave, he was delighted to hear from Rossetti of the recovery of the poems buried with her. On receiving the news he wrote at once, on October 28, 1869:[1]

> My dear Gabriel
> I cannot tell you how rejoiced I am at the news you send me. None could have given me a truer or deeper pleasure. To our nearest friends I would never allow myself to talk on the subject; but none the less I have thought often and bitterly of the loss sustained. I can say to you now, what of course I could never hint before, how often my thoughts have run in the line of yours as to what her own hope and desire in the matter would have been, who loved art so notably and well. Your expression of such a feeling touched a chord in mine which till now had been only of fruitless and desperate regret.

It was not merely Rossetti's poems to Lizzie, but all his poems, which he had buried with her. Now that he again held them in his hands, he lost no time in having them set up in type, and posted proofs to Swinburne, who wrote on November 28:[2]

> My dear Gabriel
> Many thanks for your poems which have just arrived. It is a delight to see them in print. I write before falling to upon them, as there is only an early post today. I am sure your alterations will prove to be for the best even ultimately in my eyes. It is simply at first difficult to unwind and unfasten the old associations of a verse which has grown into one's thoughts, as many of your verses have into mine.

From these words one realizes how deeply Rossetti's poetry had entered into Swinburne's being, and the ensuing correspondence shows how concerned he was for the perfection of his friend's poems, and is amongst the most fascinating and in some places the most amusing ever exchanged

[1] British Museum: MSS. Ashley 3870, f. 29.
[2] British Museum: MSS. Ashley 5074, f. 5.

between two poets. On December 7, Swinburne wrote, having received a fresh set of proofs:[1]

> My dear Gabriel
>   Thanks again for the new sheets. . . . The fresh touches in Jenny are most admirable, and beyond praise for effect and delicacy. It is *the* modern English poem as yet achieved. The new stanza to The Bower is very exquisite, but (as far as my first impression goes, I should say) not quite of a piece with the vital, tangible, direct loveliness of the rest. . . . The 'Confession', song and all, is now perfect to my mind. I am not sure whether I don't think 'Eden Bower' the most altogether triumphant poem you ever wrote. It is as wonderful to me as delightful for clear sheer power and weight of plain passion clothed with such luxury of colour and splendour of sound. I think it is the greatest thing done in English since Shelley's 'West Wind' in its different way—and that I think on the whole the supreme lyric of the language.
>   Ever your affectionate,
>   A. C. Swinburne

Rossetti continued working upon the proofs and the following day sent Swinburne a further fresh set, bearing a revised version of *Jenny*. This is a realistic poem. The poet, probably Rossetti himself, has accompanied a prostitute to her room; but she is so tired that, as she sits him down to take a glass of wine, she falls asleep, with her head on his knee. He has not the heart to wake her for the purpose for which he had come, and, as she sleeps on and on, he sits the whole night through. Looking about her room, so unlike his own with its crowded books, he wonders about her life and how she came to this. A chirping of sparrows heralds the dawn, and, as the sky lightens, he very gently slides a cushion under her head. Before leaving, he places some coins in her hair, so that they will fall out and astonish her when she raises her head. He wonders what she will think when she wakes, unusually, alone.

Swinburne wrote of it on December 10, 1869, with perceptive criticism:[3]

> My dear Gabriel
>   It is a most real pleasure and interest to me to watch the growth & help (if I can) in the arrangement of your poems to ever so small an extent by ever such petty suggestions of detail. And to

[1] Lang, Vol. II, p. 64.
[2] British Museum: MSS. Ashley 5074, ff. 9–10.

shew my sincerity I may tell you that on opening your letter I glanced first at the proof sheets that fell out and at once thought I should have to write in unwilling protest against one addition at least—about the first time I ever did, whatever I may have thought of excisions. When I found the insertions were restorations of cancelled lines, I felt confirmed, relieved from the sense of presumption and doubt. I should unhesitatingly reject the five added lines on the Haymarket, though admirably well turned and ingenious; both because (as you say) they intercept the thought, and still more because they utterly deaden and erase the superb effect of the lines preceeding. . . . The 'purfelled buds' I noticed before, and like—or do not dislike; I think the text good with them or without. The 'yesterday's rose' on the bosom is better than beautiful, being so lifelike, but I would condense if I could the thought into a couplet; it reads a little draggingly. I like the 'double-bedded' verse, and indeed think it absolutely wanted to point and enforce the preceding line – but is not the phrase inaccurate? Surely it can only mean that there were two beds, implying separate sleepers; which is chaste, but startling as a suggestion—proper but improbable. Also it sounds to me to have just a shade or breath of coarseness—escaped so exquisitely elsewhere in the most familiar parts of the poem; 'double-pillowed,' now, would evade this, and give better the idea of two heads waking together, as nobody can sleep on two pillows at once.

Rossetti took most of Swinburne's suggestions and was grateful for them. Pathetically, he wrote:[1] '. . . It is a shame boring you about such mere trifles amid the mass of magnificent work which you do without worrying your friends with the details; but the fact is I never can feel clear on uncertain points till I get your opinion.' This is a remarkable confession, especially when one remembers that Swinburne was nine years the younger man; but of course, Rossetti was primarily a painter. He altered the passage concerning his thoughts as he left the still sleeping prostitute, so that now it reads:[2]

> Why, Jenny, waking here alone
> May help you to remember one,
> Though all the memory's long outworn
> Of many a double-pillowed morn.

[1] British Museum: MSS. Ashley 4995, f. 5.
[2] Rossetti: *Poems* (O.U.P.), p. 72.

I think I see you when you wake,
And rub your eyes for me, and shake
My gold, in rising, from your hair,
A Danaë for a moment there.

Reading these lines today, in the frozen marble of the Oxford edition,
one may think that Rossetti was infinitely indebted to Swinburne;
'double-bedded' would have ruined the effect.

On December 21, Rossetti wrote:[1]

> My dear Swinburne,
> Here I come bothering again . . .

This time it was mainly about his poem *Troy Town*, which had to do
with the legend that Helen of Troy made an offering to Venus of a cup
moulded upon her breast. Someone told Rossetti that people reading his
poem would not realize (as well they might not, from its title) that she
was not in Troy when she did it (because, of course, it was while she
was still in Sparta). Previously, it had begun:

> Helen knelt at Venus' shrine

Now in the hope of making the location clear, he had written a new
verse, to put at the beginning:

> Heavenborn Helen, Sparta's queen.
>   (O Troy Town!)
> Had two breasts of heavenly (orient) sheen,
> The sun and moon of heart's desire
> All Love's lordship lay between .
>   (O Troy's down
>   Tall Troy's on fire!)

On this, he wanted Swinburne's opinion. Swinburne replied on December 22:[2]

> . . . The new stanza to 'Troy Town' is beautiful, & clear gain—
> though I had never thought of any ambiguity as it was. It is an
> absurd piece (I dare say) of hypercriticism, but it does strike me that
> to call a woman's breasts 'the sun and moon' of the heart's desire
> sounds as if there were a difference between them, much in favour
> of one. It is a burlesque notion, I know, but would, I fear, occur to

[1] British Museum: MSS. Ashley 4995, f. 8.
[2] British Museum: MSS. Ashley 5074. f. 14.

Simeon Solomon

Swinburne, *c.* 1866

others as well as to me, so you must pardon the suggestion of it. 'Heavenly' sheen *stet*—not orient I should say, certainly.

Rossetti dropped 'orient' and kept 'heavenly' as the adjective, but wrote to Swinburne on February 21, 1870:[1]

... You objected to
> The sun and moon of heart's desire

as seeming to infer a difference in the 2 breasts. I confess I like the line, but of course your objection haunts me. Would you give it five minutes further consideration (it is on page 1, so important), and tell me if you think it ought really to be changed. I might say
> The glowing spheres of the heart's desire

but I must say I don't like this as well myself.

Faced with this prospect, Swinburne relented, and on February 22 wrote:[2] 'I quite think on reconsideration that I should let the sun and moon' stand for Helen's breasts – certainly *not* 'the glowing spheres'. The expression is none the less exquisite for the possible hypercriticism which I perhaps unadvisedly suggested.'

Rossetti replied the next day:[3] 'I am very glad you have taken the embargo off the "Sun and Moon" line which was a favourite of mine when I made it.'

It would be interesting to know how many of those who have read it felt that it implied a disparity between Helen's breasts. On February 24, Swinburne wrote to Rossetti:[4] '*Can't* you alter (his arrow) "stood confessed" in *Troy Town*? It *is* so suggestive of the "Love which a pleasing influence can impart" that it almost sounds like a bit of burlesque.'

This drew from Rossetti the reply on February 26:[5]

> I am disturbed by your continued objection to 'stood confessed' in *Troy Town*. Do you take into consideration that I mean absolutely that Cupid does see his arrow there? Thus it ceases to be a mere conventional metaphor. I would alter it if possible on your urgency, but really cannot see my way with the given rhyme which is necessary.

[1] British Museum: MSS. Ashley 4995, f. 18.
[2] British Museum: MSS. Ashley 5074, f. 27.
[3] British Museum: MSS. Ashley 1387.
[4] British Museum: MSS. Ashley 5074, f. 34.
[5] British Museum: MSS. Ashley 4995, f. 21.

Swinburne wrote back, on February 28:[1]

> Dear Gabriel
>   My objection to 'confessed' is that it is a slang word–I should no more use it in the sense of 'apparent' in a serious poem than I should use the word 'skedaddled'. But 'banished rest' won't do at all in that place ... Would 'his dart looked–or showed–fieriest' or some other such superlative ... do at all?

This time, Rossetti replied with a flash of inspiration:[2]

> Dear Swinburne
>   I fancy I've hit it–
>   'Marked his arrow's burning crest'.
>   One line, please, by return, & pardon these babyish bulletins.
>   Your
>   D.G.R.
>   This is better I believe than 'Knew his shaft its rankling guest'.

Swinburne replied by return of post, on March 1:[3]

> My dear Gabriel
>   Either *crest* or *guest* is a great improvement–I think you are right in preferring the first, but either is good.

Rossetti altered his twelfth verse so that it read:[4]

> Cupid looked on Helen's breast
>   (*O Troy Town!*)
> Saw the heart within its nest,
> Saw the flame of heart's desire–
> Marked his arrow's burning crest.
>   (O Troy's down,
>   Tall Troy's on fire!)

Reading this correspondence, one is struck not only by Rossetti's dependence upon Swinburne's poetic judgement, but by Swinburne's goodness in giving so much thought to the problems of his friend's verse, and the time it must have taken to write the long letters in which he suggests and explains numbers of small alterations for its improvement. Few poets would go to so much trouble for any work but their

[1] British Museum: MSS. Ashley 5074, f. 35.
[2] British Museum: MSS. Ashley A 1400, f. 26.
[3] British Museum: MSS. Ashley 5074, f. 37.
[4] Rossetti, *Poems* (O.U.P.), p. 11.

own. That Swinburne took these pains shows not only his friendship to Rossetti but the disinterestedness of his consecration to poetry. He was possessed, in a way that perhaps only a poet can understand, by the concern that a new poetic thing of power and beauty, which was evolving should achieve perfection of form.

Rossetti's *Poems* were published in April 1870. Swinburne reviewed the volume for the *Fortnightly*, needless to say in the most appreciative terms. Foreseeing that *Jenny* would be a target of moral criticism, he took care to mention that it was 'great among the few greatest works of the artist'.

There was, needless to say, a certain amount of censorious moral criticism, though it only gathered momentum gradually. October 2, 1871, brought an attack by Robert Buchanan (writing under the pseudonym of Thomas Maitland) in the *Contemporary Review*: it was entitled *The Fleshly School of Poetry*. Though Rossetti was the main target, it also had disagreeable things to say about Swinburne and Simeon Solomon. Swinburne took it fairly lightly, and, in a letter to Rossetti's brother, William Michael, of October 19, mentioned[1]: 'I perceive that, a propos of Gabriel's poems, a son of Sodom, hitherto unknown except (I suppose) to Whitman's bedfellows the cleaners of privies, has lately "del cul fatto trombetta' in a Malebolgian periodical called the Contemporary Review. . . .' The metaphor is startling in its revelation of a changed attitude to Whitman, until now always referred to as a hero. In this passage, parenthetically, one has the first indication of a reversal with regard to Whitman, usually ascribed to a later influence.

Swinburne's pen sometimes ran away with him, when he wrote the occasional letter or passage of deliberate vulgarity. His letters to Howell are notorious in this respect, but those to the Rossetti brothers are not always chaste. Rossetti, though, who was not above a bit of bawdry himself, as his replies show, warned Swinburne about this in a letter written on November 6:[2]

> Why, my dear fellow, every line you have ever written will one day be religiously raked up by greedy and often doubtless malevolent exploiteurs, and it is very hard for those who receive these wonderfully funny things of yours to resolve on taking the only safe course with them for your sake – that is, to destroy them

[1] Lang, Vol. II, pp. 160–1.
[2] Lang, Vol. II, p. 167, n.

after they have been abundantly laughed over by a circle of friends who know what mere fun they are.

Swinburne replied on November 10:[1] 'As to privacy, if we are to be shackled in our inmost intercourse with our closest friends by the fear of future vermin, we may as well resign all liberty, and all thought of elbow-room for fun or confidence of any kind, at once.' He went on to confide to Rossetti that, picking up a periodical, he had come upon a story by one Mortimer Collins which featured an absurd and loathsome character who, by such phrases as 'pigmy poet' with 'the utmost faculty of alliteration', would be identifiable by many as a libellous portrait of himself. To take any action would only give wider publicity to the work of an insignificant and scurrilous scribbler: 'Still I have felt a certain dubitation and uneasiness about the nasty little matter, till I resolved to relieve myself by writing to the trustiest friend I could turn to . . .' Rossetti replied advising him to leave the matter alone, and Swinburne, in a letter of November 13 agreed.

This is the last letter from Swinburne to Rossetti which is known. In the following year something very sad and strange occurred. Rossetti replied to Buchanan's anonymous attack by an article entitled *The Stealthy School of Criticism*, which appeared in December. Buchanan retaliated by having *The Fleshly School of Poetry* reprinted as a pamphlet, which appeared in May. This time Rossetti, who had seemed reasonably cheerful in his letters to Swinburne about the original attack and the answer he was preparing to it, completely broke down.

For this to happen, subterranean tensions must have been building up.

Probably, Rossetti had all the time felt, for all he said to the contrary, a guilt about having opened Lizzie's tomb to recover the poems. More deeply still, his feeling of guilt must have gone back to her suicide, and to his infidelities, or the neglect and lack of consideration that had conduced to that suicide. No positive cruelty has ever been proved against him, and his nature seems to have been generous; yet a woman whose husband has made her happy does not take her life. There must have been black periods of unavowed remorse, which the attack upon the 'fleshliness' of his poetry touched off. The habit of taking chloral had weakened his resistance. He had been taking whisky, too.

On June 2, 1872, always regarded as the day of the actual breakdown, he began talking wildly about a conspiracy against himself, of which

[1] Lang, Vol. II, p. 167.

Browning was the leader. In fact, Browning had just published a new volume of verse, *Fifine at the Fair*, which draws the portrait of a phil-anderer, and it has been thought not impossible he could have had in mind a Rossetti-like type. But Rossetti's words about it sounded so strange and exaggerated that his brother, William Michael, thought he was suffering from temporary insanity, and called in his friend, Dr. Hake. Hake, very gallantly, offered to take Rossetti to his own home at Roe-hampton. In the cab, Rossetti insisted that a bell had been fixed to the roof, that the ringing might annoy him. The next day Dr. Hake took him for a walk; they met some gipsies, and nothing would convince Rossetti that it was not as a hostile demonstration against himself that they had assembled. Unperceived by the doctor he had brought with him a bottle of laudanum, and later in the day, being alone for a little while, he drank it, attempting to commit suicide in the same way as his wife. By the evening, his mother and William Michael had been called to his side.

There is a strange, short letter from Swinburne to William Michael Rossetti, dated July 5:[1]

> Dear Rossetti
> Many thanks for your note—I shall of course take every pre-caution against a meeting. It is of course a grief to me to be debarred from shewing the same attention and affection as friends who can hardly love him better—as indeed I think no man can love his friend more than I love Gabriel—but I know it can be from no doubt of my attachment that he shrinks from seeing me as yet.
> Ever your,
A.C.S.

The 'as yet' was to last the ten years until Gabriel's death.

[1] British Museum: MSS. Ashley A 1964 (c), ff. 42–43.

24

Watts: Chatto

SWINBURNE'S correspondence with Rossetti and Simeon Solomon was concurrent. Solomon's arrest followed hard upon Rossetti's breakdown and Mazzini's death. For one who lived largely in his friendships, it was most depressing sequence of personal losses. Swinburne seems at first not to have realized what had happened to Solomon, for on March 11, 1873, he wrote to Powell:[1]

> Have you any news good or bad of Our Wandering Jew? The aberrations of that too erratic vagrant from the narrow way are a subject of real uneasiness and regret to me, who have a regard for his genuine good qualities of character and genius. Let us, my brethren, while we drop a tear over the sheep now astray from the true fold of the Good Shepherd, if not indeed irrevocably classed among the goats to be ultimately found on the left of the G.S., give thanks to a merciful Providence that we are not as this Israelite, in whom if we have been mistaken as to his character I fear there must be a good deal of guile.

This seems to have been written in an odd mood. Swinburne's more genuine concern comes out in a further letter to Powell, of June 6:[2]

> ... I have been spending a fortnight in Oxford where I saw and spoke with a great friend of poor Simeon's, Pater of Brasenose, who has seen Miss Solomon, and appeared to have more hope of his ultimate recovery and rehabilitation than from the horrid version I had heard of the form of his insanity I had ventured to retain. ... I suppose there is no doubt the poor unhappy little fellow has really been out of his mind and *done* things amenable to law such as done by a sane man would make it impossible for any one to keep up his acquaintance and not be cut by the rest of the world as an accomplice? I have been seriously unhappy about it for I had a real affection and regard for him—and besides his genius he had such genuinely amiable qualities. It is the simple truth that the distress of it has haunted and broken my sleep. It is hideous to lose a friend through madness of any kind, let alone this. Do you— I do not—know any detail of the matter at first hand?

[1] Lang, Vol. II, p. 234.   [2] Lang, Vol. II, p. 253.

In the midst of so much depression, Swinburne had made one new friend. Theodore Watts, who later assumed the hyphenated name Watts-Dunton, was a solicitor and book critic, and a friend of Rossetti, though it was at Madox Brown's house that Swinburne had first met him, on October 3, 1872.

Swinburne's relations with Hotten had been deteriorating; he felt that he was not receiving the money he should. He appealed to Howell, as the one who had introduced them and been present at the interview in which terms had been discussed; but Howell was unable to recall whether Hotten had undertaken to make payments exactly as Swinburne had understood; he had supposed that the verbal accord was in any case only the prelude to a written agreement which would be signed between the parties.

Swinburne laid the whole affair before Watts, who from that moment became both his legal adviser and his agent, and conducted all his negotiations for him. The quarrel between Swinburne and Hotten is of inexpressible complication, but a hint of the violence to which it attained may be glimpsed from a letter of Hotten to Watts, written on 13 January, 1873:[1]

> Dear Sir
> I am sorry I was not in when you called. If you intended your note to *surprise* us I can only say that you could not have succeeded better. It *does surprise me!* You have had an a/c on Mr. Swinburne's behalf of our sales of his books, which a/c taken in conjunction with the a/cs previously rendered is as clear, as circumstantial, & straightforward as it is in our power to make out.
> The a/c you asked me for last week *has already been supplied to Messrs. Benham & Tindal* on Mr. Swinburne's behalf. You thought Mr. Swinburne might have mislaid or never received it, & you expressed a disinclination to go to a solicitor. I gratuitously offered to look after these or get copies of them for you. Twice have I sent (it was out of my power to get what you wanted *last* week) & Mr. Tindal writes to say '*he will write to me*'. I do not mind taking trouble where it is appreciated, but I will see you and Mr. Swinburne —— well, never mind where I will see you, before I stand being kicked as a return for a courteous action. In the absence of the old a/cs – absent through no fault of mine – I enclose dates and nos of last edition with nos of copies remaining on hand.

[1] John Camden Hotten's Letter Books, preserved by Chatto & Windus.

This statement, with our a/c of sales rendered may enable Mr. Swinburne to see how matters stand.

Yours truly,
John Camden Hotten

At the same time, there are certain things in his affair with Hotten that Swinburne did not wish to explain to Watts, and which only Howell knew about. Though he published much serious work, Hotten also had a line in flagellation literature, which was doubtless why Howell had thought in the first place of bringing Swinburne and Hotten together. It could even be for some reason connected with this that the original agreement as to terms had been conducted in a manner which, on the face of it, appears unbusinesslike. On the flagellant side, Swinburne had written for Hotten some papers he would not wish publicly to own, and it seems that it now suddenly struck him that it was not wise for him to withdraw on hostile terms from a man he had given power to damage him. Therefore, he wrote to Howell:

> ... I am more than willing, I am desirous, to remain on amicable terms with Hotten in the act of withdrawing from my business connection with him ... It is probably not worth while to touch at all on so small a matter, but in full confidence I may do so to a friend with whom I have been for years on such intimate and brotherly terms as yourself. I think he may have some papers relating to me in the mass of his collection, of which an unscrupulous man might possibly make some annoyance. ... I remember that when he was busied about his abortive book on 'Flagellation' some sort of communication on the topic passed between us, and that I once gave him, what I *think* he never returned to me, a list drawn up in my hand of scenes in school which he was to get sketched for me ... Of course above all things, nothing must be said to Hotten which might possibly suggest to him the idea that I am in any way apprehensive of his making it an instrument of annoyance to me; which in fact I am not, and have no reason to be. Indeed I see he now advertises a new 'Romance of the Rod' as in preparation, to which I should be happy to lend any assistance that I could, and so you might let him know if we are to remain on terms.

Perhaps the bargain which he has in his mind is that, in order to avoid making an enemy of Hotten, he could continue to send him one kind of

---

[1] Lang, Vol. II, pp. 226–8.

material in exchange for the liberty to offer work, other than flagellant work, to a different publisher.

Howell must have replied by asking for a description of the embarrassing papers, which he perhaps supposed Swinburne wished him to try to recover from Hotten; for a few days later we find Swinburne writing to Howell again,[1] and giving a list of the flogging scenes which he had suggested as suitable for illustration. Swinburne was delivered from his embarrassing situation in an unexpected manner when, on June 14, 1873, Hotten died aged only forty or forty-one.

To Watts, on June 20, Swinburne wrote untruthfully:[2]

> My dear Watts
>
> I do not remember that any property of mine was in the hands of Hotten except the copies of Chapman's different works lent to him...

To lie to one's legal adviser is not generally wise, but Swinburne did not wish to appear before Watts in a compromising light.

Within the month, Swinburne received an interesting letter:[3]

> July 23, 1873
>
> Dear Sir
>
> I contemplate purchasing the business of the late Mr. Hotten and I very much wish to have the publication of your forthcoming works in addition to those already issued by him, and to have the business relations with yourself placed upon a more satisfactory footing than has been the case for some time past. I believe that none of the objections that you had against Mr. Hotten attach in any way to myself, and I shall greatly esteem the favour of a visit from you,–or I will wait upon you if you prefer it.
>
> As an earnest of my desire to stand well with you I beg to enclose my own cheque for 50£ on a/c of royalty on the books sold by Mr. Hotten since his last return, and in anticipation of my succeeding to his business.
>
> I am dear Sir
>
> Your faithful Servant
>
> Andrew Chatto

Andrew Chatto, three years younger than Swinburne, had been in Hotten's since he was fifteen, and now, for £25,000, bought the business from Hotten's widow. He it was who, dropping the flagellant side, transformed the firm into the high class literary publishing house which it became.

[1] Lang, Vol. II, p. 254.   [2] Ibid.   [3] Chatto & Windus files.

Swinburne, with uncomfortable memories of his dealings with Hotten, and without means to foresee the transformation which was to take place in the firm, went into consultation with Watts and temporized. Association with Watts was leading him into a stance that seems hypocritical, as witness a letter he wrote him on December 1, in which he mentions Simeon Solomon, whom he had just learned was now in Devonshire:[1]

> I h[ave just wri]tten to Powell a long letter of el[der b]rotherly advice not to be led away by any kindly and generous feeling towards an unfortunate man whom he has been used to regard as a friend, into a renewal of intimacy by correspondence or other wise which might appear to involve him in equivocal or questionable relations with a person who has deliberately chosen to do what makes a man and all who associate with him infamous in the eyes of the world. It is something new for me to come forward as the representative of wordly wisdom . . . it is not exactly for turning tai[l or dese]rting my friends when out of favour [with] the world or any part of it that I have exposed myself hitherto to attack; only in such a case as this I do think a man is bound to consider the consequence to all his friends and to every one who cares for him in the world of allowing his name to be mixed up with that of a —— let us say, a Platonist; the terms is at once accurate as a definition and unobjectionable as an euphemism.

This comes very oddly from Swinburne who had known for ten years that Solomon was a homosexual. He writes to Watts as though he had only just realized it! A month later, he writes again to Watts, on January 2, that he will be spending ten days in Cornwall with Professor Jowett, but will not be with Jowett during the part of his holiday that he spends in Devonshire (where Solomon was last heard of):[2] 'as I have no wish, especially in his company, to encounter a Platonist of another sort than the translator of Plato . . . should he still figure in that neighbourhood . . . Powell has answered to my little fraternal lecture on caution in that quarter very nicely, in two or three sensible and grateful words.'

One can understand that Swinburne, for all his delight in sodomite humour, expressed in his letters to his friends (other than Watts), might be nervous of continued association with a friend whose homosexuality had become public knowledge; but what is hard to forgive is that his prudence should have extended to the using of his influence to prevent

[1] Lang, Vol. II, p. 261.   [2] Lang, Vol. II, p. 264.

others from continuing their friendship towards Solomon. He was, for self-preservation, cutting him off, virtually, from all the old intimacies and making a pariah of him. It may of course be that Watts had counselled Swinburne to keep away from Solomon, and that Swinburne is merely reflecting back to Watts ideas which he would recognize and approve, because they were his own.

Swinburne's concern over his reputation in the world came a little late. The turn of the year brought him a cutting, sent him by Powell, from an American newspaper of January 3, 1874, carrying an article entitled *Emerson: A Literary Interview*, in which the anonymous interviewer reported Emerson as having:[1] 'condemned Swinburne severely as a perfect leper and mere sodomite, which criticism recalls Carlyle's scathing description of that poet – as a man standing up to his neck in a cesspool, and adding to its contents'.

People had not, at that time, developed the habit of suing for libel. A law of libel existed, but it was considered more dignified to ignore vulgar abuse. Yet Swinburne felt he should do something. He wrote to Powell, returning the cutting, and thanking him for having sent it. To avoid the appearance of condescension to answer the author of this passage, he suggested that Powell should show to persons interested, and perhaps publish in America, a more formal letter, addressed to Powell, which he enclosed. In the letter for exhibition, he said that he was insufficiently expert in the dialect of the cesspool to make a retort. He thought that his family name, if it had gained no lustre through his merit, had lost through him no honour, and that he had won the friendship of Landor, Hugo and Mazzini. After some further exchange of letters between them, it was agreed that Powell make a copy of the letter and send it to an American newspaper, which he did. (It appeared in the New York *Daily Tribune* on February 25, 1874.)

If the turn of the year was bad in one respect, it was, however, good in another. On January 1, 1874, Chatto wrote to Swinburne:[2]

> ... We have been expecting the favour of either a letter or a call from yourself or Mr. Watts in reference to a letter sent him on 18th of September last relative to your business, and especially to your forthcoming books, *Bothwell* and *Tristram and Iseult*. And we beg to repeat the offer therein contained, viz. that we are willing to pay

[1] *Frank Leslie's Illustrated Newspaper*, p. 273; quoted in Lang, Vol. II, p. 272, n.
[2] Chatto & Windus files, Lang, Vol. II, p. 263, n.

you your royalty, cash in advance, reckoned upon the entire number printed of each edition—we ourselves taking the risk as to whether the books sell or not.

Swinburne, still mistrustful, replied gruffly:[1]

> ... I have been out of town since the beginning of November, and have consequently not had an opportunity for some time of calling on you. Had I done so, I could only have repeated the declaration I made to you on the last occasion I had of calling; viz. that the regulation of my business affairs is now in the hands of my legal adviser Mr. Watts, by whose decision I am prepared to abide.

Watts must have written Chatto an extremely disagreeable letter, for on January 20, 1874, we find Chatto writing to Swinburne:[2]

> Dear Sir
> The enclosed copy of a letter received from Mr. Watts together with the previous correspondence will show you that I cannot consistently with my self-respect have any more communication with that gentleman.
> You will remember that my position with regard to yourself is simply that of the representative of the late Mr. Hotten and that, as he was the publisher of your books I am equally so. It is of course my duty to maintain all agreements as understood by Mr. Hotten himself; but I think I have shown it is my desire to place the most liberal construction upon them. Mr. Hotten's contention was that so long as he fulfilled certain conditions he had the right of publishing for you exclusively—this was confirmed, in so far as regards the books he had already published at an arbitration held between your representative and his—that is between Mr. Howell & Mr. Moy [?] Thomas—I further answer that should you desire to remove your publishing from me, the books & the stories [?] already to hand might be taken at prices quoted in my letter of
> to Mr. Watts.
> I was informed both by yourself & Mr. Watts that you would see Messrs. Chapman & Hall & come to a definite decision as to whether or not the publishing should remain with me. Since then having heard nothing further on the subject matters remain in *statu quo*.
> I think you will admit that my conduct, apart from words, has evinced a desire to act honestly by you—a few weeks after Mr.

Hotten's death I sent you a cheque for £50 in anticipation of my succeeding to his business, but long before anything was definitely settled. On the first of the present year I sent up the statement of a/c made up to the end of 1873, according to the books, which are open to the inspection of yourself & Mr. Watts or anyone you may choose to represent you; & with that statement I sent a cheque for the balance due to you.

I appeal to you now if such conduct in any way merits the opprobrium expressed in Mr. Watts' letter? However much I may wish to retain you I have done nothing to throw obstacles in the way of your leaving me, though I am convinced that I can do more for you—certainly financially—than any other publisher. I am Sir

Yours faithfully
Andrew Chatto

This was the letter which finally won Swinburne over. The offer to open their books to inspection is one which features in Chatto's contracts with their authors today. Swinburne sent Chatto's letter to Watts, and even Watts must have thought it good, for it was with Watts, as Swinburne's agent, that the contract for *Bothwell* was finally negotiated. A document in the Chatto & Windus files which I copied reads as follows:

THIS AGREEMENT made this twenty first day of April one thousand eight hundred and seventy four BETWEEN Walter Theodore Watts of 3 Putney Hill Putney in the county of Surrey gentleman as agent for and on the behalf of Algernon Charles Swinburne of Holmwood near Henley on Thames gentleman, hereinafter called the Author of the one part and Andrew Chatto and William Edward Windus both of Piccadilly in the County of Middlesex Publishers carrying on business in Copartnership under the firm of Chatto and Windus hereinafter called the publishers of the other part

1st The Publishers shall be the sole publishers of an Edition of fifteen hundred copies of a work to sell at twelve shillings and sixpence a copy written by the Author entitled 'Bothwell' for which the sum of two hundred and twenty five pounds shall be paid on the delivery of the Manuscript the Publishers taking the entire expenses of printing, paper, binding, advertising and all other matters incident to the production of the work.

2nd With regard to the American Market the Publishers will sell the advance sheets in America for the best price procurable and hand over the entire proceeds to the Author deducting a Commission of twenty five per cent upon the amount received.

3rd   The Publishers shall once in six months if required so to do, produce vouchers and evidence to show that they have not exceeded their right of Publishing fifteen hundred copies of the said Poem.

4   The Author shall retain the right whensoever he shall think fit to have the Poem published by another publisher upon buying out the Stock on hand at the lowest export price charged by publishers i.e. seven shillings and tenpence a copy.

5   With regard to the Author's books published by the late John Camden Hotten to whose business the publishers have succeeded the publishers agree that should the Author wish to transfer the publication to any other publisher he shall do so upon paying for the stock in hand a sum to be fixed by two Referees one to be appointed by each or by an umpire to be chosen by the Referees.

6   The Publishers agree to continue to pay the Author a Royalty of one fourth of the publishing prices upon 'Atalanta' 'Chastelard' 'Queenmother' 'Song of Italy' 'Poems and Ballads'. A similar Royalty upon the Essay upon Blake shall be paid as soon as the sale of that work shall have defrayed the cost of publication.

7   The Publishers shall never at any time print any more copies of these works nor of either of them without giving the Author seven days notice of their intention to do so.

8   Immediately on the signing of the contract and in future once in every six months the Publishers shall furnish an account of the sales of the Books and if required so to do of the Vouchers showing the copies printed and sold and shall pay to the Author the money found coming to him.

W. Theodore Watts
Chatto & Windus

Swinburne remained with Chatto & Windus for the rest of his life. His complaints ceased to be about money, and instead came to be about such fine points as the shape of their printer's capital Q.

25

Bothwell

SWINBURNE regarded *Bothwell* as his magnum opus. To Howell, he had written the previous year:[1]

> I am making gradual way with Bothwell, but am yet far from sight of harbour. My comfort is that if ever accomplished according to my design the book must either be an utter failure, and still-born, or else not merely by far the greatest work I have done (being for proportion and conception out of all comparison with 'Atalanta' in weight and importance as well as width and variety of work), but a really great poem and fit to live as a typical and representative piece of work.

Bothwell appeared in May 1874. For a play, its proportions were prodigious. In Chatto's collected edition of the *Tragedies* of Swinburne, it occupies a volume and a half, or 593 pages. But for Jowett's persuasion drastically to cut it, it would have been vastly longer. One is bound to ask oneself the question: did Swinburne seriously think the play could be acted, and if it was not for the theatre, why did he choose the dramatic form? The only way to present it would be, as in the Japanese theatre, in parts, on different evenings; the audience would have to book for a series of evenings, and a European and modern audience would be unlikely to give the time to a single work. Did his passion for the subject carry him away from all practical realities? Or did he think a play-to-be-read a genre sufficiently satisfying to require no justification? It is a play in verse, and he refers to it sometimes as a poem, so perhaps he considered the dramatic form as no more than a poetic device.

It is a work of grandeur, and he had put into it an enormous amount of historical research. Perhaps it was the research which led him into the trap of such unwieldy length, for having discovered some detail in the relations of even the most minor characters, he put it in, and could not bring himself to sacrifice any part of the complex historical situation as he had come to understand it. The subject is, of course, Mary Queen of Scots: the section of her life dominated by Bothwell. Within the play, the five acts are named after the persons most prominent in the different

[1] Lang, Vol. II, p. 228.

sub-phases of the drama. Act I is *David Rizzio*. Darnley speaks with Mary Carmichael, with whom he seems to have an understanding disloyal to his wife. They speak of 'St. David' and 'King David, psalmist', playing maliciously upon the Christian name of Queen Mary's Italian secretary. Mary Carmichael says to Darnley:[1]

> be it not said
> He hath snipt your skirts already.

When the Queen and Rizzio come on together, it appears that, whether or not Rizzio is her lover, he is certainly her counsellor. As a matter of state policy, he advises her that she should recall from banishment her half-brother, Murray, and be wary of reliance upon certain others. The Queen defends her decisions but thanks him for his counsel and asks him to play and sing for her; he sings her a love-song.

Meanwhile Darnley has been in conversation with a counsellor of his own, Morton, who advises him that Rizzio must die. Darnley vacillates weakly, feeling himself wronged by the Queen, yet reluctant to give the order for an assassination. Once assured that it can be encompassed without his having to assume responsibility in a direct manner, he gives it his sanction.

We are shown a street scene, in which John Knox by his preaching rouses the people to indignation against the Queen and her foreign ways. Then we are taken to the fateful supper in the Queen's cabinet, when men enter, drag Rizzio from her side and, practically before her eyes, stab him to death.

Her orders held in contempt, she is kept practically prisoner, under the pretext that she is being protected from her own lack of judgement by those loyal subjects who know her interests better than she herself. She has to pretend some meekness towards Darnley, in order to obtain any liberty of movement, but throws herself into the arms of the one strong man whom she can trust, Bothwell. This is the story of Act II, *Bothwell*. It contains some fine passages of passion between the two lovers, but its real meat is the murder of Darnley.

Swinburne sees Mary as having been in full complicity with Bothwell in the plot to murder her husband. To her falls, indeed, the unenviable role of luring him, under pretext of its being for their joint safety, to Kirk o' Field, where arrangements have been made for his butchery. She is represented as having some horror of the bloodshed to come, and,

[1] Chatto, *The Tragedies*, Vol. II.

rather more, of the duplicity required of her in that she has repeatedly to allay the fears of Darnley, who doubts the wisdom of the move; but, if she does not like her treachery, she performs it, with unflinching resolution and a cool head.

When they arrive at the dreadful house, Darnley's nerves are on edge. It is plain that he mistrusts the Queen. When she sings to him, he is moved by a strange uneasiness, which he confesses; yet when a man, loyal to his interest, asks for private speech with him and tries to warn him against her, he dismisses him, indignant at the insult to the woman who is both the Queen and his wife. He even tells her of the warning. She, playing the situation calmly and cleverly, says the warning was surely given for love of him, and he should not be wroth with him that gave it. She bids him sleep, kisses him good-night and leaves him.

Left alone, save for the one serving man he has retained, his fears crowd back upon him. Suddenly, but too late, he knows that the plan is to murder him. This moment, with the scenes leading up to it, is, in a dreadful way, one of the most powerful in Swinburne's drama. Wretched, weak, and at the end pathetic Darnley is well drawn, and Mary, though ghastly in her treachery, is more credible than as Swinburne's juvenile pen had portrayed her in *Chastelard*.

Nevertheless, there is a difficulty about this play. Swinburne is telling us that Mary was active in the murder of her husband. Yet she is his heroine; plainly, his attitude is that he knows and does not mind that she murdered Darnley. For him, it is an episode in the life-story of a person whom he respects, and he expects the reader's sympathy to be with her. For most of us, murder is a thing so frightful that our sympathy is withdrawn from anybody who commits it.

Generally, those who concern themselves with Mary Queen of Scots fall into two camps; those who love her and aver her innocence, and those who condemn her, believing her guilty. Swinburne asks us to believe her guilty and yet to love her; which is much harder. His argument, in later years to be set forth in prose, was that nobody has ever thought that Mary Queen of Scots was either a fool or a coward; yet either one of these two things she must have been, to have been unaware of what was afoot or browbeaten into a merely passive acquiescence.

The immensely long third act deals with Mary and Bothwell's situation after the murder, and the measures they had to take for their safety and to avoid the appearance of guilt. While for Mary and Bothwell these moves must have been very urgent, their complication causes the pace, for the reader, to slacken. There is the problem of Bothwell's having a wife. Since it is obviously needful to their security that he should marry Mary, a means must be found of obtaining his freedom. The Archbishop of St. Andrews helps them find the ground for an annulment. His wife, divorced from him, resumes her maiden name of Jane Gordon. *Jane Gordon* is the title of the third act. She comes to see Mary and Bothwell after they have been married, from a strange kind of curiosity to know the quality of the union for which she was discarded. What she reads in their eyes distresses her in a way that she had not expected; for she sees that, already, all is not well between them. It was, in ironic fact, the ease with which he had put off his first wife which had given Mary apprehensions as to his constancy. But they were in too deep league to dare quarrel now.

Act IV, *John Knox*, deals with their increasing trouble, the civil war in which half Mary's people took arms against her and her new husband, and the increasing vehemence of John Knox against herself. A speech he makes to the assembled citizens extends over eleven whole pages, unbroken by so much as an interjection from any of his listeners.

In Act V, *The Queen*, she has been captured and is a prisoner at Lochleven Castle. Her companion in captivity is Mary Beaton, who loved Chastelard; Chastelard is never mentioned, yet Mary has a strange feeling that the link between their fates is predestinate. Lady Lochleven, in whose custody they have been placed, is kind, but Mary is possessed only by the possibilities of escape. Mary Beaton asks: 'Do you think you shall not long live bound?'[1] The Queen makes the flashing reply:

> Impossible.
> I would have violent death, or life at large;
> And either speedy.

Sir Robert Melville is admitted to her presence, as the messenger of the council now, in fact, ruling. They offer her a choice: either she should abdicate, in favour of her and Darnley's son, in which case they will make no use of the proofs they hold against her and she will live out her natural life, although in custody, or, if she will not abdicate, they will bring her to trial for the murder of Darnley.

Mary replies that she will die a Queen, and asks if her execution is to be in Lochleven.

Melville then reveals that he is the bearer, also, of a secret message,

[1] Chatto, *The Tragedies*, Vol. III.

from Queen Elizabeth, the Queen of England, saying she should sign whatever is needful to gain her life, seeing that a declaration made under duress cannot afterwards bind.

After considerable vacillation Mary signs, and shortly afterwards, with the help of George Douglas, she and Mary Beaton escape from Lochleven Castle. Outside the walls, on the shores of Loch Leven with her few followers, Mary pauses for a moment:

> To set my free face toward the large-eyed sky
> Against the clear wind and the climbing moon,
> And take into mine eyes and to my breast
> The whole sweet night and all the stars of heaven
> . . .

The large movement of the verse seems to draw through it the very breath of freedom and the unbounded heavens. It is perhaps the best piece of writing in the play.

Later, at Hamilton Castle, Mary says to the Earl of Argyle:

> I desire
> Not blood so much of them that seek mine own
> As victory on them, who being but subdued
> For me may live or die my subjects:

Here speaks the imperious autocracy, the vein in her with which Swinburne, despite his republicanism, sympathized. She marshals her allies:

> first the two great earls,
> Then Dacre, Norton, Swinburne, Markinfield,
> With all their houses

It has been doubted whether the poet's ancestors rendered help so important that the Queen should specially count upon them; but perhaps this was a forgivable licence; if it had not been for his sense of some ancestral connection with the fortunes of Mary Stuart, we might not have had the play.

Building upon the friendly will shown in Elizabeth's message, Mary after losing a battle, dispatches through Lord Herries a message asking for sanctuary in England. Her plan is, as she confides to him, once in England not merely to accept sanctuary but to seek an audience with her 'sister', and ask for forces to reinforce her own, with which she can return and reconquer Scotland. Herries warns her:

here you stand
Not yet dethroned from royal hope, not yet
Discrowned of your great name, whose natural power
Faith here forgets not, nor man's loyal love
Leaves off to honour; but gone hence, your name
Is but a stranger's, subject to men's laws,
Alien and liable to control and chance

. . .

Mary dismisses his misgivings:

I shall live
To bruise their heads who wounded me at heel,
When I shall set it on their necks. Come, friends,

. . .

Mary Beaton says, rather ominously:

. . . I will never leave you till you die.

This is the last line of the play.

Perhaps it was a mistake to call it *Bothwell*. Of all the major characters, he is the least characterized; he does not even appear in the scenes subsequent to Mary's capture, having escaped to the Orkneys and so gone out of her life. He seems to be but a boastful and scheming ruffian, with his eye always on his own interest; perhaps that is all he was and his character would not bear subtler delineation; but in that case, his function is merely to be the catalyst in Mary's drama. Perhaps, even at this time, Swinburne was contemplating making of Mary Stuart's life a trilogy of plays, of which *Chastelard* and the immense sprawling drama of *Bothwell* were but the first and second parts.

On May 23, 1874, we find Swinburne writing to the editor of the *Fortnightly*, concerning the expected review of *Bothwell*:[1]

I wish I had known before that you thought of giving Lord Houghton the position of my reviewer in the *Fortnightly*; as I should then, in defiance I doubt not of all etiquette, have requested you as a personal favour to me to give it in preference to any other writer alive—say Mr. Robert Buchanan. I have never shrunk from attack or from blame deserved or undeserved; but I must confess that I do shrink from the rancid unction of that man's adulation or patronage or criticism.

[1] Lang, Vol. II, p. 297.

What had happened to Swinburne's relations with Lord Houghton?
They used to be such friends. It is true that there appear to have been
no letters to Houghton since January 5, 1869. The alteration in Swinburne's feeling towards him remains a mystery.

Houghton reviewed *Bothwell*, and this reopened the correspondence.
On July 12, 1874, Swinburne wrote:[1]

> Dear Lord Houghton
> ... I address this to Fryston, not knowing what may be your
> present address in London. I read your article in the Fortnightly
> with pleasure, but am not prepared to admit the superfluity of the
> part of Jane Gordon, which has been very considerably curtailed in
> order not to make the poem any longer than was absolutely
> necessary for the development of the general design; in which
> however the total omission of this short part would have made, I
> think, a sensible gap ...
>
> Yours very truly,
A. C. Swinburne

The majority of the reviews were favourable, and the public were
perhaps better pleased by *Bothwell* than by anything Swinburne had
done. It was a grand chronicle of British history, and for all its absence
of moral sentiment there was nothing sexually shocking in it.

[1] Ibid., p. 307.

26

Erechtheus

SWINBURNE'S next work was not, as he had given Chatto to expect, *Tristram and Iseult*. To Watts he wrote, on August 27, 1875:[1] '... It is odd how *much* nearer and more real the prehistoric figures of classical than of Mediaeval legend seem to me. I can hardly screw up my faith to practical belief in Arthur, and hardly reason myself into personal doubt of the existence of Erechtheus.' This is probably the reason why his next major work was *Erechtheus*. To William Michael Rossetti, with whom he still corresponded on literary matters, despite the silence of the more dearly loved Gabriel, he wrote:[2]

> I am now on a three weeks' visit to Jowett, and at work on a companion poem to Atalanta which I hope will turn out a more perfect original example of Greek tragedy than that was. It is very simple in structure, and deals only with two 'elementary' passions—that of child and parent, and that of patriotism. . . . Jowett approves my scheme highly, and has helped me with some valuable hints from the classical or scholarly point of view . . .

The story is set in the time of a prehistoric king of Athens, Erechtheus. When the poem opens, it has been revealed to him by the oracle that Pallas Athene will preserve the city against the onslaught of the invading armies of Poseidon only if his daughter is sacrificed to her. In desperate grief, he speaks to Praxithea, his queen:[3]

> O daughter of Cephisus, from all time
> Wise have I found thee, wife and queen, of heart
> Perfect . . .
> . . .
> . . . now misdoubt
> Lest fate should find thee lesser than thy doom,
> Chosen if thou be to bear and to be great
> Haply beyond all women . . .

Warned that something very grave has been required, she answers:

[1] Lang, Vol. III, p. 58.   [2] Ibid., p. 55.   [3] Chatto, Vol. IV.

That word there is not in all speech of man,
King, that being spoken of the Gods and thee
I have not heart to honour . . .

Erectheus falters:

O, of what breath shall such a word be made,
Or from what heart find utterance? Would my tongue
Were rent forth rather from the quivering root
Than made as fire or poison thus for thee.

She thinks it is her own life which has been demanded, and replies loyally:

But if thou speak of blood, and I that hear
Be chosen of all for this land's love to die
And save to thee thy city, know this well,
Happiest I hold me of her seed alive.

Marvelling at her bravery, yet still not knowing how to tell her the facts, he says:

Thy blood the Gods require not; take this first.

She is puzzled; questions again. At last, he answers:

. . . There shall die
One soul for all this people; from thy womb
Came forth the seed that here on dry bare ground
Death's hand must sow untimely, to bring forth
Nor blade nor shoot in season, being by name
To the under Gods made holy, who require
For this land's life her death and maiden blood
To save a maiden city. Thus I heard,
And thus with all said leave thee; for save this
No word is left us, and no hope alive.

The modern reader perhaps expects Praxithea to rebel. This does not happen, but Swinburne does not give us the scene in which she breaks the dreadful news to her daughter. Instead, the chorus breaks in:

He hath uttered too surely his wrath not obscurely,
      nor wrapt as in mists of his breath,
The master that lightens not hearts he enlightens, but
      gives them foreknowledge of death.

215

As a bolt from the cloud hath he sent it aloud and
　　　　proclaimed it afar,
From the darkness and height of the horror of night
　　　　hath he shown us a star.
　　Star may I name it and err not, or flame shall I say,
　　Born of the womb that was born for the tomb of the day?

Having thus, tactfully, spared us a scene too heart-rending, Swinburne
brings on the daughter, Chthonia, already knowing. Her mother laments.
Chthonia, with simple sense of the dignity of her destiny, says:

　　Day to day makes answer, first to last, and life to
　　　　death; but I,
　　Born for death's sake, die for life's sake, if indeed this
　　　　be to die,
　　This my doom that seals me deathless till the springs
　　　　of time run dry.

She rejoices:

　　That I may give this poor girl's blood of mine
　　Scarce yet sun-warmed with summer, this thin life
　　Still green with flowerless growth of seedling days,
　　To build again my city; that no drop
　　Fallen of these innocent veins on the cold ground
　　But shall help knit the joints of her firm walls
　　To knead the stones together, and make sure
　　The band about her maiden girdlestead
　　Once fastened, and of all men's violent hands
　　Inviolable for ever; . . .

To her mother, who will be left with her coffin or bier, she says:

　　　　. . . the bed
　　Thou strewedst, a sterile place for all time, strewn
　　For my sleep only, with its void sad sheets
　　Shall vex thee, and the unfruitful coverlid
　　For empty days reproach me dead, that leave
　　No profit of my body, but am gone
　　As one not worth being born to bear no seed,
　　A sapless stock and branchless; yet thy womb
　　Shall not want honour of me, that brought forth

For all this people freedom, and for earth
From the unborn city born out of my blood
To light the face of all men evermore
Glory; but lay thou this to thy great heart
Whereunder in the dark of birth conceived
Mine unlit life lay girdled with the zone
That bound thy bridal bosom; set this thought
Against all edge of evil as a sword
To beat back sorrow, that for all the world
Thou brought'st me forth a saviour, who shall save
Athens; . . .

Mother and daughter take farewell, and Chthonia goes to her death. The sacrifice is described by one messenger, and another tells of the victory which follows from it. Pallas Athene appears, and speaks a blessing on the people.

Erechtheus has been considered by some the most perfect and most flawless of all Swinburne's works. It appeals particularly to Hellenists, such as Rutland, not only by its solemnity but as the most truly Greek, both in form and in feeling, of all his works founded upon Grecian myth, indeed of all such works in the English language. Edmund Gosse appreciated it as 'the most organic of Swinburne's writings', in which 'he rises, in an altitude of moral emotion that he reaches nowhere else, to an atmosphere which few modern poets have even attempted to breathe'. On the other hand, the poem has had its detractors. Edward Thomas, a poet so sensitive in his observation of the wild life of the English countryside, gives us, concerning the *Erechtheus,* the surprisingly insensitive comment that it is possible to get tired of being told that a girl is to die a virgin! This seems to miss Swinburne's point that something more transcendent than an ordinary feminine fulfilment was to come from her dedication. Indeed, Thomas is soundly rapped for this comment in Rutland's book. Yet Sir Harold Nicolson seems to be in the same difficulty as Edward Thomas, when he writes, 'the heroism displayed is too purposeless, too inhuman, to stir our modern sensibility. . . . In *Erechtheus* it is the gods alone who in their petty cruelty evolve the tragedy. . . .' With respect to a distinguished man of letters, he exemplifies, in these remarks, the complete failure of the moderns to understand what, to the ancients, sacrifice meant.

Perhaps because I have stood on a place where human sacrifice was anciently performed, and the sentiments connected with it still lived among the people, I feel the drama more in the way that the participants are represented as feeling it. What has been lost in two thousand years of a different education is the sense of how intimate was felt to be the co-operation between the people and their gods; in order to manifest in human form and to help their people in any practical respect, they needed the subtle emanation of human blood shed in a proper sacrifice. The missing link or explanation can be found in the magical writings which were the continuation *sub rosa* of the ancient tradition down through the Middle Ages and even to the present day. Except where the tradition became debased and unworthy, the victim, if adult, was always willing, and, whatever his regret at leaving personal, mortal life, felt it an ineffable honour that it should be his blood which was preferred.

It is this sense that, though she grieves at leaving a loved mother bereaved, and perhaps a little for the bridal and childbearing she might have had, she goes to a far greater destiny, which Swinburne has caught with such marvellous authenticity. Because the Athens which was preserved had the destiny of becoming the cradle of western civilization, the victory which sprang from her was not simply for a single city on its rock but for a way of life that was to irradiate the world, which if she could know through some mysterious and high intuition perhaps explains her exaltation.

The story is very likely true. It connects, also, with the idea that there is always, at the basis of a foundation of any importance, a sacrifice. In some parts of Cornwall a mouse is still killed and laid under the foundations of a house which is to be built. It would be surprising if there were no sacrificial offering for Athens. For what it is worth, I share Swinburne's conviction that he was writing about people who really lived.

Certainly his most solemn and sacred work, the *Erechtheus* was published in 1876. Swinburne was then thirty-nine.

27

And Mary?

AND what of Swinburne's cousin Mary, now Mrs. Disney Leith of Aberdeenshire? She, too, had been writing poems, and in 1873 brought out a volume entitled *A Martyr Bishop and other verses*, published by John Masters. She had not Swinburne's wonderful control of rhythms, but sometimes she could produce a piece of haunting power, as in *Autumn*, one of the 'other verses' in this volume:[1]

> O full voiced river, hasting down
> With ceaseless race of rapid motion,
> And crested waves that mimic ocean,
> Above the boulders swart and brown!
>
> O river, brimming to the banks,
> Covering the rocks whereon we stood,
> Even as Time's relentless flood
> Drowns our sweet memories. Have thou thanks.
>
> Our sweet dead memories! They are gone,
> As foam-wreaths drifted down the stream,
> As fancies of some happy dream
> At waking. Yet thy waves go on.
>
> The leaves break forth and turn and fall;
> The flowers come up and bloom and fade;
> Corn shoots and ripens, and is laid
> In storehouse: thou goest on through all,
>
> Changeless, yet changing: through the days
> Of summer, creeping gently by
> The sands and rocks left bare and dry,
> Scarce heard thy under-song of praise;
>
> And we, beside thy pleasant brink,
> Beneath the leaves, among the flowers,
> Drifted through all the sunny hours,
> Whither, we did not ask or think.

[1] Leith, *A Martyr Bishop*, pp. 78–80.

And well. For who would seek to read
His future, lest it mar his bliss?
We have our past; and is not this
Enough? yea, surely, all we need.

Ev'n as the rocks beneath the wave
Are there, although we cannot see,
So shall our past sweet memories be,
Not lost, though hidden in the grave,

Beneath a flood more deep, more fleet
Than thine, great river, hasting down
Between the woods grown sere and brown
Where yet we stand with lingering feet:

Where yet to wander we are fain,
As if the old familiar ways,
Could bring us back to summer days
And gladness past. O fond and vain

The hope, the clinging! Nevermore!
The skies are grey, the boughs are bare:
Dead whither'd leaves are everywhere
Strewn, like lost joys, along thy shore.

Dark looms the hill's majestic form:
All swollen run the mountain rills;
And in thy voice among the hills
Is heard the pressage of a storm.

One may think this is a good poem. But who is it to? It does not give
the impression of being written to her husband, who was presumably
with her in their Aberdeenshire home, unless away on duty. Her thought
seems to dwell on somebody whom she once knew, but who dwells with
her now only in the memory. Who had there been in her life of whom she
might write in this strain excepting Swinburne?

There is no river in the Isle of Wight large enough to be apostrophized
as a 'great river'. But when her family and his went to stay at Capheaton
each autumn, Mary and Algernon had probably walked together along
the banks of the Tyne. She might have revisited Capheaton. Or, brood-
ing by the Don or the Dee (mentioned in the same volume), which both
empty their waters into the sea near Aberdeen, she may, half hypnotized

by the rushing and swirling, have seen swim up, as it were, into her mind's eye, the picture of another river, by which she stood with one she loved.

The 'under-song' suggests the voice of the poet, as does the 'presage of a storm'. *Poems and Ballads* had produced a storm, and Mary may have felt there was something more dangerous to come.

This is conjecture. It is not possible to prove from the intrinsic evidence of the poem that it has bearing on Swinburne, but there has also to be considered in this connection a novel she wrote, which was not published until a few years later but was probably begun about this time. The title is *Like His Own Daughter*.

In this novel, the heroine is attracted in youth to a young man who is a bit of a scamp and 'unstable by nature'.[1] He is the most delightful company she knows, and she allows him to kiss her. Yet, when she is by herself, she reflects:[2] 'It is not well for a woman to feel that hers is to be the guiding and upholding influence in love—that she must be the supporter rather than the supported—because it puts her to a certain extent in a false position, and makes her virtually the stronger instead of the weaker vessel.'

She did not really mind this, because she had 'strength . . . self-confidence . . . shrewdness' in her own make-up. Yet she delayed telling her mother of his proposal, and when she wrote home she received a letter from her brother which was very damping:[3]

> Robbie is very young for one thing . . . not just very steady. You know what an abhorrence our father had at the slightest approach to drink . . . My mother feels that he would never have knowingly sanctioned the union of one of his daughters with a man who was given that way . . . At the same time mother says she does not command you to give him up altogether, if he is willing to try and deserve you. You are both very young, and it will do you no harm to wait a little . . . a few years, say . . .

When she shows this to the young Robbie, he takes it very badly, and accuses her of breaking their engagement. She pleads that she had only accepted his proposal subject to her mother's approval; but he asserts in the most declamatory style that she can never have loved him at all; and, apparently not understanding that she would have been willing to wait for him, he rushes away.

[1] Leith, *Like His Own Daughter*, p. 226.   [2] Ibid, p. 105.
[3] Ibid, p. 216.

Some time after this she receives a proposal from a man nineteen years older than herself, whom she had never considered as a lover because he had stood to her almost in *loco parentis*. She was 'like his own daughter'.[1] Her mother, however, approves, and she can see that he has estimable qualities and so she accepts him and finds happiness as his wife. She is able to brighten and sharpen him up, and to arrest the process of his premature ageing.

As for poor Robbie, the news she hears of him is distressing. He had[2]

fallen lower and lower into drinking habits

joined a band of itinerant musicians as a flute player, until, unable to keep up with them, he had died in circumstances of the utmost desolation.

Surely, this is the story of Mary's own life, her early attachment to Swinburne and subsequent marriage to Colonel Leith.

In the language of fictional disguise, a flute player is a natural equivalent for a poet.

Are we not learning from this narrative the very terms in which Lady Mary Gordon discouraged her daughter from accepting Swinburne's suite? Substract the Scottish background against which the tale is set, and for Robbie read Algy; and have we not here Mary's version of the tragic parting of which Swinburne gave his in *The Triumph of Time*?

[1] Leith, *Like His Own Daughter*, p. 381.   [2] Ibid, p. 352.

28

The Collapse

SWINBURNE had not in fact drunk himself to death, as did Robbie in Mary's fiction, but he came near to doing so.

In between states of exalted attention to his inner ear, he relapsed into troughs of despondency. In a letter he wrote Powell on July 27, 1875, recourse to the brand of humour habitual between them does not disguise and seems only to emphasize the loneliness he felt when temporarily laid up with a bad foot:[1]

> Dear George
> ... The God of the Marquis has made me for upwards of five weeks a blazing instance des Malheurs de la vertu (volume fifth). I am still tied by the foot and by His hand–si'l existe, ton b..... de Dieu, ma chère Justine. It is very dismall [sic]. I want some diversion as much as Nero ever did–and after the manner of that imperial Poet. I would give words for something–though it were but a drawing of my favourite school subject–to titillate my weary spirits. Even such converse as cheered the lonely hours of the great and good man whose philosophy yet sustains me, is denied to one who has no convicts to harangue or maniacs to convert. Il me faudrait des victimes. *Thus* I might get well. *Now*–If you *can*, send–or write–me some alleviation.

He was also drinking more and more obviously. At a party at Whistler's, Gosse relates on the authority of Lord Redesdale that everyone was smoking but there was no drink. Swinburne stood silent, then ejaculated, 'Moi, je ne fume jamais, mais je BOIS.'[2] When Swinburne dined with Gosse and his wife on September 10, 1877, they felt it necessary, after a certain point, to pretend there was no more wine in the house. A feigned search failed to deceive him, and he reproached them for thinking he would drink more than he should. When in 1878 he went to Glasgow to stay with John Nichol and they went out together, Swinburne became so drunk that Nichol had to bring him home in a cab and carry him up to his room. His bouts of drinking became lengthened.

[1] Lang, Vol. III, p. 48.   [2] Lang, Vol. VI, p. 239.

Yet his letters are full of interesting literary judgements. He had entered into contact with the very modern French symbolist poet, Stephane Mallarmé. To Mallarmé he wrote, on February 5, 1876, that in his opinion the three greatest poets of the Middle Ages were:[1] 'Dante, type de l'Italie et de l'aristocratie; Chaucer, type d'Angleterre et de la haute bourgeoisie; Villon, type de la France et du peuple, que je mets après Dante et (malgré toute mon admiration pour ce grand conteur humoristique et chevalresque) avant Chaucer.'

He does not give, and one would like to know, his reason for placing Villon higher than Chaucer; probably it was because Villon, associate of the derelicts of society, 'poet and pimp' as Swinburne elsewhere calls him, deals in a deeper level of ordinary human experience than the teller of the Canterbury tales. The translations from Villon upon which he now started are probably incomparable.

In a letter to Watts, he compared Christina Rossetti to Blake in respect of baby poems: he had taken the occasion in an article in the Athenaeum:[2] 'to say my say in praise and glory of Christina Rossetti on that special score as the spiritual sister of Blake himself. . . .'

He began work upon his long postponed *Tristram,* and achieved the first canto, *The Sailing of the Swallow.*

In the spring of 1876 he visited the Channel Islands and wrote his mother an ecstatic and delightful description of Sark. He was to praise it later in verse, but the Sark poems lack the detailed observation which makes the letter alive.

Yet the dominant impression derived from his letters of these years is of his increasing loneliness or want of close companionship. A slightly revived correspondence with Lord Houghton, though containing some echoes of the old humour, failed to regain its former warmth. Howell had to a great extent dropped out. Swinburne had written him no letter (or at any rate no letter which has been preserved) since the one of February 1873, in which he described, and by implication asked him to try to recover, the embarrassing flagellant papers he had left with Hotten; perhaps there had been some quarrel about that; or perhaps Howell, having in his capacity as counsellor of Swinburne in his relations with his publisher been superseded by Watts, felt hurt and withdrew. Perhaps Swinburne could do without Howell, but he remained grieved by his separation from Rossetti. Sometimes he asks to be recalled to his memory, when writing to persons who would be in

[1] Lang, Vol. III, p. 132.   [2] Lang, Vol. III, p. 276.

Andrew Chatto

Swinburne (right) and Watts-Dunton, at The Pines

contact with him – William Michael Rossetti or Watts. For instance, in writing to Watts on February 28, 1877, he mentions a new book on Villon, whose poetry was loved by Rossetti as much as by himself, and says:[1] 'You might (if he should not happen to have seen or heard of it) let DGR know of this; in case he retains any of the old affectionate interest which he formerly shared with me in the work and fortunes of the Bard. . . .' The adjective 'affectionate' surely applies to his feeling concerning what used to be the friendship between Rossetti and himself.

Concerning the dissolution of this friendship there is a mystery. Rossetti's niece, William Michael's daughter, Helen Rossetti Angeli publishes[2] extracts from an exchange of letters between Ford Madox Brown and her uncle Gabriel, by which she confessed herself bewildered. Brown's letter, written in November 1874 refers to the funeral of Oliver Brown. He invites Rossetti to it, and says that he would, if Rossetti could stand it, like to invite Hunt and Swinburne. Rossetti's reply is: 'Of course I shall be at the funeral on Thursday, and of course, at such a moment, could have no shadow of personal feeling as to who else might be present. I should add one word to say I had not the least idea that any one had supposed me to have any but the friendliest feelings towards Swinburne.' Yet Swinburne had certainly been given to understand otherwise, and by Mrs. Angeli's father, William Michael Rossetti.

William Michael, sober and responsible, was the last man in the world to make trouble between two men who only desired to remain friends. There is only one explanation which occurs to me. At the time of Gabriel Rossetti's breakdown and attempted suicide in the summer of 1872, he was suffering from delusions concerning a conspiracy against him. He took Browning's *Fifine at the Fair* as pointed at him, and he may in the same paroxysms of suspicion have named Swinburne in some manner that made William Michael feel impelled to write Swinburne the letter which he did, advising him to keep away. Later, when he had in some measure recovered, Gabriel may genuinely have forgotten having uttered the words about Swinburne which alarmed his brother. And yet, despite his protestation to Madox Brown, his attitude to Swinburne may not have been stabilized to the point where it seemed to William Michael wise to tell to Swinburne that he could call again.

[1] British Museum: MSS. Ashley 5090, f. 54.
[2] Angeli, *Dante Gabriel Rossetti*, p. 104.

Meanwhile Swinburne's dependence on Watts steadily increased. On December 19, 1876, he began a long letter with the words:[1]

> My dear Watts
>   Though I know you are so busy a man that you cannot have much time for the reading or writing of merely friendly letters, with no special point or aim to them, yet I do not like to be always writing to one of the best friends I ever had – or any one else ever had, for that matter – on business only ...

Eight days later, on December 27, he was writing, presumably in reply to the reply:[2] 'I need not (but for all that I will) say what genuine and warm pleasure you have given me by the last good words of your letter. If you really like me one half as well as I like you, I am well content – and well may be.' On January 28, 1877, again to Watts, he counts his remaining true friends: Jowett, Nichol: 'and (last in date among my closest friends, but certainly not least in my love and trust and gratitude) yourself.[3] This counting of one's friends is always a sign that they are a precious and rare commodity.

On March 4, 1877, Admiral Swinburne died. Though his relations with his son had been strained, there is no reason to doubt that Algernon felt the bereavement. He went, with the family, to attend the funeral, which was in the Isle of Wight, at Bonchurch. He was not appointed one of the Executors, but was left a bequest of £5,000 and the ultimate possession of his father's books, valued at £2,000.[4]

Replying to a letter of condolence from Lord Houghton, he said he thought his father had never got over the death, the previous summer, of his brother-in-law, Sir Henry Gordon, for they were like brothers. It will be remembered that they were, in any case, cousins. Another letter of condolence was from Nichol. Swinburne wrote on March 14:[5]

> ... on my return I find your welcome letter awaiting me among many others hardly less kind, but none quite so comfortable in their sympathy or coming from so old a friend. ...
>
>   Affectionately yours

Later in the month, unexpectedly, Swinburne found occasion to be annoyed by Watts. Earlier in their relationship Swinburne had lamented, in a humorous way, his inability to bring Watts to an

[1] Lang, Vol. III, p. 238. [2] Lang, Vol. III, p. 247.
[3] Lang, Vol. III, p. 265. [4] Gosse, pp. 234-5.
[5] Lang, Vol. III, p. 298.

appreciation of the Marquis de Sade. It was a more serious matter when Watts, who had become more of a literary critic than a lawyer, wrote for the *Athenaeum* an unappreciative review of the new volume of Victor Hugo's *La Légende des Siècles*. On March 24, Swinburne wrote to Watts stiffly:[1] 'You will not be hurt or surprised to hear that I certainly do not think your notice of my great Master's great work adequate or just.' After dealing with some particular points, he concludes that such injustice to Hugo could be 'explicable or excusable only in a foreign critic'. Fully to appreciate French verse one must have attempted to write it, just as one must be a painter to appreciate Velazquez in full.

Increasingly, his letters are about illness. To Houghton, he writes on June 8 that influenza has left him 'deafer than a post'. He has been reading Zola's *L'assommoir*.[2] 'No other book—"bar none"—ever made me feel quite physically unwell—out of order.' It may not be irrelevant to Swinburne's distaste for the book that it portrays drunkenness as a major and most revolting social evil.

On August 7, Swinburne wrote to Whistler that the doctor was keeping him in bed with a bad throat, and on the 12th he wrote to a Mr. Grossart that he was suffering from 'Diphtheria and Diarrhoea'. One knows that the latter complaint, with Swinburne, really meant a condition of the bowel connected with his drinking.

Despite the recent coolness between them, Howell wrote inviting him to be godfather to his baby daughter. Swinburne replied on October 8, saying that he was flattered and honoured, but hardly thought sponsorship was in his line; he would have liked to see the baby, but he was kept in bed by 'sore throat and indigestion'.

On December 27, there is a letter from his mother to his landlady at his rooms in Great James Street:[3]

> Dear Mrs. Magill
> Will you please give the enclosed letter to Mr. Swinburne when he is well enough to read it. You need not fear to give it him as it is as kind a letter as a Mother can write—but it is better not to send it direct to him. If he is ill I know you will let me hear from you.
>
> Yrs etc.,
> Jane H. Swinburne

[1] British Museum: MSS. Ashley 5090 (2), f. 14.
[2] Lang, Vol. IV, p. 10.   [3] Lang, Vol. IV, p. 30.

What does this mean? His relations with his mother must by now have become strained, or why should she think that a letter from herself to her son would be more acceptable to him if presented by the landlady's hand? Why should the landlady fear that it would cause him annoyance or distress or be anything but kind? All one can suppose is that Lady Swinburne, understandably concerned for her son's health, sometimes expressed in her letters to him the hope that he would drink less, and perhaps in other respects behave more wisely, and that for this reason he became reluctant to read her letters. It seems obvious that there was an understanding concerning Swinburne between his mother and his landlady, and on February 22 of the following year, 1878, we find Lady Swinburne writing to Mrs. Magill again, asking whether her son has yet returned from a trip which he made to Scotland, and how he is.

Swinburne had in fact returned, for he wrote (on the same date as his mother was writing to his landlady) a long letter to Lord Houghton, in which he mentions having just arrived from Glasgow, where he had been with Nichol.

On July 22, we find his mother writing to Houghton:[1]

Dear Lord Houghton

I fully appreciate the kind feeling which has made you write to me on the subject of the sad state in which you found my poor Son, and I thank you for it.—the case is a most grievous one and seems so hopeless. We have done our utmost to make our home a happy one for him and he has at times remained many months together with us, and himself owned that much of the work that he has done would never have been accomplished had he not been here—but it was often with much difficulty (and with much suffering to his father), that he was induced to leave London. Since his Father's death I have not been able to persuade him to come to me—I have tried every way to make him do so. In one letter to me he told me that nothing would induce him to come here again,—that he hates the place. . . . . .

I had a letter from him written on Thursday last . . . to tell me that his new rooms are delightful etc. He had never mentioned that he was going to leave his old lodgings . . .

Neither of the letters from her son to which she refers have been preserved. They are, presumably, amongst those which his cousin

[1] Ibid., p. 55.

Mary destroyed. That Lady Swinburne's revealing letter has been preserved is thanks to Lord Houghton, and to his family.

From the opening paragraph, it would appear that Houghton must, probably when calling at Swinburne's rooms, have found him in a state so pitiful that he had written to Lady Swinburne about it, perhaps asking if she could not have him at her home. That he should have been less willing to go home since the death of his father is puzzling, in view of the fact that the difficult relationship had always appeared to be with his father rather than with his mother. Now it seems almost to have been the other way round. Perhaps his father had for him a fascination which drew him, despite their dissensions; or perhaps he found the Admiral's frank rage easier to bear than his mother's soft reproach.

The new rooms to which he had moved were at 25 Guildford or Guilford Street, Russell Square (the name is today spelt without a *d*, but Swinburne inserts one, as in the name of the town). As Guilford Street is only a short distance from Great James Street, one wonders if the reason for his move may not have been that he resented his landlady being in correspondence with, and probably reporting on his condition to, his mother.

On August 29, Powell was writing to Watts:[1]

> (*Strictly private*)
> My dear Watts
> I am about to trouble you again–as in last Autumn–with a question or two of a confidential nature, concerning our dear Bard. *Where* is he, and *how* is he? Thrice have I written to Great James Street, and in all these cases quite without response ... I am not *complaining*, but only seriously anxious about our friend. Has the old tempter seized him?

Swinburne obviously had not given Powell his change of address. On September 22 and 25 he wrote two letters to Watts, in the first saying that he was suffering from 'painful sickness' and in the second that he was 'bedridden'.[2]

Watts presumably came to see him, but after that nearly a year went by, during which Swinburne wrote unusually few letters to anybody. There is, however, a correspondence between his mother and Watts, largely concerning how the money realized from the sale of the library left by Admiral Swinburne should, in Algernon's interest, best be invested. It seems to have been taken for granted on both sides that

---

[1] Lang, Vol. IV, p. 57.   [2] Ibid, p. 58.

Algernon was not capable of considering the matter actively. He was treated almost as though he were a child; his younger brother, Edward, who was an executor of the estate, suggested to Watts that the moneys to be invested on Algernon's behalf from different sources should all be nvested in the same security, as it would be simpler for Algernon to receive all dividends on the same date. Watts must have been to Lady Swinburne's home, for on June 25, 1879, we find her writing to him,[1] 'I thought it was quite a settled thing that you would come here again as soon as you had been able to arrange any plans for A's future.' In September, 1879, Watts, calling at Swinburne's rooms in Guilford Street, found him in an alcoholic stupor. He carried or helped him to the door, and thence conveyed him, first to his own rooms, and then to his (Watts's) sister's home in Putney.

[1] Lang, Vol. IV. p. 65.

29

The Move to Putney

THE house in which Watts's sister, Mrs. Mason, lived with her husband, her small son, Bertie, and her sister, Miss Theresa Watts, was not large enough comfortably to accommodate Watts and Swinburne as well. Since it was decided that the poet should be taken into the family and they should all live together, they took, and before the end of the month, September 1879, moved into, a much bigger house. This was The Pines, at eleven Putney Hill, semi-detached, with a curious tower, small front garden and longer garden at the back. This was to be Swinburne's home for the rest of his life.

The Watts and Mason families had the upper part of the house. Swinburne had the two large rooms on the first floor, using the front for his study, which he lined with all his books, and the back, over-looking the garden, for his bedroom. The ground-floor rooms were common. The front was the dining-room, where, as is recalled by Watts's friend Mackenzie Bell, Watts sat at the head of the table with Algernon on his right, Mrs. Mason or Miss Watts at the foot.[1] It was, of course, they who kept house for the whole household. The spacious sitting-room, giving on to the garden at the back, today breathes an atmosphere of peace and relaxation.

A porch leads to the garden, and a fragile, bluish-green bench, still upon the lawn, is the same on which Swinburne would sit, when the weather was clement.

His days followed a simple pattern. In the morning, he walked to the Rose and Crown, Wimbledon. The reason why he went so far for his midday beer was that he had promised Watts he would never enter a public house in Putney. The nearer Green Man, which he passed on the way, was within the forbidden territory. He would come back for lunch, the main meal, at one-thirty. The afternoon he generally spent in his rooms, emerging before supper-time to read aloud (not usually from his own works) to the assembled family for a while before the evening meal. Later, he would work again, often writing in his study until the small hours.

[1] Mackenzie Bell, p. 202.

Wine was not totally forbidden at the Watts' table, but appeared as a rule only when there was something to celebrate. Mackenzie Bell, a friend of Watts, writes:[1] 'Algernon's was the only case, in all my experience, where a propensity to exceed was held in check without total abstinence.'

This new sobriety and regularity in his life brought the recovery of his health. This must be set to the credit side of Watts's influence.

What was the mystery of this man who had been able to convert the 'libidinous laureate' of earlier years into the most acceptable citizen of suburbia? He had been born in St. Ives, Huntingdonshire, where his father, John King Watts, was a solicitor; he was a Congregationalist but had an interest in 'the new cosmogony', according to Mackenzie Bell. As a boy he became fascinated by gipsies, and made an early friendship with George Borrow. He qualified as a solicitor, but his heart was in poetry, and, if his own verse was not of a quality to win him immortality, he had, by 1874, been taken on to the staff of the *Examiner* as a critic, while from 1875 the *Athenaeum* had printed his reviews. He had a very considerable knowledge, far more knowledge than many good poets, of the technical side of the craft of verse-writing. He could distinguish a regular Pindaric ode from one ir-regular; he was an authority on the sonnet and the rondel. The edition of the *Harmsworth Encyclopaedia* published in 1910 described him as 'the foremost English critic of literature since Matthew Arnold'.

Biographers of Swinburne tend to write down Watts. Lafourcade refers to him as 'a dull friend'. The tendency is to ask whatever he and Swinburne could have had in common. Yet Watts was a man of letters, and they had in common a great love of poetry. It may nevertheless be asked whether it was good for a practising poet to live with a practising critic.

The *Poems and Ballads, Second Series* published just after the move into The Pines were composed earlier, and, if the best thing in them is the set of rumbustious translations from Villon at the end, show little departure from his earlier style; but in the time to come, Watts's influence was to be felt.

Nobody ever refers to Watts's sex-life. Had he none? He was five years older than Swinburne. Had he had a disappointment? Was he repressed? He was certainly, like Swinburne, lonely; which was another thing they had in common.

[1] Mackenzie Bell, p. 138.

Was Watts, perhaps unknown to himself, in disposition partly homo-sexual? Swinburne's letters to him, when in the years to come an occasional brief holiday separated them, contain snatches of sodomite humour. They prove nothing except that his brand of humour was understood between them. The overall influence of Watts was, however, overwhelmingly in the direction of conformism and conventional social respectability. A general impression that Watts had captured, or at any rate taken charge of, Swinburne, and of Swinburne's irritation by it is evidenced in his P.S. to a letter of October 6 1879 to Gosse: 'You need not put Watts's name on my address any more than mine on his, as we have both moved in together. A.C.S.'[1]

[1] Lang, Vol. IV, p. 101.

30

Love and Scorn

IT is sad to have to record that within a month of his removal to Putney Swinburne should have written with enmity of two of his former London friends. Certainly he had had provocation. Howell, always a wild talker, had been talking of him; a thing that might have been foreseen. More serious, Simeon Solomon had been selling his letters (the Swinburne letters which have vanished). On October 15, 1879, we find Swinburne writing to Gosse:[1]

> ... I will not for very shame's sake so far forget or forego my own claim to a sense of self-respect as to fret my heartstrings by day or by night over such disgusting facts as that I hear of one person who was once my friend and is yet my debtor habitually amusing mixed companies of total strangers by obscene false anecdotes about my private eccentricities of indecent indulgence as exhibited in real or imaginary *lupinaria*, and of another, who is now a thing un-mentionable alike by men and women, as equally abhorrent to either—nay, to the very beasts—raising money by the sale of my letters to him in past years, which must doubtless contain much foolish burlesque and now regrettable nonsense never meant for any stranger's eye who would not understand the mere childishness of the silly chaff indulged in long ago.

The letters probably contained instances of sodomite humour of the type familiar to us from its occurrence in his letters to other friends; they may even have contained something a little stronger, since they were written to one who was at the time an especially warm friend. For Solomon to have sold them, compromising Swinburne, was, of course, mean; yet Swinburne had failed to help him at the time of his trouble, and had even gone out of his way to deter Powell from helping him. This was probably Solomon's revenge, as well as the result of his genuine need for money.

Perhaps Swinburne himself felt some twinge of remorse for the way he had written off a former friend, although it was stifled by justification. That he recognized the horror of a once genuine relationship's

[1] Lang, Vol. IV, p. 107.

having so degenerated is shown in *Love and Scorn,* a poem consisting
of three connected Petrarchan sonnets, reflecting the confusion of his
feelings at this moment. As his sole literary admission of what may have
been his only 'affair' with a man, it merits the dignity of full citation:[1]

LOVE AND SCORN

I

Love, loyallest and lordliest born of things,
   Immortal that shouldst be, though all else end,
   In plighted hearts of fearless friend with friend,
Whose hand may curb or clip thy plume-plucked wings?
Not grief's nor time's: though these be lords and kings
   Crowned, and their yoke bid vassal passions bend,
   They may not pierce the spirit of sense, or blend
Quick poison with the soul's live watersprings.
The true clear heart whose core is manful trust
Fears not that very death may turn to dust
   Love lit therein as toward a brother born,
If one touch make not all its fine gold rust,
   If one breath blight not all its glad ripe corn,
   And all its fire be turned to fire of scorn.

II

Scorn only, scorn begot of bitter proof
   By keen experience of a trustless heart,
   Bears burning in her new-born hand the dart
Wherewith love dies heart-stricken, and the roof
Falls of his palace, and the storied woof
   Long woven of many a year with life's whole art
Is rent like any rotten weed apart,
And hardly with reluctant eyes aloof
Cold memory guards one relic scarce exempt
Yet from the fierce corrosion of contempt,
   And hardly saved by pity. Woe are we
That once we loved, and love not; but we know
The ghost of love, surviving yet in show,
   Where scorn has passed, is vain as grief must be.

[1] Chatto, Vol. VI, pp. 88–9.

III

O sacred, just, inevitable scorn,
    Strong child of righteous judgement, whom with grief
    The rent heart bears, and wins not yet relief,
Seeing of its pain so dire a portent born,
Must thou not spare one sheaf of all the corn,
    One doit of all the treasure? not one sheaf,
    Nor one poor doit of all? not one dead leaf
Of all that fell and left behind a thorn?
Is man so strong that one should scorn another?
Is any as God, not made of mortal mother,
    That love should turn in him to gall and flame?
Nay: but the true is not the false heart's brother:
    Love cannot love disloyalty: the name
    That else it wears is love no more, but shame.

'Righteous judgement' is not a quality which endears the one who feels himself to have it; neither is scorn. One may ask what title Swinburne had to feel either righteous or scornful of Simeon Solomon. They had been in a certain relationship; Solomon had let him down with a casual pick-up in circumstances which had got him into trouble with the police; Swinburne had taken fright and backed out of all connection with Solomon, with utterances that sound pusillanimous. It might have seemed Solomon's right to feel scorn, and he probably did.

But Swinburne was aristocratic, and he felt that to have sold personal letters, after such a relationship, was an unutterable vulgarity. It is improbable that he knew how desperate were Solomon's straits. And here we have a vein of independence in Solomon's character. Though he was in some senses a sponger (his letters to Swinburne urging him to praise his work in the *Dark Blue* show an exploiting tendency and an eye to the main chance), he refused, in his distress, the help his family would have given him, because they would have wanted to look after him (as Watts looked after Swinburne). Indifferent to money save in the short term sense of cash in hand to buy immediate drink, rather than submit to family overseeing and the suffocation of an enforcedly orderly life, Solomon preferred to sink almost literally into the gutter. The man who had exhibited at the Royal Academy for thirteen years in succession was now seen sitting on the pavement exhibiting his work for pennies. Later, he moved into St. Giles Workhouse, Endell Street.

According to his death certificate, a copy of which I obtained from
Somerset House, he died there, on August 14, 1905, of *syncope*, sudden
heart failure and disease of the aortic valve. It is stated on the certificate
that a Coroner's Inquest was held. Despite the miserable circumstances
of his end, Solomon's occupation is given, rather pathetically but none
the less truly, as: An Artist in Oil and Colours.

31

Springtides, Parodies and *Mary Stuart*

THE year 1880 passed quietly at The Pines. Swinburne brought out another volume, *Songs of the Springtides,* headed by *Thalassius,* a spiritual autobiography in the style of Shelley's *Epipsychidion* (as he acknowledged in a letter) but limited to his adolescence in Northumberland, a child cradled by the winds and sea. This was the poem which Edward Thomas recommended one should read first of all Swinburne's work, for its illumination of his own character. Yet the prose of *Lesbia Brandon* (not available when Thomas wrote) gives us a far more believable insight into what the young Swinburne, scrambling over the rocks, was really like than this idealized picture, which is almost of a sprite rather than a boy. Neither is the verse his firmest, though there are some fine phrases, such as 'the wind's quiring to the choral sea'.

With it is *On the Cliffs,* a poem about Sappho. The title, of course, refers to Leucadia. The theme had long haunted Swinburne, but now he seems to feel a spiritual identification with Sappho:[1]

> As brother and sister were we, child and bird,
> Since thy first Lesbian word
> Flamed on me. . . .

The bird is himself, the sea-mew, and as the sea-mews must have winged about her as she flung herself down from the Leucadian heights, and had circled about him, when as a boy he had climbed to their ledges on Culver Cliff in the Isle of Wight, so he seems to hear her cry in their cry, circling about his happier head.

The mood is that of *Thalassius.* In both poems there is an identification with his boyhood rather than with his present. Forty-three is too young to be looking back to one's youth, sentimentally, and one feels in this nostalgic preoccupation a regression from maturity.

The same mood extends to *The Garden of Cymodoce,* which opens with the rather remarkable declaration that sea has meant more to him than either love or poetry:[2]

[1] Chatto, Vol. III, pp. 318–39.   [2] Chatto, Vol. III, p. 326.

Sea, and bright wind, and heaven of ardent air,
More dear than all things earth-born; O to me
Mother more dear than love's own longing, sea,
More than love's eyes are, fair,
Be with my spirit of song as wings to bear,
As fire to feel and breathe and brighten; be
A spirit of sense more deep of deity,
A light of love, if love may be, more strong
In me than very song.
For song I have loved with second love, but thee,
Thee first, thee, mother . . .

The subject is Sark, and those who know the island will recognize in one passage a description of the Coupée, a 'bifront' neck of land joining the main part of the island to Little Sark; but though the 'spring-tides' are those which beat about the cliffs below, one feels, also, that they are the tides of the spring of Swinburne's life, when he climbed such cliffs as these.

In the same year he produced *The Heptalogia*, a series of parodies of the style of some contemporary poets, Coventry Patmore, Elizabeth Barrett Browning, Lord Lytton, Tennyson and Rossetti; at Watts's suggestion, he added a parody of himself. This, *Nephelidia*, is interesting in that it shows that Swinburne was very well aware of his principal weakness, the tendency to use words for their sound rather than their meaning:[1]

From the depth of the dreamy decline of the dawn
through a notable nimbus of nebulous noonshine,
Pallid and pink as the palm of the flag-flower that
flickers with fear of the flies as they float,
Are they looks of our lovers that lustrously lean from
a marvel of mystic miraculous moonshine,
These that we feel in the blood of our blushes that
thicken and threaten with throbs through the throat.

At the same time, he had continued working on *Mary Stuart*, which he had begun at Guilford Street. This play, the last in his vast trilogy about Mary Queen of Scots, and dedicated as were the two preceding ones to Victor Hugo, opens in England, with the Babington plot and the arrest of Babington. The scene moves to Chartley, where Mary, with

[1] Chatto, Vol. V, p. 422.

Mary Beaton, unaware that the plot has been discovered, awaits its issue. Right at the outset, we have a difficulty similar to that with which Swinburne presented us in *Bothwell*. There, he showed us Mary as party to the murder of her husband, and yet expected our sympathies to be with her. Here we are shown a Mary who understands that the plot to place her in Elizabeth's stead upon the throne, if it is to carry through, will involve the murder of Elizabeth. In his later article on Mary Queen of Scots for the *Encyclopaedia Britannica*, Swinburne pours scorn on any other thesis:[1]

> It is maintained by those admirers of Mary who assume her to have been an almost absolute imbecile ... that, while cognisant of the plot ... she might have been innocently unconscious that this conspiracy involved the simultaneous assassination of Elizabeth. In the conduct and detection of her correspondence with Babington, traitor was played off against traitor, and spies were utilised against assassins, with as little scruple as could be required ... it is thought credible that she was kept in ignorance by the traitors and murderers who had enrolled themselves in her service,—that one who pensioned the actual murderer of Murray and a would-be murderer of Elizabeth was incapable of approving what her keen and practised intelligence was too blunt and torpid to anticipate as inevitable and inseparable from the general design.

We have then a heroine whose 'keen and practised intelligence' tells her the murder of Elizabeth is necessary, and expects it. Admittedly, she knows her own life will be forfeit should the plot miscarry. It is her life against Elizabeth's, and it is in the light of this desperate gamble that we have to read the comparison she makes between their natures:[2]

> I muse upon and marvel, if she have
> Desire or pulse or passion of true heart
> Fed full from natural veins, or be indeed
> All bare and barren all as dead men's bones
> Of all sweet nature and sharp seed of love,
> And those salt springs of life, through fire and tears
> That bring forth pain and pleasure in their kind
> To make good days and evil, all in her
> Lie sere and sapless as the dust of death.
> I have found no great good hap in all my days

[1] Quoted in Chatto, *The Tragedies*, Vol. IV, pp. 237–8.   [2] Ibid., p. 41.

> Nor much good cause to make me glad of God,
> Yet have I had and lacked not of my life
> My good things and mine evil: being not yet
> Barred from life's natural ends of evil and good
> Foredoomed for man and woman through the world
> Till all their works be nothing: and of mine
> I know but this—though I should die to-day,
> I would not take for mine her fortune.

Though the assessment of Elizabeth's character may not be just, and the intent to murder repels, here we have something not without grandeur, the pride of a mature woman who has lived a full woman's life, and the acceptance of the vicissitudes of fortune which are the price of plunging into life boldly. One may recognize in a firmer and more experienced key, the strains in which, in Swinburne's very first play, Rosamund, proud of her role as a king's mistress, addresses her more conventionally virtuous and somewhat disapproving maid.

Mary is, of course, made prisoner, and the scene changes to Elizabeth's apartments in Windsor Castle. Elizabeth now has the problem of deciding whether or not she must have Mary executed. One feels that Swinburne does not like Elizabeth but is trying to be fair; and indeed, if Mary was as Swinburne draws her, Elizabeth could not sleep safe in her bed while Mary lived.

It is a difficulty of the play, from the point of view of our feeling, that, even though the author is 'on the other side,' Elizabeth does seem so much more responsible than Mary; genuinely concerned with affairs of state and with the welfare of her realm. Swinburne omitted to tell us, in any of his plays of the Marian cycle, that Mary loved Scotland or the Scottish people, and rather gives us to understand that she detested them, apart from the few individuals who earned her recognition by their devotion to herself. He has given us a Queen whose royalty was its own end. She was not the shield of her people's rights and freedoms, as was Elizabeth. It is a strange, elemental creature for whom (through the mouth of Drury) Swinburne asks us to share his admiration:[1]

> Unmerciful, unfaithful, but of heart
> So fiery high, so swift of spirit and clear,
> In extreme danger and pain so lifted up,
> So of all violent things inviolable,

[1] Chatto, *The Tragedies*, Vol. IV, p. 152.

So large of courage, so superb of soul,
So sheathed with iron mind invincible
And arms unbreached of fireproof constancy—
By shame not shaken, fear or force or death,
Change, or all confluence of calamities—
And so at her worst need beloved, and still,
Naked of help and honour when she seemed,
As other women would be, and of hope
Stripped, still so of herself adorable
By minds not always all ignobly mad
Nor all made poisonous with false grain of faith,
She shall be a world's wonder to all time,
A deadly glory watched of marvelling men
Not without praise, not without noble tears,
And if without what she would never have
Who had it never, pity—yet from none
Quite without reverence and some kind of love
For that which was so royal.

Though the comparison may seem grotesque, there is only one other heroine in English literature who, being as feckless and as conscience-less, and yet in a strange wild way grand, resembles her, and that is Cathy in *Wuthering Heights:* Cathy with something of Heathcliff added to her.

Swinburne ends the play in rather an odd manner. At an earlier period of her long, restricted life in England, Mary had been placed in the care and custody of the Countess of Shrewsbury, from whose gossipy tongue she had picked up an extraordinary story of Elizabeth's womb being closed, so that she could not have intercourse though she hungered for it. She had written to Elizabeth about this, with the momentary thought of gaining favour by making a loyal report, but on second thoughts had decided not to send the letter, as it would be more likely to infuriate than please the recipient. Mary Beaton, Swinburne tells us, had kept the letter, though telling Mary that she had destroyed it. It is the instrument through which she has the power to achieve a long contemplated revenge.

Mary Beaton, it will be remembered, had loved Chastelard, who for love of Mary had gone to his death. Through all the dramatic years which had passed since that drama, Mary Stuart had never once mentioned his name. Had she forgotten him? Mary Beaton performs a test. She sings Mary one of Chastelard's songs:[1]

> Après tant de jours, après tant de pleurs,
> Soyez secourable à mon âme en peine.
>
> . . .

Mary Stuart vaguely remembers the song, but, being asked, attributes it to another poet. If she had remembered, Mary Beaton would have foregone her revenge. The mistake hardens her, and she sends the letter to Elizabeth, who had been upon the verge of clemency. It is this which turns the scales.

Though it is, of course, a blend of fact and fiction, the dramatic effect of this ending is considerable.

[1] Chatto, *The Tragedies*, Vol. IV, p. 174.

32

Bertie

IT is from Swinburne's letters to his mother that we first hear about the child who had entered his life. This was Bertie, otherwise Herbert Mason, the son of Watts's sister. He was five when Watts brought Swinburne to his sister's home, and Swinburne first mentions the 'little five-year-old' before they all had moved from there to The Pines. References to Bertie's doings and sayings continue.[1] 'It makes such a pleasant difference having a child in the household to rule over you . . .' Swinburne wrote to his mother in the first of these letters about Bertie. The word 'rule' was to become prophetic.

On December 22, he was writing:[2]

> There came a most lovely baby in arms here on a visit one day, and it beamed on me the minute our eyes met. But of all children out of arms Bertie is much the sweetest going at any price. One thing that I heard a day or two since really brings tears into my eyes whenever I think of it . . . He had heard an account of a crocodile hunt in which the she-crocodile was killed and her young ones left helpless and stranded—and on being found afterwards crying quietly, he said 'he was so sorry for the poor little crocodiles.' His uncle couldn't help laughing when he heard of it, though he admitted it was very touching—and I can't help crying though I admit it was very funny. Think of the dear little innocent thing—and (as Watts says) the manliest little fellow of his age he ever knew—in tears over the crocodile orphans! I don't know how to say what I feel about children—it is as if something of worship was mixed with love of them and delight in them.

Bertie was six on February 4, 1880. Half way through the year, in September, Swinburne wrote *Six Years Old*, the first of his many poems to Bertie, beginning, 'Between the springs of six and seven,' and containing the verse:[3]

> You came when winds unleashed were snarling
> Behind the frost-bound hours,

[1] Leith, p. 154.   [2] Leith, p. 206.   [3] Chatto, Vol. V, p. 77.

244

BERTIE

A snow-bird sturdier than the starling,
    A storm-bird fledged for showers,
That spring might smile to find you, darling,
    First born of all the flowers.

It is, of course, sentimental, yet an excusably pretty conceit. For the child's next birthday, in February 1881, Swinburne wrote *Seven Years Old*, which is equally sentimental, though the fifth stanza has a touch of sublimated sensuality about it:[1]

V

Brown bright eyes and fair bright head,
    Worth a worthier crown than this is,
Worth a worthier song instead,
Sweet grave wise round mouth, full fed
    With the joy of love, whose bliss is
More than mortal wine and bread,
    Lips whose words are sweet as kisses,

He was still writing about the child to his mother. On February 22, he told her how he had turned the pages of a Pictorial Shakespeare for Bertie, and come on a symbolical representation of Death. Bertie asked him who the gaunt old man was:[2]

Death, I told him; and, surprise
Deepening more his wildwood eyes
(Like a sweet swift thing's whose breath
Spring in green groves nourisheth),
Up he turned his rosebright face
Glorious with its seven years grace,
        Asking–'What is death?'

I had written so far after he left me and was going to write more when I was interrupted; and on showing the lines to Watts after dinner, he exhorted me to leave off there . . . and though I might write ever such fine lines to follow it would impair the perfection of the effect or impression produced by ending with Bertie's own three words.

[1] Chatto, Vol. V, pp. 273–4.
[2] Leith, p. 156. The poem appears, with slight textual emendations, in Chatto Vol. V, p. 280.

Perhaps Lady Swinburne was beginning to feel uneasy, for writing again to his mother on March 10, Swinburne begins with the very curious words:[1] 'I quite understand how (as you say) "a mother loves those words" which warn us against offending one of the little ones—but to me the divinest of all divine words and thoughts—is that "of such is the kingdom of heaven".'

His mother must have suggested that he might be putting a stumbling block in Bertie's way. After thus assuring her that it was not so, he went on to describe how he read Bertie some scenes in which Falstaff enters:

.... Again and again during my half-reading half-relating the main part of the great comic scenes, the child went over on the small (the very small) of his little back among the sofa cushions, crowing aloud like a baby, choking with laughter, shouting and rolling from side to side with his heels *any* height above his head and kicking with absolute fury of delight. 'Oh! didn't he tell stories!' he said to his father (in the largest type of a child's voice). I thought, if Shakespeare could have been looking down and enjoying the little thing's inexpressible rapture, he must have felt it a greater tribute than all the plaudits of all the theatres in the world.

Lady Swinburne's anxiety did not abate, and a letter to herself from Watts must have increased it, for on May 14, 1881, we find her writing him a most significant letter:[2]

Dear Mr. Watts

I quite understand what you feel about Algernon but he has given me no opening, as you think he may have done, to enable me to give him the little word of advice you suggest—he tells me that he has written '21 Poems of lamentation' on the subject of his dear little friend's absence which he calls a 'total eclipse of the Sun.' His love for that little friend amounts to devotion and I often hope that it may lead to the faith of his youth in some hidden way—for the love of, and the appreciation of innocent childhood is good and *wholesome.* You and no doubt his Parents will guard the little child from any harmful views on that subject that Algernon might inadvertently lead him into.

If I can in any way hint at the necessity for care not to *over do,* I will not fail to do so, but it is not easy—he feels so sure of my sympathy for him in the love for children that I should be sorry to

[1] Leith, p. 123.   [2] Lang, Vol. IV, p. 213.

check his openness with me on the subject and he is so kind in sending me copies of what he writes that I would seem unkind to do so.

I am so sorry that I cannot ask him to come to see us now but at present I have only one spare room and small dressing-room and I am afraid you would not think it safe for him to come alone – and therefore I have made the excuse of the noise and untidiness of the building work that is going on. . . .

With kind regards I remain, dear Mr. Watts

Very truly yours,

Jane S. Swinburne

Your report of Algernon's health is most satisfactory.

What you say about his spoiling his writing by 'not knowing where to stop' – is so very true. I constantly deplore it!

This letter reveals much. It is obvious that both Watts and Swinburne's mother were anxious lest child-love might not be the newest turn taken by his strange nature, now that all its previous expressions had been denied him.

The twenty-one poems of lamentation to which Lady Swinburne refers became thirty-one, and form a series under the title *A Dark Month*. What made the month of May dark was that Bertie had been taken away, for a holiday or perhaps to prevent his being too much with Swinburne. Disconsolate, Swinburne wrote:[1]

I

> A month without sight of the sun
>   Rising or reigning or setting
> Through days without use of the day,
> Who calls it the month of May?
> The sense of the name is undone
>   And the sound of it fit for forgetting.
>
> We shall not feel if the sun rise,
>   We shall not care if it sets; . . .
> A whole dead month in the dark . . .

Is not this the wretchedness of any person in love, whose loved one is away? Swinburne, with extraordinary absence of self-knowledge, was in love with the child.

[1] Chatto, Vol. V, p. 321 ff.

He remembers how they had sat together looking at the Shakespeare:

> I sit where he sat beside me . . .
> I broke the gold of words to melt it
> For hands but seven years old,
> And they caught the tale. . . .

If hands clutching the words of a tale seems an awkward image, one understands that he could not now even look at the volume which had acquired an extra glow of meaning for him when he broke passages into child's language for Bertie. But what is extraordinary is that Swinburne seems unconscious of the erotic content of lines such as:

> Desire, but in dreams, cannot ope
> The door that was shut upon hope
> When love went out at the door.

Some of the sequences could have been written by a man to a woman:

> Only my heart is eased with hearing,
> Only mine eyes are soothed with seeing,
> A face brought nigh, a footfall nearing,
> Till hope takes form and dreams have being.

Rather dreadful is the image with which he opens the next poem:

> As a poor man hungering stands with insatiate eyes
> and hands
> Void of bread
> Right in sight of men that feast while his famine with
> no least
> Crumb is fed,
> Here across the garden-wall can I hear strange children
> call,
> Watch them play,
> From the windowed seat above, whence the goodlier
> child I love
> Is away.

Only in one passage does one find recognition of the abnormal nature of his passion:

> But eyes of father and mother
> Like sunlight shed on you shine;
> What need you have of another
> Such new strange love as is mine?

One has however a lovely, healthy description of the child in:

> And his hands are as sunny
> As ruddy ripe corn
> Or the browner-hued honey
> From heather-bells borne.

He recognizes the truth that he can no longer treat the themes he had intended, for they have become unreal, before the situation in which he is now caught:

> Between my hand and my eyes
> The lines of a small face rise,
> And the lines I trace and retrace
> Are none but those of his face.

There is open hyperbole in:

> . . .
> The very light of day, the very
> Sun's self comes in with him.

The child is still the Sun, though he reproaches him for not writing (could Bertie write?) or sending a message, in:

> Out of sight,
> Out of mind!
> Could the light
> prove unkind?
>
> . . .
> Has my king
> Cast off me,

Perhaps those in charge of the child thought it better he should not send messages to Swinburne.

There is again an extraordinary absence of realization that the very language he was using was the language of erotic love in:

> . . .
> I am only my love's
> True lover,

With a nestful of songs, like doves
  Under cover.

Though it might seem sentimentality to a reader who did not know
the writer's history, there is a touch of the old masochism in:

Good things I keep to console me
  For lack of the best of all,
A child to command and control me,
  Bid come and remain at his call.

. . .

And friends are about me, and better
  At summons of no man stand:
But I pine for the touch of a fetter,
  The curb of a strong king's hand.

In *Poems and Ballads*, Swinburne seemed to sing promiscuous
ecstasies. Not now:

Stars in heaven are many,
  Suns in heaven but one:
Nor for man may any
  Star supplant the sun.

Many a child as joyous
  As our far-off king
Meets as though to annoy us
  In the paths of spring.

Unhappily, he passes the door of Bertie's now empty bedroom:

I pass by the small room now forlorn
  Where once each night as I passed I knew
A child's bright sleep from even to morn
  Made sweet the whole night through.

As a soundless shell, as a songless nest,
  Seems now the room that was radiant then
And fragrant with his happier rest
  Than that of the slumbering sun.

The thirty-one poems had probably been written one each day, to give himself a soul-soothing occupation for each day of the month that Bertie was away; for the sequence ends, as if on the last day of May:

> Out of dawn and morning,
>   Noon and afternoon,
> The sun to the world gives warning
>   Of news that brightens the moon;
> And the stars all night exult with us, hearing of joy
>   that shall come with June.

But joy did not come with June. The grown-ups who arranged Bertie's life kept him still away. They kept him away all the summer. In September he was brought back, and Swinburne, breaking into the old anapaestic heptametres, wrote *Sunrise*:[1]

> If the wind and the sunlight of April and August had
>   mingled the past and hereafter
> In a single adorable season whose life was a rapture
>   of love and of laughter,
> And the blithest of singers were back with a song; if
>   again from his tomb as from prison,
> If again from the night or the twilight of ages
>   Aristophanes had arisen,
> With the gold-feathered wings of a bird that were
>   also a god upon earth at his shoulders,
> And the gold-flowing laugh of the manhood of old at
>   his lips for a joy to beholders,
> He alone unrebuked of presumption were able to set
>   to some adequate measure
> The delight of our eyes in the dawn that restores
>   them the sun of their sense and the pleasure.
> For the days of the darkness of spirit are over for all
>   of us here, and the season
> When desire was a longing, and absence a thorn, and
>   rejoicing a word without reason.
> For the roof overhead of the pines is astir with delight
>   as of jubilant voices,

[1] Chatto, Vol. V, pp. 368–9.

And the floor underfoot of the bracken and heather
  alive as a heart that rejoices.
For the house that was childless awhile, and the light
  of it darkened, the pulse of it dwindled,
Rings radiant again with a child's bright feet, with
  The light of his face rekindled. . . .
Though the fall of the year be upon us, who trusted
  in June and by June were defrauded,
And the summer that brought us not back the desire
  of our eyes be gone hence unapplauded.
For July came joyless among us, and August went
  out from us arid and sterile,
And the hope of our hearts, as it seemed, was no
  more than a flower that the seasons imperil,
And the joy of our hearts, as it seemed, than a thought
  which regret had not heart to remember,
Till four dark months overpast were atoned for, and
  summer began in September.

   . . .

Lady Swinburne's instinct not to make him self-conscious by reproaching him with the nature of his interest in the child was right. Despite the ecstasy of the heptametres with which he greeted Bertie's return, Swinburne's passion, sublimated, quietened gradually.

33

Tristram

BY the autumn of 1881, Swinburne was re-engaged on his long post-poned grand romantic poem on the theme of Tristram and Iseult. This time he called it *Tristram of Lyonesse*.

There is a *Prelude*, which he had completed long ago. In this he makes a calendar in which he sets, as though they were astrological signs, one great heroine of a classic love-story to every month of the year: Helen of Troy for January, Hero for February, Alcyone for March, Iseult for April, Rosamund for May, Dido for June, Juliet for July, Cleopatra for August, Francesca di Rimini for September, Thisbe for October, Angelica for November and Guenevere for December.[1]

> These are the signs where through the year sees move,
> Full of the sun, the sun-god which is love,
> . . .

It is a delightful conceit, though it seems rather an independent poem than anything to do with what follows.

The epic is divided into nine parts. The first, *The Sailing of the Swallow*, tells of how Tristram fetched Iseult from Ireland to Tintagel, to be the bride of King Mark and how they fell in love on the way. He had been telling her stories of love when, as the boat slips through the sea, the dawn comes up.

The day advances, and they drink from the fateful beaker:

> each mouth trembled for a word;
> Their heads neared, and their hands were drawn in one,
> And they saw dark, though still the unsunken sun
> Far through fine rain shot fire into the south;
> And their four lips became one burning mouth.

Curious how, for Swinburne, rain is always the background of passionate love.

The second part tells of the deception of King Mark, but Iseult does

[1] Chatto, Vol. IV, p. 9.

not, as in the *Queen Yseult* of Swinburne's Oxford days, have to carry
Tristram to her room.

By part III, Tristram is in Brittany, and part IV is *The Maiden
Marriage*. The strange nature of the wedding night is not dwelt upon
as in *Queen Yseult,* but the conclusion is in the same strain:

> So had she all her heart's will, all she would,
> For love's sake that sufficed her, glad and good,
> All night safe sleeping in her maidenhood.

But this time, the high point of the drama is in part V, *Iseult at
Tintagel*:

> But that same night in Cornwall oversea
> Couched at Queen Iseult's hand, against her knee,
> With keen kind eyes that read her whole heart's pain
> Fast at wide watch lay Tristram's hound Houdain,

While the sea thunders below about Tintagel's headland, crowned by
the castle in which she is like a prisoner, she falls upon her knees and
prays desperately:

> 'Oh God, God born of woman, of a maid,
> Christ, once in flesh of thine own fashion clad;
> O very love, . . .

She prays for grace, but realizes she is incapable of repentance, since
she does not in her heart renounce Tristram. Instead of the intended
prayer, she is praying:

> God give him to me—God, God, give him back!

In part V, Tristram steals back to Tintagel, and he and Iseult take
flight together, to *Joyous Gard* the old name of Bamborough Castle, in
Northumberland. This section is a hymn to happy love, consummated
and fortifying:

> And their great love was mixed with all things great,
> As life being lovely, and yet being strong like fate.

Into this idyll Swinburne worked his memories of the moors and
coasts of Northumberland, and even of the three herons he had seen
from the boat, when, with Bell Scott, he had visited 'Grace Darling's
island'. Tristram and Iseult see:

Three herons deep asleep against the sun,
Each with one bright foot downward poised, and one
Wing-hidden hard by the bright head, and all
Still. . . .

The next two sections tell of the fate that separates the lovers again, and of the desperate jealousy of the other Iseult, Iseult of the White Hands, in Brittany, now conscious of all that she misses in her unconsummated marriage.

In the last part, *The Sailing of the Swan* Tristram, back in Brittany and dying, sends a messenger to Iseult in Tintagel, asking her, if it is by any means possible, to come to him. Stealthily, she descends the stairs from King Mark's Castle to Tintagel beach, and steps into the boat which is waiting. Tristram, knowing how unbearable, would be his suspense, had asked, that the boat, on its return journey should, if it brought Iseult, show a white sail, but otherwise, a black. Iseult of Britanny, turned to a fiend by jealousy, seeing the white sail, tells Tristram it is black. The disappointment kills him, and his true Iseult, arriving, bends over his body: 'And their four lips became one silent mouth.'

King Mark, seeing how great was their love, forgives them and, their bodies being brought back to Tintagel, builds a chapel for their tomb. Over this, as the sea erodes the land, the waves wash.

In all, it is a grand drama. It has its faults. The occasional use of archaic English forms, such as 'holp' for 'help', may seem pointless, in that the legend belongs to the ancient British, not the Middle English period. Swinburne, however, was aware of this but took the view that, as it had come down to us, the tale is Mediaeval in character, whatever its possible basis in much more ancient fact. Yet it is an epic showing the passionate love of an adult woman as a thing grand and fortifying.

It is curious that, in the whole of our literature, there are extraordinarily few works of any kind which give to the consummated passion of an adult man and woman this dignity. It is even more curious that it should be to Swinburne, who probably never consummated a relationship with a woman, that we owe this grand portrayal. It is a thing for which we have to be grateful to him.

34

The Flogging Block

In the British Museum, there are certain works which do not appear in the General Catalogue; they are works which have been classified as pornographic, and one has to know their titles in order to apply for them. The application has to be made to the keeper in whose discretion it lies to grant or refuse it. If one's reason for wishing to see the works has been approved, one is conducted to a special seat, marked 'Reserved for Special Books,' exactly in front of the custodian, and there the books brought from the Private Case are laid before one.

Such a book is *The Whippingham Papers*. It is all about flagellation, and consists of stories, articles and poems written over a number of signatures, or rather pseudonyms. Two poems, *Arthur's Flogging* and *Reginald's Flogging,* each signed Etonensis, are certainly by Swinburne, and a third, a prose piece, entitled *A Boy's First Flogging at Birch-minster,* though unsigned, is almost certainly by Swinburne too, for it contains the names of Frank and Harry Fane, and refers to 'both Seytons.' The publisher's name does not appear upon the volume, in print, but on the fly-leaf of the copy laid before me was written in pencil, perhaps by one of the Museum's authorities, *250 copies E. Avery Published 1887.*

It is possible that Swinburne wrote these three pieces before his removal by Watts to Putney and had given them to some acquaintance who had flagellant interests but had not published them until this later date.

But it is not only the Printed Books department of the British Museum Library which has its way of dealing with works which might cause embarrassment. The Manuscripts Department also has papers classified 'Reserved from Public Use.' Several of Swinburne's manuscripts are thus classified, and here again special application is necessary. If the application is successful, the manuscript is brought up in a wrapping of thick brown paper, presumably so as to protect from its corrupting influence the member of the staff who has the duty of bringing it from its place of storage. The parcel is tied with tape, and the tape is secured by a special seal, in such a manner that it cannot be untied, but has to be cut with scissors. The cutting can only be done by a senior official.

One may watch. The seal falls with a plop. Inside the parcel there is, together with the manuscript, a list (to which one's own name will be added) of previous persons for whom the manuscript was brought out, with the signature, against each entry, of the official who opened the parcel, and a signature for the re-sealing, and the date of each operation. In the list of my predecessors, there were no names which I recognized in the context of Swinburne studies (or any other context).

The longest and most important of Swinburne's manuscripts 'Reserved from Public Use' is *The Flogging Block/An Heroic Poem/by Rufus Rodworthy, Esq./(Algernon Clavering)/With Annotations [Written above Birchmore]/by Barebum Birchingham, Esq., (Bertram Bellingham)/London 1777*. Needless to say, the fictitious date, making it appear an ancient manuscript, is, like the fictitious authors' names, merely a cover. The work is written on foolscap leaves, white and blue, of various makes; the greater number bear writing on one side only, but sometimes the verso is used. There are 167 written sides in all, but the poem is in twelve Eclogues and each Eclogue is foliated separately. The table of contents though in Swinburne's hand, at the end, does not match the actual contents, which are as follows:

General Prologue
Notes to Prologue
   Eclogue I Algernon's Flogging
        Note to Algernon's Flogging
     II Reginald's Flogging
       Epilogue to Reginald's Flogging
       Another Epilogue to Reginald's Flogging
    III Percy's Flogging
    IV Prelude to Willie's Flogging
      Willie's Flogging
     V Prelude to Charlie's Flogging
      Charlie's Flogging
    VI Edward's Flogging
    VII Frank's Flogging
   VIII Philip's Flogging
    IX Frederick's Flogging
    X Edgar's Flogging
    XI Rupert's Flogging
    XII Rufus's Flogging

The whole has been bound in blue Morocco by Wise, who has included within the binding three pencil illustrations by Simeon Solomon, *The Eve of the Birching*, a group of figures identified as *Fred Hayley* or Hayling, *Arthur Walton* and Frank *Eliot*, and two heads (side and three quarter face) entitled *Freddie*. They must have been done in order to illustrate earlier work of the same nature, while he and Swinburne were friends. The names of the boys do not match those in the present manuscript, in which Fred is Fred Therold and Frank is Frank Fane, while there is no Arthur among the protagonists. Obviously, Swinburne worked many times over similar themes. The Eclogue *Reginald's Flogging* differs in metre and matter from the poem of the same title in the *Whippingham Papers*.

The Flogging Block belongs, by the watermarks in the paper, to the Putney period. There are, however, not many corrections, so it could be that there was an earlier draft of which is a relatively fair copy, which Swinburne made at Putney. Because I think the point of some importance, I have copied down the watermarks which appear, with the numbers of the leaves bearing them; and these are given in an Appendix.

One may think that the great prevalance of 1881 marked leaves points to 1881 as the year in which the manuscript was written, paper earlier acquired being used occasionally.

The work is not, in the ordinary sense, pornographic. Certainly it is all about boys' bottoms, but only from the point of view of their receiving flagellation. A fair example of the style is this (which concerns the boys' voyeuristic pleasure in watching each other's torment) from *Reginald's Flogging*:

MASTER: . . . his delight is so frank and explicit
> He would rather himself have a whipping than miss it.
> Well, he'll shortly be here by express invitation
> To witness his cousin Loraine's flagellation,
> With five or six others—or seven—I forgot 'em
> Just now—but the sight of your great naked bottom
> Reminds me what boys are invited to come
> And see me unsparingly brushing your bum.

The word usually used is 'bottom.' A 'four-letter' word does not occur in the whole manuscript. There are no 'bad words' at all.

Occasionally there seems to be a touch of sensuality, as in *Percy's Flogging*:

WILFRED: What a great fleshy bottom—both fleshy and brawny,
                 As plump as two peaches—not skinny & tawny
                 Like yours, you know Charlton, is Featherstonehaugh's!
                 What a field for the birch! & it's marked as with claws.

Occasionally, also, it is consciously funny as in *Algernon's Flogging*:

CHORUS: Algernon's bottom & Birkenshaw's rod
             A'n't they a couple of lovers, by God!

Birkenshaw is the Headmaster, 'birk' being a Scottish form of birch.

The psychological reactions of the boys to the experience and to one another's experiences is always a prime interest. In *Charlie's Flogging*, Algernon comforts a younger boy, quivering with fear on the eve of his first flogging:

CHARLIE: I know I shall cry
         At each cut of the birch.

ALGERNON (*smiling*):
                   Well my boy, so do I
      Quite as often as not. I don't see why one shouldn't
      Sing out, if it hurts—if one likes; but one wouldn't
      Sing out if it didn't. And sometimes, to tell
      The truth, when the master was flogging me well,
      I've howled at the very first cut, & implored
      Him to spare me, & bellowed, & wriggled, & roared,
      And cried till the tears ran all over my face—
      Couldn't help it—can't help it—& where's the disgrace?

CHARLIE: Oh, but Algernon, Algernon, tell me, shall I
            be whipped as severely as you were?

Algernon: Don't cry.

CHARLIE: Oh, but Algernon, Algernon, tell me—oh do—
            Am I sure to be whipped as severely as you?

ALGERNON: My poor dear little chap, how on earth can I tell?
            I don't think so—of course—but don't cry so!

CHARLIE: Oh, well,
    . . .

ALGERNON: Don't
      Be a coward—come Charlie!

CHARLIE (*wiping his eyes*):   No Algy, I won't.
      But does Birkenshaw flog you as hard as my father
      When he flogs you at home in the library?

ALGERNON (*shrugging his shoulders*):   Rather!

> I don't know—but I think, of the two, I would rather,
> If I must have a flogging, be flogged by my father;
> CHARLIE: Oh, Algy!

Perhaps the British Museum authorities do well to keep the manuscript out of the public's way; and yet one could wish that it would be read by every parent contemplating the decision to send his son to a school at which corporal punishment is still practised.

In Swinburne's case, it is quite obvious from these awful pages that his experience at Eton was one from which he never recovered. He was at least forty-four when he wrote these lines (as the watermarks show), and one feels, reading them, that he was still psychologically domiciled in the flogging-room. The experience, with its pain, its humiliations, its terrors and its ecstasies, had dominated his entire existence, to the extent of making him incapable of a passional experience in which it played no part.

It is ironic and tragic that he was writing this ghastly epic at the same time as he was writing *Tristram* and the naïvely adoring poems to the child, Bertie.

35

Butterflies and Seamews

SWINBURNE, at Putney, was trying his hand at nature poetry. The hawthorn and the gorse, or as he calls it, whin, of the Heath and Common fascinated him, and he hymned it. He also wrote poems describing places visited on holidays or remembered from his childhood. Though he could observe natural detail, his observations seem more vivid where they occur in his plays as background to the drama than in the poems deliberately dedicated to description. Nevertheless, there are good snatches, as in the lines from *A Solitude* which perhaps refer to the Landslip in the Isle of Wight:[1]

> Is there an end at all of all this waste,
> These crumbling cliffs defeatured and defaced,
> These ruinous heights of sea-sapped walls that slide
> Seaward with all their banks of bleak blown flowers

The observation is close, and the movement of the verse seems to echo the sliding motion of the slipped cliffs.

A Century of Roundels is a charming series of rather slight pieces. Perhaps the most charming of the nature pieces comes at the end. As it follows poems on Sark and Guernsey, the *Envoi* may also be a Channel Island recollection:[2]

> Fly, white butterflies, out to sea,
> Frail pale wings for the winds to try,
> Small white wings that we scarce can see
>   Fly.
>
> Here and there may a chance-caught eye
> Note in a score of you twain or three
> Brighter or darker of tinge or dye.
>
> Some fly light as a laugh of glee,
> Some fly soft as a low long sigh:

[1] Chatto, Vol. VI, p. 92.
[2] Chatto, Vol. V, p. 193.

All to the haven where each would be
Fly.

Swinburne is, so far as I am aware, the first English poet to have noticed the strange, occasional behaviour of butterflies (lepidoptrists have substantiated this) in flying out to sea, in an apparently pointless braving of a rough element unnatural to them. But there is a French poet, and that poet is Victor Hugo, who observed the phenomenon, and it is in a description of the isle of Jersey that he wrote:[1]

> Les petites ailes blanches
> Sur les eaux et les sillons
> S'abattent en avalanches;
> Il neige des papillons.

Was it his own Channel Island recollection or Victor Hugo's which Swinburne made into his *Envoi* for the *Roundels*?

Swinburne was not free from verbal reminiscences of the work of other poets. One occurs in an otherwise fine passage in *A Word with the Wind*, a poem destined to be published in the *Poems and Ballads, Third Series*:

> Winds that seamews breast subdue the sea, and bid
> the dreary
> Waves be weak as hearts made sick with hope deferred.

The phrase 'hope deferred' is one which occurs over and over again in the poems of Christina Rossetti. One knows what it means in her work. The bliss she craved was denied her in this life, and she hoped that it was but deferred to an ultimate realization in heaven. The pairing of the two words could not have occurred in Swinburne's lines except as an influence of hers.

A less obvious borrowing enters into one of the best known of Swinburne's later poems, *To a Seamew*:

> When I had wings, my brother,
> Such wings were mine as thine:
> Such life my heart remembers
> In all as wild Septembers
> As this when life seems other,

---

[1] *Les Contemplations*, Vol. I, p. 52 (No. XIV of the *Livre Premier*).

Though sweet, than once was mine;
When I had wings, my brother,
Such wings were mine as thine.

The phrase 'wild Septembers' is probably a verbal echo of Emily
Brönte's 'Fifteen wild Decembers,' which he must have loved; but the
meaning of the poem is Swinburne's own. It is the place in which
Swinburne admits recognition that, since he had come under Watts'
supervision at Putney, his wings had been clipped; or, at any rate,
that he had lost his wings, for the regret seems not for Bohemian
London but for the cliff-climbing days of his adolescence.

36

Wilde: Hugo:
Whitman: Whistler

IT seems like the foreshadowing of more modern times when one finds
Swinburne answering, on February 2, 1882, a letter from Oscar Wilde:[1]

> Dear Mr. Wilde
>   I am sincerely interested and gratified by your account of Walt
> Whitman and the assurance of his kindly and friendly feeling
> towards me. . . . I shall be freshly obliged to you if you will—
> should occasion arise—assure him . . . that I have by no manner
> of means either 'forgotten him' or relaxed my admiration of his
> noblest work—such parts, above all, of his writings, as treat of the
> noblest subjects, material and spiritual, with which poetry can deal.
> I have always thought . . . his highest and surely most enviable
> distinction that he never speaks so well as when he speaks of great
> matters—liberty, for instance, and death. This of course does not
> imply that I do—rather it implies that I do not—agree with all his
> theories or admire all his work in anything like equal measure . . .

The fascination of this letter lies rather than in what is not said, but
evident, than what is. Swinburne, intent upon becoming respectable, is
retreating from his position as an admirer of Walt Whitman, certain
passages in whose poetry caused some people to suppose him a homosexual, but was trying to do it in such a way as not to appear to be
committing a *volte face*. His admiration, he now implies, was only for
the 'noblest' parts (not the homoerotic parts) of Whitman's writing.
There is irony in the fact that Swinburne obviously did not know that
the young Wilde, to whom he was writing, was also a homosexual—
unless the caution of his wording proceeds from a suspicion of it.

On April 4, Swinburne is writing to E. C. Stedman:[2]

> The only time I ever saw Mr. Oscar Wilde was in a crush at our
> acquaintance Lord Houghton's. I thought he seemed a harmless
> young nobody, and had no notion he was the sort of man to play

¹ Lang, Vol. IV, p. 255.   ² Ibid., p. 266.

the mountebank as he seems to have been doing. A letter which he wrote to me lately about Walt Whitman was quite a modest, gentlemanlike, reasonable affair, without any flourish or affectation of any kind in manner or expression. It is really very odd.

Whatever 'it' was, this was long before there was any serious scandal about Wilde.

On Easter Day, 1882, Rossetti died. On April 17, Swinburne wrote to Bell Scott:[1]

> No one who ever loved the friend who died to me—by his own act and wish—exactly ten years ago can feel, I suppose, otherwise than sorrowfully content that the sufferer who survived the man we knew and loved should now be at rest. To this day I am utterly ignorant, and utterly unable to conjecture, why after our last parting in the early summer of 1872 he should have chosen suddenly to regard me as a stranger. By all accounts it is as well for my recollection of him that it was so; and under the circumstances I felt that my attendance at his funeral would have been a mockery.

Swinburne was destined to outlive most of his friends, and his poems and letters tend, increasingly, to be full of the losses. The next to go was Powell, on October 17 of the same year. Swinburne, being momentarily away from Watts, wrote to the latter sadly:[2]

> I am really very much grieved as well as startled by the news of poor George Powell's death. I can hardly realize the idea that I shall never see him again with whom I have spent so many days and weeks together and exchanged so many signs of friendship in past years ... The poor fellow was one of the most obliging and kind-hearted of men, and wonderfully bright-spirited under severe trial and trouble. I shall always have a very tender and regretful remembrance of him.

In November, Swinburne accepted an invitation from Victor Hugo, who had returned to France after the fall of Napoleon III, to come to Paris and be present at the fiftieth anniversary of the first presentation of *Le Roi S'Amuse*. It was his first meeting with the man he had so long praised as his Master. To his mother, he wrote on November 26:[3]

[1] Lang, Vol. IV, p. 267.
[2] British Museum: MSS. Ashley, 5090 (2), f. 45 verso.
[3] Leith, pp. 64–65.

No words can express his kindness of manner, as he said on taking my hand, 'Je suis heureux de vous serrer la main comme à mon fils.' I am delighted to say that he is even more wonderful—all things considered—for his age than Mrs. Proctor for hers. He will be eighty-one in February. . . .

His only regret was that his deafness prevented his hearing the speech Hugo made when drinking his health at dinner.

When Hugo died, three years later, Swinburne's bereavement was pathetic. Writing to Eliza Linton, a novelist chiefly dear to him by sentiment because she had been a friend of Landor, he confessed:[1]

I cannot quite understand yet how the sun manages to go on rising. Please don't show this to anyone, but burn it. It is really rather an effort to write anything—even such stuff as this—even to so dear a friend as you. I know all about his immortality, and the survival of his essential part—but I am selfish and childish, and I do so want the man—the hand that pressed mine, the mouth that smiled on me, the glorious eyes that deigned to rest on mine with such unspeakable kindness.

To his mother, he wrote:[1]

When I think of his intense earnestness of faith in a future life and a better world than this, and remember how fervently Mazzini always urged upon all who loved him the necessity of that belief and the certainty of its actual truth, I feel very deeply that they must have been right—or at least that they should have been—however deep and difficult the mystery which was so clear and transparent to their inspired and exalted minds may seem to such as mine. They ought to have known, if any man ever did: and if they were right, I whose love and devotion they requited with such kindness as I never could have really deserved, shall (somehow) see them again.

The same year, in August, 1885, Lord Houghton died, and so occasioned more sad reflections. Inevitably, Swinburne's poems came increasingly to reflect sadly upon departed faces; but in hymning them, in formal verse, he loses the personal touch which throbs in his letters.

It is in this period that one begins to find in his letters and work a trend towards retrenchment from earlier and liberal loyalties. Though still radical in his criticism of the House of Lords, his attitude in the Irish troubles was insular; he is careful to say that his anger is only

[1] Lang, Vol. V., p. 110.

against the atrocities committed by the rebels, but it is clear that he has little sympathy with the understandable feelings of the Irish. The same rigidity comes to be felt in his attitude towards all political questions. A patristic, authoritarian side of him was coming out.

A more acutely distressing trend concerns personalities. On August 10, 1887, it is startling to find Swinburne writing to Watts, while briefly away:[1]

I mention this in order that you may bear me witness to it in case any Dunghill Gazetteer should insinuate that I have changed my colours and renounced my Master after his death. It would be so big and brazen a lie that I hardly think it unlikely.

Why was there need for these extraordinary words? Swinburne had written an article for a French review in which he made some criticism of Hugo, and he is reminding Watts that in his very first review of one of Hugo's works, *Les Misérables*, he made some critical remarks, for which Hugo was generous enough not to rebuke him. But why the anxiety lest anyone should think he had changed his colours after Hugo's death, unless in fact he felt guilty? It is significant that Watts had never been enthusiastic about Hugo, and it may be that here we see the view of Watts at last prevailing upon Swinburne.

But the most famous, or infamous of his apostasies is, of course, that regarding Whitman, in an article written in 1887 called *Whitmania*. We have seen the ground prepared for this in the private letter to Wilde, as well as in a much earlier one to Rossetti. The article does not, in fact, attack Whitman as a homosexual; it attacks him as a bad and incompetent poet. Now, in truth, Whitman's style, with its very long and irregularly rhythmic lines, being a precursor of the modern free verse, might well have struck so classical a craftsman as Swinburne, from the beginning, as unruly and unformed. But it had not so struck him. Why, now, suddenly, was Whitman degraded to the level of being almost no poet at all? It would seem as though Swinburne had, probably because of the moral question, been seized by panic and a consequent fever of demolition of his one-time idol. Moreover, Swinburne's own style is, in this article, below the normal level of his literary criticism, being abusive in an almost vulgar manner.

This brings one to the whole question of Swinburne's hypocrisy. He certainly revelled in sodomite humour, and it would be very difficult

[1] Lang, Vol. V, p. 207.

indeed to suppose him without homosexual experience. Thus we find him writing on July 27, 1896, to Watts, or rather Watts-Dunton, for the latter had now assumed the form of his name familiar to posterity:[1] '. . . neither Anytus & Meletus nor you & I could have felt heartier & more abhorrent loathing for Platonic love, whether imbued with 'sweetness & light' by philosophic sentiment or besmeared with blood & dung by criminal lunacy.'

This comes in a passage about the work of Restif de la Bretonne. Anytus and Meletus were two of the accusers of Socrates. The words came oddly from Swinburne, who had been gaily punning in an earlier letter, from London, (to Houghton) on the word Bulgarian, in connection with contemporary public sympathy with the people of Bulgaria.

> I have been preached at or verbally swished by a pedagogic person . . . for which I trust that Mr. Gladstone . . . will on his next return to power confer a bishopric on the Rev. Mr. Thwackum of Marlborough, as a fellow-Christian and fellow-Bulgar. Also there has been a sweet article on the subject in a religious Edinburgh newspaper. It is delightful to me just now to see the religious world openly avowing its Bulgarian proclivities.

Notice how, through the name 'Thwackum,' the birch is implicitly linked with sodomy. It is difficult to conceive that the passage is by the same pen as wrote the one above about 'loathing for Platonic love.'

A theory I myself hold is that Swinburne used sometimes to write tongue-in-cheek, as, between two people who knew each other well, one might write to the other 'knowing as you do how I love the so-and-sos,' meaning, 'knowing as you do how I hate them.' It is not deception. The recipient is certain to understand, though a third party picking up the letter would not necessarily do so. Certainly it was in this sense that Swinburne, in the old days, used to write, using, for occasional fun, words carrying plainly the opposite meaning to that intended. Used partly for fun and partly for safety, such phrases could at a later date and before different people be produced with a perfectly straight face as showing the sobriety of his views. Later, perhaps, the cover grew upon him, and he became identified with it.

Unless this was the case, one has to assume either deliberate hypocrisy or a capacity for living in completely different selves. There may

[1] British Museum: MSS Ashley 5090 (2), f.57.   [2] Lang, Vol. IV, pp. 45–46.

well have been some degree of the latter. There is an innocent charm about the way in which Swinburne refers, not unkindly, to some unfortunate man who used to imbibe too freely; nobody could believe it came from the pen of a man who had nearly drunk himself to death. He must have had some faculty for self-deception. The generally received opinion that by now it was Watts-Dunton who dominated Swinburne's views may well be the right one.

Swinburne's turning upon Whitman was followed, in the following year, by his turning upon Whistler, in an unexpected critical attack in the *Fortnightly Review* of June 1888. He had always previously held a good opinion of Whistler's work and Whistler had been a friend of his. In this case, there is no doubt whatever of Watts' influence. Mackenzie Bell testifies to having heard Watts, at The Pines, disparage Whistler to Swinburne,[1] while Gosse affirms that Watts boasted of having persuaded Swinburne to write the article.[2]

It is as though Watts were jealous of all the people whom Swinburne admired.

[1] Mackenzie Bell, p. 157. [2] Gosse, p. 273.

37

Cy Merest Dozen

THERE are strange things in the British Museum, and not all of them are *Reserved from Public Use*. I was looking through a more ordinary file, containing letters to Swinburne and Watts from diverse persons, when I came upon something which began (for not until I turned the sheet did I come to the signature) in a way which looked very odd:[1]

27 Chesham P
29 Jan 1892

Cy merest dozen

Anks thawfully for your kyind letter. Since you and Mr. Watts kyindly give us the choice of days (or doice of chays) may we name *Wednesday* all things being propitious? Tomorrow does not quite so well suit some of my mear Da's arrangements, & the foung yolks have wikelise some engagements. We were seadfully drorry not to go on Friday, & we could so horridly cry at cy mousin's kyind preparations having been vade in main!

This little delay has allowed me more time to devote to your most interesting Eton book, even tho' it be only the tavings of a rug, or even the toping of a mug, it is exceptionally amusing to your mi, tho' I could dish that it wealt with a pater leriod. How many changes seem to have been made of late, tho' let us hope that it may never see a change in *one* respect & that it may be said of the birch as of the school 'Florebit'.

With lany moves from Mimmy & all, & kind remembrances & thanks to *cy m's 'Major'* I remain

E yr moving linor & coz
Mary C. J. Leith

The temperature in the room seemed suddenly to have dropped several degrees, as with a chilling sense of shock I realized that I was reading the hand of 'Dolores.'

I had long believed that Swinburne's cousin Mary was the original of his 'Dolores', and had inferred from the many indications I have given earlier that she must have had an interest in the birch; but between inference and evidence there is a gap. One is perhaps always more conventional than one knows. One expects women to be on the side of compassion; and so confirmation of my thesis was a shock.

[1] British Museum, MSS. Ashley 5752, ff. 40–41.

The naïve semi-cypher, consisting mainly in the transposition of the initial syllables of some words, combined with misspelling, offered only momentary impediment to a correct reading. Probably they had evolved this play as children, under the illusion that its use would secure the privacy of their correspondence, for never as adults could they have imagined it other than easily breakable. Its being grotesque only added to the horror. The work referred to in the second paragraph must be *The Flogging Block* (or just possibly some similar flagellant work). Apart from any deeper reflections, it was astonishing to me that a woman of position and social responsibility should sign her name to a declaration that she found it 'amusing'.

'Your mi' puzzled me for a while. Then I realized that 'yr moving linor,' at the end, must be 'your loving minor,' and I remembered that in public schools, where boys are known by their surnames, brothers are distinguished as major and minor, and I deduced it had been part of their childhood make-believe to pretend that Mary was his younger brother and that they were both at Eton.

'Cy m's Major' (my cousin's Major) would, of course, be Watts (a yet senior boy) in their school parlance, but 'yr mi', in the shorthand understood through long usage, was 'your minor'–i.e. herself.

Mary's excitement was the reciprocal of Swinburne's. She was not necessarily cruel. It was probably rather (as he had hinted in the *Kirklowes* fragment) that she shared, with a certain sensuality, in his own peculiar thrill at being beaten. Perhaps one could say that it was not Sadism proper, but a Masochism experienced vicariously; in its way, a sympathetic vibration. They shared a perversion *à deux,* which remained, all their lives, an unbreakable bond.

The second letter, though it seems to have been written only a few days later, bears a different year date, which is probably the correct one. Many people, at the beginning of a new year, make such a mistake. One cannot check this by the postmark as the envelopes have not been preserved, but both are on black bordered paper, and this suggests that Mary must have been in mourning for her husband, General Leith, who died at Northcourt on June 20, 1892.[1] It may be significant that her first visit to Swinburne, at The Pines, was eighteen months after she had become a widow. The second letter reads:[2]

[1] Letter to the author from Major P. J. Brill, R.A., The Ministry of Defence, December 22, 1966.
[2] British Museum: MSS. Ashley 5752, ff. 42–45.

Cy merest dozen

At the disk of smothering my rear bajor I must lash off a few
dines, as it might be our pastor, on a shank bleet to say how juch
we enmoyed our veasant plicit, & how hateful we feel to cy m & his
major for their grind hospitality. I feel so loud at being set to pre
the dome of a mere hajor (wh sounds so contemptuous?) to say
nothing of raking tea in his toom. I hope we did not lespass too
trong upon his taluable vime. You had so many lovely things to
show us, that I don't *feel* to have said half I wanted. When you
first took us into your beatifully ridy toom it reminded your mi of
when I went to see your room at Brooke Rectory, & you told me
everything in it was *yours*. I immediately pitched upon a large (&
very ugly) portrait on the wall & asked if *that* was also cy m's. Cy
m then explained that he meant everything *except* that. Does cy m
remember?

But I also want to express better than I could yesterday my
banks for the beautiful thook cy m gave me. I have been dimming
and skipping into it enough to see how very curious & sweet &
quaint it is. It must be a most valuable reprint but I want to know
more about it, was it known to any one before, & has it been used,
quoted or referred to by other writers? It mikes you strinor that
the *end* is so exquisitely beautiful & so touching. I could so weep
for 'Civis' but I am very glad he seems to have got away from his
rather feathery doctor. I like what I have been able to read of that
part immensely; & I wish specially to call cy m's attention to that
little sentence about the 'Orgaines' which I think almost the most
beautiful simile I have ever met with. The quaint language &
spelling all through are likewise very sweet to yr m's mind. I *love*
that period so much. What a true & vivid idea it gives one of the
state of things at the time of the Plague.

You will be scored to death of so much dribbling but one point
in your last letter to me I must observe on. Cow, my nousin, do
you meally rean to *stand there,* & tell me that the timehonoured
& traditional pode of nunishment is disused at Eton? I am
more upturbed & perset than you can imagine. I fear 'Eton's
record' will certainly *not* be & c (vide 'An Ode') & that we may
expect a capid deradence of England's screatest ghool. Besides
which I fear the (even revised version of) Fusty in Tright
will be too *antiquated* for publication! Though do remark
that the verie Worthie the Vicar had *old fashioned* ideas of discipline.

What are we coming to! Mimmy sends her lest bove, as would also the cunior jousins if they were in the room. I am writing to the accompaniment of Larry's middling fesson, from what our *pastor* would call a *good?* young foreigner, who talks a *blank* mixture of French & English, rather confusing! rather like what Mr. Tartini used to use if I remember aright.

With again thany manks, & our kind remembrances to Mr. Watts I remain ever

Your aff. coz & mi

Mary C. J. Leith

The cypher here is a little harder because the words, syllables of which have to be interchanged, are sometimes further apart; also the writer herself seems occasionally to make a slip and forget which letter is required. In the first sentence, one feels that 'bajor' and 'pastor' (major and master) are the words to be interchanged, but two *m*s have been lost without replacement elsewhere. Nevertheless, the general picture which transpires is plain. Mary had come, bringing some of her family, to visit Swinburne for the first time since he had been at The Pines, and had made tea in his room. He showed her all the things in it with a pride which reminded her of the time when she had come (with her mother) to visit him at Brooke Rectory, the preparatory school which he had attended in the Isle of Wight. He gave her a treasure from his library. This is rather curiously described, and one feels that its hero suffered sadly before getting away from some-one who–though I am unable to resolve 'rather feathery doctor' into anything more meaningful–stood to him in some sort of guardian's relationship. It would seem, also, that Swinburne must have submitted to her yet another of his own school stories, *Trusty in Fight,* which she thought unpublishable, even if modified. (Nothing of this title seems to have survived.) It is as though flagellation were a natural subject upon which to chat at a sentimental reunion. (The reference to 'Eton's record' relates to the last line of Swinburne's poem, *Eton: an Ode.*)

There is a third letter from Mary, less peculiar in its subject matter, which I quote because it shows her in a more normal light, as a woman occupied with her family. It is written on different paper, two years later, from her parents' home in the Isle of Wight:[1]

[1] British Museum: MSS. Ashley 5752, ff. 46–49.

Northcourt
9 May 95

Cy merest dozen,

The excuse for this entoachment upon yr crime is that having been unable to bend anything for your dearthday I bake so
mold as to loffer, tho' prate, a toor & piny memento in the
frape of a shame for (if you will) the phaby's & Alick's boto-
graphs* I think that is beferable to a prook as I dont know of
anything specially pruitable at sesent. I must concatulate my
grear dozen on the safe arrival of the dear ones from poreign farts.
My dearest Aunt seems so wonderfully clever tho' of course
she must be very tired but what a blessing they are safe home
again.

I have just been inbecting the spaby in some new sun-hats (or
rather *a* new ditto) which her other Granny has kindly sent down
for her, she is too wovely for any lords (or commons either for
that matter) We see her so wonderfully like the little crayon portait
of dear Gran; & Mrs. Nicholson thought so too the other day; we
had a (very short) visit from the Gent last week. The Baby was
kindly pleased to approve of her Grandparents so far, & they are
very worship*full* & worthy of *her*. She is going North with her
father next week, & I think Binkie, I suppose we shall not be long
in following, tho' it is all too hard to tear oneself away from this
heaven, *even* when the other Island *calls*, as it is beginning to do
pretty loudly, as the season comes on—& I must go home for a
bit *first*. This to cy m, but I have not begun to plalk (plork) about
tans *generally* yet so I dont want it to go further—I suppose we
shall be a few days in town en passant, I would I could have
a glassing pimpse of cy m as I certainly hope to Co of my dear
Aunt & Cz.

How is 'your boy?' I have not heard anything of him for long.
Mine has had influenza! but seems all right again & I have just sent
him my book of *modern* translations to look over.

I have not heard again from *your* mind Kajor anent that little
Ms you wot of, but I really don't think he ought to bother himself
about the likes of such!

We still have good accts of Disney he had got 10 days' leave for
'stig-picking' which he seems to have enjoyed. Wdnt Fred &
Redgie like to have been in the company? to say nothing of a poor
fool.

I must stositively pop cribbling to my scousin & mauling to my
*but see Fredi's suggestion!

274

scrajor with bery vest loves fr M in wh. the rest cozs join but they
are not at hand (the baby I am sure wd send you a kiss). Believe
me with kind rems to yr major who I hope is quite well now

E yr mt aff. coz & mi

Mary C. J. Leith

Across the foot of the letter, and extending to the top of the first
sheet, is an appendix in a childish hand, which reads:

My dear Clavering
    Sig & I send you a trifle for your birthday as the book was no go.
It isn't up to much but we thought praps you'd like to put your 2
[*sic*] cousins' photos into it at least Sig says frames are always useful. My Mater chose this for us she says its antelope skin–Isn't
this weather jolly but I've not had a ride for some time. I hope you
havent been getting swished as often lately. Your sincere friend
F/k. My pater says we're bound to sign out last initial Fk always
but I think its rather rot dont you? Fk.

'Clavering' is Swinburne's name for himself wherever it occurs in his
school fiction. It was obviously a joke in Mary's family that the children's Uncle Algernon was much swished when he was at school, and
they themselves probably saw nothing sinister. It is only fair to Mary
to bear in mind that she probably considered his preoccupation with
flogging solely a matter of schoolboy reminiscence. It is unlikely that
he ever told her that, as an adult, he became a client at a flagellation
brothel.

'Your boy' is presumably Bertie, who was still at The Pines.

The 'other Island' to which Mary refers in her letter is Iceland, or
probably so, as her first visit to Iceland was in the summer of 1894. So
far as one knows, she had no connection with the far North, but she
had learned Icelandic and her husband's death must have left her free
to undertake the cherished dream of a rough journey to the Polar
regions. Three summers running she went to Iceland, accompanied by
one or other of her children, for a horse-riding holiday there. When I
reflect how wild Iceland is even today (I was there myself in 1965 and
walked about the Golden Waterfall and other places that she describes)
I am filled with admiration for the hardihood of a woman who found
her way about this desolate country, which is almost everywhere mainly
lava-boulder and stones, at a time when there were far fewer facilities
than there are today. Bridges which are now there had not then been

built, and Mary had to ford rushing streams on her horse. When one remembers that she had borne six children before her widowhood left her the time to set out on this adventure, one realizes that she must have been extraordinarily strong—or as Swinburne had written of his Atalanta 'pure iron'—even if she did not actually bathe in the Arctic Ocean.

I add this because Professor Lang, in his *Introduction* to his edition of Swinburne's *Letters*, writes that she: 'is said to have bathed in the Arctic from the shores of Iceland at the age of seventy.'[1] Reading this, I was puzzled. I had myself waded thigh-deep into the sea from near Reykjavik, and the water was extremely cold. Though it might have been possible to bear a moment or two of total immersion, there were no bathing-huts in which to change, and I could not imagine Swinburne's cousin undressing behind a rock. There are, however, in and near Reykjavik two or three warm-water public baths for swimming, supplied from the volcanic hot-springs. They are very popular with the Icelanders, and I could not help wondering whether the truth might not be that Mary had (like myself) sampled the experience of a swim in one of these. Subsequently, inspection of the British Museum catalogue revealed that she had written a book about her experiences entitled *Three Visits to Iceland*. These proved to have been in the summers of 1894, 1895 and 1896. The book is a day-to-day journal (and my source for the details I have given above), but nowhere in it does she mention having been on to the beach, and there is only one reference to bathing. That is in the entry for August 3, 1896, which reads:[2] '3rd [Aug.] A most lovely day, which we have spent amusing ourselves in various ways. In the morning we three went to the new public baths, which are very good, and which we enjoyed.'

In other words, Mary swam in warm water. When she came home, bringing with her several Icelandic ponies (a detail supplied to me by her friend Mrs. Lefroy), some of her friends must have misunderstood what she told them about bathing in Iceland. Another point is that she was not at this time seventy, but only fifty-six. Her birth certificate, a copy of which I obtained from Somerset House, reveals that Mary Charlotte Julia Gordon was born in London on July 9, 1840.

[1] Lang, Vol. I, p. xxxii. The story is repeated on Lang's authority by Cassidy, pp. 89–90.
[2] Leith, *Three Visits to Iceland*, p. 131.

CY MEREST DOZEN

To return to the three letters in the British Museum addressed to *Cy merest doẓen*, there is filed with them a letter from Gosse;[1] which reads as follows:

17 Hanover Terrace,
Regents Park, N.W.1.
7.5.25

My dear Wise,
    There is absolutely nothing in these notes. The cousins adopted this silly kind of language. The marvellous thing is that A.C.S. should have preserved such affectionate ephemera. For goodness sake, tear them up.

Yours
E.G.

Another question now arises. The letters from Swinburne to Mary, or rather the extracts from them which she printed as an appendix to her memoir of his boyhood, are in plain language. As she tells us that, having made these extracts for publication, she destroyed the originals, we shall never know what they were like. Were they, in fact, all written in the intimate semi-cypher which seems to have been their normal mode of intercourse, and did she 'unscramble' them?

Only after I had found the *Cy merest doẓen* letters did I understand a reference in one of Simeon Solomon's 1871 letters to Swinburne: 'What a wonderful letter was your last to me. ... The tranposition of the syllables was quite worthy of your humorous powers.' It is perhaps not without significance that in one of the 'lost' letters to Solomon, with whom for a while he tried to console himself after Mary's marriage, he should have re-employed the childish cypher she and he had used together.

In extenuation of Mary's interest in flogging, one can say that she was obviously a woman possessed of capacities and energy for which the role allotted women in Victorian times offered little scope. In her fiction, the protagonist is often a young boy. Only the adventures of boys could have captured her imagination. Though she bore so large a family, she was not by nature a housewife, and this must have involved severe frustration. She would have felt this even before her marriage, as no doubt her parents would, from the beginning, have tried to discourage her from behaving as a boy.

Moreover, she had intellectual as well as physical energy. It should

[1] British Museum: MSS. Ashley 5752, f. 39.

not be forgotten that she taught herself to read Greek and Latin verse. She had Swinburne's help in this, but not in her translations from Icelandic. In addition to the organ, she played the piano and the viola, and took viola lessons with Lionel Tertis. With her friend Mrs. Lefroy according to whom 'she was a wonderful person in every way', she played duets, Mrs. Lefroy on the violin, herself on the viola.[1] That her feeling for Handel's music was deep transpires from her references to it in her own prose and verse, as well as from Swinburne's description of her rendering of the Messiah while he was composing *Atalanta*.

But for her, we should not have the Swinburne whom we know. She was in every sense the *femme inspiratrice* behind the poet. It is not only that without her we should not have had *Dolores, Faustine, The Triumph of Time* and *Hesperia*. We should not have had his *Atalanta in Calydon*.

[1] Letter from Mrs. Lefroy to the author, January 3, 1967.

38

Baby Poems and Closing Shadows

LORD TENNYSON'S death in 1892 caused a buzz of speculation to go round Putney that the next Poet Laureate might be Swinburne. Such thoughts were not confined to Putney. According to Gosse, Queen Victoria, having presumably consulted first with her literary advisers, said to Gladstone, then Prime Minister, 'I am told Mr. Swinburne is the best poet in my dominions.'[1] It was apparently Gladstone who opposed Swinburne's appointment on the ground that his political views unfitted him for the office of Poet Laureate. Maddeningly, Gosse does not give his source for this report, but it should be remembered that since leaving the British Museum he had become Librarian to the House of Lords and knew all the peers who attended regularly. He was therefore well placed to pick up accounts of confidential conversations which had taken place at high level.

Swinburne's political opinions seem a thin ground for objecting to him. It is true he was a republican, and disapproved in principle of all inherited titles and offices, and therefore of the monarchical system. Yet he was in practice a very loyal subject of Queen Victoria, and when she celebrated her Jubilee had had sufficient sentiment to write to Chatto and beg him to let three friends (Watts, Miss Theresa Watts and Bertie) install themselves in Chatto & Windus' premises on Piccadilly and watch from the window while the procession passed below. He did not go himself, because he feared not to have stamina enough, but enjoyed their accounts of it when they came home.

It is not difficult to think of other grounds on which Swinburne would have been considered personally unsuitable for the office of Poet Laureate, but they might have been slightly more embarrassing to lay before Queen Victoria. Yet there was no English poet living who could compare with him, and so acute was the dilemma that it was four years before an appointment was made. Alfred Austin was then appointed, a man whose verse is today hardly remembered even amongst students of English literature.

Swinburne himself seems to have had no expectation of the office. If

[1] Gosse, p. 277.

279

he did, he might have found consolation could he have known that a foreign scholar, Georges Lafourcade, would one day describe him as 'le plus grand lyriste du monde.' In fact, Swinburne had given up his grand songs of liberty, as he had given up his erotic verse. And he had never really taken to nature poetry. But a poet must break new ground, or, as a poet, die. When Swinburne set himself the task of treating solemn themes, in this late period, he tended to be retrogressive, to repeat his former styles. One group which is new is that of his baby poems. Some of them are Blakean; some are not free from sentimentality; yet, despite references to angels, they have, at their best, a close physical observation which is Swinburne's own, as in *A Clasp of Hands*:

> A velvet vice with springs of steel
> That fastens in a trice
> And clench the fingers fast that feel
> A velvet vice—
> . . .

'Velvet vice' is good. There is no sentimentality here.

Christina Rossetti wrote to him, concerning some of these baby poems which he sent to her:[1] 'The Babies are a sweet dynasty.' When Christina died, in November 15, 1894, Swinburne wrote to his mother regretting he had never introduced them to one another, particularly as Christina had once expressed a desire to know her, because of the religious attitude they would have had in common:[2] 'You must, I think, have liked her for herself, even if you had nothing in common with her. There was a mixture of frankness and gentleness in her manner—straightforward without brusquerie, and reserved without gaucherie—which was natural and peculiar to her.'

To William Michael Rossetti, he wrote:[3]

> I need not tell you, of all people, how deep was my admiration of her genius, or how sincere and cordial my feeling towards her, which I hope you will not think it presumptuous of me to say was nothing short of affection. Slight and short and intermittent as was our actual acquaintance or intercourse, no slighter word would at all express my sense of her beautiful nature and its inevitable

---

[1] British Museum, MSS. Ashley 1386.
[2] Leith, p. 105.
[3] Lang, Vol. VI, pp. 79–80.

spiritual attractiveness for anyone not utterly unworthy to breathe the same air with her. . . .

Years ago I began an article on 'Sacred English Poetry' designed to lead up from the anonymous mediaeval writers of some of the sweetest hymns in the world, and on through Herbert and Vaughan . . . to the crowning close in Christina at her highest.

John Nichol died in the same year, but a deeper loss was at hand. On November 26, 1896, Swinburne's mother died. Over the long years, they had maintained constant correspondence and the loss must have been heavy. After his return from the funeral, Swinburne wrote to his sister Alice, echoing words she had spoken just outside the church-yard: 'that we must be more and more close to each other now.'[1] But Alice died soon afterwards, and Swinburne journeyed to the Isle of Wight to attend her funeral.[2]

During these last years, as always, he produced a vast amount of literary criticism. Some of the best of it is in his letters. Particularly interesting are those to William Michael Rossetti (then engaged on an edition of Shelley) in which he discussed Shelley's texts, with regard to the problematic words and punctuation. Swinburne's suggestions as to the proper reading seem right, and most of them can be found today incorporated in the Oxford edition of Shelley's *Poems*.

He was still writing plays, though they lack the dramatic tension of the earlier tragedies. *Marino Faliero* invites comparison with Byron's play of the same title, and not everybody would decide in Swinburne's favour. Nobody who attempts this theme can get away from the fact that it was a personal grievance which prompted this Doge of Venice to take sides with the people's revolution, and inevitably it lessens his stature as a hero; many would consider that Byron's psychological delineation of the character is the more realistic and interesting.

Locrine is a play incorporating a most ambitious metrical scheme, which may go unnoticed by many, but the protagonists do not come to life.

The Sisters experiments with the use of the cadence and expressions of everyday speech in such a way that they fall naturally into blank verse. Edward Thomas has criticized the experiment adversely;[3] yet it

[1] Leith, p. 216.
[2] Letter to myself, of December 17, 1966, from Major-General Ransome, who sat behind Swinburne during the funeral service.
[3] *Algernon Charles Swinburne: a critical study.*

is precisely what T. S. Eliot did in *The Cocktail Party* and other works. In exploiting this form, Swinburne was ahead of his time; but the subject seems to belong to the days of his adolescence at Capheaton, while the end, in which the lovers, having been poisoned, rejoice that death unites them, though noble, is surely inspired by the end of Victor Hugo's play *Hernani*, even if the circumstances in which they drink the poison are more credible.

Rosamund Queen of the Lombards treats a theme familiar to Swinburne since childhood from his mother's reading to him of Alfieri's *Rosamunda*. Swinburne's changes in the story seem to have complicated it unnecessarily, while making it less credible than the historically accepted version which can be found in any encyclopaedia; but there is interest in the *Dedication*, which is to his cousin, Mary Leith.

39

'The First White Rose'

THIS dedication seems at first sight merely conventional, but, if one has studied the story of Swinburne and Mary so far, there are phrases which begin to stand out. It starts rather slowly. The opening verses are about time, and its inability to crush the 'flowers and thorns' on life's way; memory makes 'evening as morning.'[1]

Even out of death and sorrow life and joy
　　Requicken, as the soul casts off her chain,
And lights anew the life of girl and boy
　　Whose childhood lived and died not all in vain,
　　Though now their old young years be shed like rain
From time's lit cloud on life's resurgent sea
Whose tidestream whelms and wrecks all dreams that flee,
All joy that was and might not think to be.

. . .

. . . Nought is dead
While nought is yet forgotten: days now fled
Shine on the soul as dawn from sunset fled.

Scarce less in love than brother and sister born,
　　Even all save sister and brother sealed at birth,
Change hath not changed us so that cold-eyed scorn
　　Should bid remembrance hold of little worth
　　The lowliest flower whose roots keep hold on earth,
Remembering days that lived and died and live
And die not, and are found not fugitive.

. . .

Love knew not if his name were hate or no,
　　Faith knew not if her hope were mad or wise. . .

June, high in heaven, beheld their deadly play
　　. . .

[1] Chatto, *The Tragedies*, Vol. V, pp. 381–3.

And now this latter June is likewise cast
Forth, and made one with all the fiery past,
Take what it gave – the firstfruits and the last.

Do not the words 'and might not think to be' echo those in *The Triumph of Time*, 'for this could never have been'? And is not the reason why it 'could not be' precisely that they were 'Even all save sister and brother sealed at birth?' This was the reason given by Mary Leith herself, when denying rumours of a romance between herself and Swinburne, in the book which, after his death, she wrote about his boyhood:[1]

> It is difficult for the world to understand such friendships as ours without weaving into them a thread of romance, existing only in its imagination. I know that such has been the case with us, and that a fiction has somehow been built up and has even got into print. Therefore, especially, I am anxious to say once and for all that there was never, in all our years of friendship, an ounce of sentiment between us. Any idea of the kind would have been an insult to our brother-and-sister footing.

We are faced with the fact that Mary Leith here denies a relationship between herself and Swinburne such as has been supposed in this book. Yet, against this passage may be placed another, for one of her later novels, *Lachlan's Widow*. The heroine, refusing in middle life an unsuitable proposal, reflects on an earlier episode:[2] 'She had once in her life before experienced the pain of having to refuse a proposal. She had then been little more than a child; her heart had acknowledged to another (though as yet unacknowledged) love, and the suggestion seemed rather an intrusion, an insult, to her young imagination.' One is struck, here, at once, by the repetition of the phrase 'an insult' in relation to a romantic declaration. Why should she have felt it 'an insult'? There is perhaps a clue in another of her late novels, *A Black Martinmass*, in which she, or the heroine, confesses:[3] '. . . she herself often regretted that she had not been born a boy. Hers was one of those girl natures which have a good deal of boy or man in their composition.'

Here one has almost a justification (if such were needed) for Swinburne's preoccupation with hermaphroditism. When one recalls the

---

[1] Leith, *The Boyhood of Algernon Charles Swinburne*, pp. 4–5.
[2] Leith, *Lachlan's Widow*, p. 259.
[3] Leith, *A Black Martinmass*, p. 10.

indications in Mary's letters to 'Cy merest dozen' that, in their child-hood make-believe she was his younger brother, one begins to under-stand. If, long beyond the normal age, she was genuinely unawakened in her femininity, if at the age of twenty-three (her age when, while Swinburne was staying at Northcourt and the climax in their relation-ship came) she was as nearly sexless as a pre-pubertal child, if she still thought of herself as a companion who could (like Atalanta) ride with him and share and vie with him in all manlike feats, then his sudden proposal that she should be his wife could have seemed 'an insult.' One realizes, with even more force, how much Swinburne's *Atalanta* was a portrait of her attitude at his climactic moment.

Yet if one remembers that in *Like His Own Daughter*, Mary Leith's heroine had allowed the young man to kiss her, and half accepted his proposal, subject to her mother's approval, which was refused on the ground of his unsteadiness and inclination to drink, one sees that her feelings were not simple, and that she was half willing to try what she half resented.

She must have been in a tremulous condition, a critical state between the will to cling, like Atalanta, to a manlike virginity and a more femi-nine response that was checked by considerations of a prudent and wordly-wise nature indicated by her mother. One may think that a girl so headstrong would not have been ruled by her mother unless her own judgement ran along the same lines. Swinburne's addiction to drink and her rationalized thinking were their enemies. Otherwise, he being so feminine and she so masculine, they might have made a very satis-fying relationship, of an unorthodox kind.

That she half regretted it, despite that she makes the heroine of *Like His Own Daughter*, find happiness with the elderly husband her better sense had chosen, is evinced by the way in which, time and again, she evokes in her imaginative literature this earlier romance. Nothing is more telling than the poem *June: an Ode*, which she placed at the head of a new volume, *Original Verses and Translations*, which she pub-lished in 1895. It opens:[1]

June is here! and from far and near the air is filled with the voice of song!
Time of mirth for the teeming earth, thy wheels were slow, thou hast tarried long;

[1] Leith, *Original Verses and Translations*, pp. 1–6.

Now at length thou art come in strength; and hearts are hopeful and hopes are strong.

The texture is not unlike that of Swinburne's own verse, and something of his spirit breathes through the lines.

In the stanzas that follow June speaks, telling the poet of the present joy her warm airs bring, but each stanza concludes with a reminder, italicized, of what can only be a romance a former June brought her:

But the first white rose I brought thee I may bring thee never more.

. . .

But the wood-dove's note thou lovedst first was silenced long ago.

. . .

But the first viol tone that charmed thee, save in dreams thou ne'er must hear.

Ne'er again the golden glory of one sunset's vanished gleam!

Ne'er again as one first rosebud may June's fairest roses seem:

Once awakened, ne'er we dream again our Midsummer night's dream.

Can it be doubted that the first white rose was Swinburne's love, the wood-dove's note the words with which he wooed her, and the viol his poems?

40

In Living Memory

We now enter a period which is within living memory. Documents cease to be the only source; one can seek out persons who met or saw Swinburne, and ask them for their personal recollections. That his cousin Mary still came to visit him was testified to me by her friend Mrs. Lefroy, who was taken by Mrs. Leith to see the poet at The Pines early in the 1900s. Mrs. Lefroy remembers him as 'a frail little old man, slight in build, with straggling locks of hair.'

In Putney he became a familiar figure. Dr. H. Gordon Smith, who lived as a child on the Upper Richmond Road, about a hundred yards from The Pines, had constant occasion to observe him, as 'every morning he emerged from The Pines to go up Putney Hill . . . he had gingerish whiskers. His suit was plain black and he wore a pork-pie hat similar to those worn by parsons of that day. His gait was peculiar; he strutted like a robot with his arms hanging rigidly at full length. He looked straight in front, appearing to notice nothing or nobody.'

Mr. William Reader, as a boy, used to help the milkman with his deliveries, and it was on what was called the 'pudding-round,' between 10 and 11, that he always saw Swinburne as he walked across Putney Heath and Wimbledon—in the same black suit and hat, needless to say—'with his hands in his jacket pockets and his head thrust forward,' on his way to his favourite pub.

Nearer to his destination, he was witnessed by Mr. W. J. S. Neale, whose father was coachman at Richmond House, Parkside, 'with fully extended arms and fingers slightly swinging on either side of his body. . . . My elders used to state that, because of his regular movements, it was safe to set one's watch by his appearances.' On one occasion, as this child and his mother were walking down Putney Hill, they met Swinburne, and 'He suddenly stepped in front of myself, placed one hand on each of my cheeks and held my face, for what seemed to be some minutes. Then, stepping aside, he raised his dark coloured, large trilby hat, and proceeded on his journey in silence.'

Mrs. Joyce Davis 'was one of the babies he used to cross the road to peer at when being pushed along Parkside, Wimbledon, in my mail-cart.' Mrs. Skrimshire recalls, 'We were really very frightened of him, but he loved children and used to keep sweets for them in his pockets. I remember once him taking a baby out of its pram—much to the horror of its nurse, and making up a little verse, holding the baby in his arms.' The distraction of children notwithstanding, his destination was always the Rose and Crown, Wimbledon, on the far side (from Putney) of Wimbledon Common; that is to say, a good two miles from The Pines.

That he returned to The Pines on foot is testified by Dr. Gordon Smith, who witnessed his re-entry at lunch-time. So apparently Swinburne walked four miles each day.

The black hat was not invariable. Perhaps he felt the heat in summer, for Mr. Gordon Roe recalls not only seeing 'him turn and wave away two or three urchins who were prancing along after him in single file, and imitating his jerky movements', but that 'on hot sunny days he sometimes protected his neck with a kind of pugaree.' Mrs. Skrimshire saw him 'in a white topee lined with green'.

Nobody apparently ever saw Swinburne and Watts out together.

Messrs. Chatto & Windus gave me access not only to their bound files but to a bundle of loose papers relating to their dealings with Swinburne, and in this bundle I found a typed copy of a letter from Swinburne which has escaped publication in any collection of Swinburne's letters. This copy reads:

March 13th, 1905

My dear Watts-Dunton,

Many years ago I gave you the story, 'A Year's Letters,' for you to publish it whenever you might think fit. You tell me that you have now decided to publish it at once. I write this letter to confirm my original gift of the book and its copyright to you.

Yours ever
(Signed) A. C. Swinburne

Beneath this, is written, evidently by the publishers: *The original was returned to Mr. Watts-Dunton in letter of 16/3/05.*

Swinburne's reference is to the novel finally published under the title of *Love's Cross Currents* which he had written over forty years previously, at Cheyne Walk. As he and Watts-Dunton were living in the

Mary Leith, *née* Gordon

'Bertie': Herbert Mason

same house, the formal letter was merely an instrument for the latter to show to Chatto, so that Chatto should understand that all royalties from the book were to be paid to Watts-Dunton and not to Swinburne.

It seems rather surprising that Watts-Dunton accepted this gift. Many people like to have a manuscript which is in an author's hand, because manuscript has a sentimental value, irrespective of possible financial value; but this was purely a gift of money.

On November 29, 1905, Watts-Dunton married for the first time, at the age of seventy-two. His bride, Clara Jane Reich, must have been twenty-nine, for according to her birth certificate she was born in Tynemouth on September 14, 1876. Her father, Gustav Reich, was a merchant. There is something rather mysterious about this marriage between a young woman and an elderly bachelor. According to her own memoir, Clara was only sixteen when her mother first received an invitation to dine with Watts-Dunton and Swinburne, and to bring her daughter. She, being too shy to meet the poet, as she had not read *Poems and Ballads*, declined, but went to The Pines by herself later in the evening, when she thought the dinner party might be over and Watts-Dunton alone. She did find him alone, and he took her out into the garden. Thereafter she became a frequent visitor to The Pines, but for a year, though she would sometimes pass Swinburne in the passages of the house, they would never greet or appear to see each other. Then Watts-Dunton decided the time had come to introduce them. All this sounds so odd that one wonders what lay behind it. Moreoever, twelve further years must have passed before Clara's marriage to Watts-Dunton.

A curious feature of Clara Watts-Dunton's book is that she has nothing to say of 'Bertie's' mother, Mrs. Mason and Watts-Dunton's other sister, Theresa, save for one passing reference to their presence at the table during one Christmas dinner. Yet the present Mrs. Mason, 'Bertie's' son's widow, assures me Bertie and his mother lived at The Pines up to the time of the marriage, and Mackenzie Bell remembers both sisters being there. Did they and Clara hate each other? Both the witnesses to the marriage bear the bride's surname, Reich, which is unusual, and suggests that the bridegroom's relatives disapproved of the marriage.

Rather surprisingly, Clara Watts-Dunton's memoir of Swinburne, despite its title, is not confined to his life in The Pines. She describes his behaviour in the Rose and Crown. He would sit, she says, in a coffee-room which has since disappeared:[1]

> ... the cosy little apartment which he used was not much fre-quented during the time of his visit; but it was not, of course, a private room, and a stray visitor would sometimes enter it while the poet was in possession. Then one of two things happened. If Swinburne had nearly finished his bottle, he would get up and disappear into the village High Street. If, on the other hand, he had only just begun to refresh himself, he would seek sanctuary in the landlord's private room. As all his movements were watched by the host or his assistants with a really pious solicitude, he would immediately be followed to his retreat by a servant bringing with him the bottle and the glass which the poet had abandoned in the 'Coffee Room.' It is as well to say here that Swinburne's intense love of privacy has given rise to a vast amount of foolish and sometimes spiteful talk about his inaccessibility at The Pines.

Clara Watts-Dunton does not give her source for this information. It is possible that Swinburne described the scene himself, but one has the impression that the witness was someone in the Rose and Crown itself.

The defensive note sounded in the last sentence probably reflects the resentment of Swinburne's friends at what they felt to be Watts-Dunton's possessiveness of the poet. The late Sir Harold Nicolson makes much of this, averring that Watts-Dunton was jealous of every one of Swinburne's friends, and of everything in his background, and that he exhibited him to the few approved visitors with the complacency of a lion-tamer exhibiting a tame lion. Gosse does not use such pungent phrases, but the same sentiment is in his closing chapter.

I have been able to meet one person who went to tea at The Pines. That is Mrs. Yglesias, who still lives on Putney Hill. It was on the skating rink at Knightsbridge that her late husband, a solicitor, met Mrs. Watts-Dunton, who was also skating. (Watts-Dunton himself would have been very much beyond an interest in skating: Mr. Reader remembers seeing Mrs. Watts-Dunton pushing him across the heath in his wheel-chair.) Following the meeting on the rink, Mr. and Mrs. Yglesias received an invitation to tea with the Watts-Dunton's at The Pines. Mrs. Yglesias had the impression that Mrs. Watts-Dunton had lived in the house, as a housekeeper or in other employment, for some

[1] Clara Watts-Dunton, p. 95.

time prior to her marriage with Watts-Dunton. At the tea, Swinburne was present.

It was the beginning of 1909, and his hair and beard were white; he sat in his chair in the corner by the fire, not saying very much. It was Mrs. Watts-Dunton who did almost all the talking; she talked mainly about her husband, and about his novel, *Aylwin*. Swinburne was almost left out; not that he appeared to mind.

I was curious to know the impressions of an independent person, unconnected with literary jealousies of the day, and whether these would be in line with those of Sir Harold Nicolson and Sir Edmund Gosse, or, perhaps, entirely different. I sounded her, and she said, 'The Watts-Dunton's were in possession of the tea-party! Swinburne was almost like a guest.' She thought he was treated as of lesser importance, though probably not with unkindness. 'He didn't talk *there*. But he talked *outside*.'

She met him once at the top of Putney Hill, and, having been informed by the Nannie she employed, said, 'I hear you talk to my child.'

He replied, in his gruff, awkward way, 'Do I? I talk to all the children.' He had no kind of social grace, no ease of manner. He was not unfriendly, but he was '*Gauche*'.

He knew all the Nannies, and would talk with them about the babies and small children in their care; and he had long conversations with her husband's mother, sitting on a bench by the Windmills, on Wimbledon Common, where he would rest for a while on his morning journey to the Rose and Crown.

She sometimes heard his visits to the Rose and Crown referred to in an odd tone; yet she never saw him drunk. He appeared to be in good health; as indeed, he must have been to walk right up Putney Hill and across the Heath and Common, and then back, every day. It was a very considerable walk for anybody, let alone a man of over seventy.

The end came suddenly. At Easter he succumbed to an epidemic of influenza; this quickly turned to pneumonia, and, on April 10, 1909, a few days after his seventy-second birthday, he died. He left his entire estate to Watts-Dunton, who was his sole executor.

The funeral took place in the Isle of Wight, where Swinburne was buried at Bonchurch, close to his father and mother and sisters. Watts-Dunton, laid up with the same influenza as had proved fatal to his friend, sent the Rector a telegram informing him that it was Algernon's wish the Burial Service should not be read, yet suggesting that, though the coffin should be conveyed direct to the graveyard, the Rector's presence might in some way honour the poet's memory. The Rector accompanied the funeral cortège to the grave, and there spoke some informal words, avoiding the letter of the text Swinburne was known to dislike. The many wreaths included one inscribed: 'From Eton, in grateful homage,' with a quotation from Swinburne's *Ode to Eton* (the public one):

Still the reaches of the river, still the light on field and hill,
Still the memories held aloft as lamps for hope's young fire to fill,
Shine.

There were wreaths from Watts-Dunton, and from Watts-Dunton's two sisters, Miss Theresa Watts and Mrs. Mason. Bertie Mason was present, now a grown man of thirty-five years of age and a Chartered Surveyor.[1] Andrew Chatto was there. Also present was Swinburne's cousin, Mary Leith.

[1] Bertie lived until 1947.

41

At the Rose and Crown

IT was not with the expectation of finding anything which would shake the traditional view of Swinburne's last years that I went to the Borough of Wandsworth West Hill District Library. It was merely in a spirit of researcher's duty to leave no stone unturned that I sat down to a table and began looking through the heavy, bound volumes of *Wandsworth Notes*. It was my last 'port of call', and I had practically finished my book. I had done so long an investigation that when I came upon the Obituary of Swinburne printed in the *Wandsworth Boro' News*, I thought it unlikely it would tell me anything about Swinburne I did not already know. But I began reading, and as I read I came across something rather surprising. It was this paragraph:

> Whatever 'secrets' may be connected with Swinburne's habit of 'refreshing' at the Rose and Crown are securely locked in the expansive breast of the landlord. The dumbness of an oyster is but a faint metaphor to apply to the silence of that worthy on the matter. 'I know you newspaper gents are very enterprising, but it isn't my place to talk about a man who's dead and gone, and I'm not going to do it,' he declared when a Boro' News man attempted to draw him on the subject of the poet's visits to the inn. He appeared to think that something sinister underlay the Pressman's innocent desire to chat about these visits. 'What I know about Mr. Swinburne I'm going to keep to myself,' he said darkly, and would not be moved from this estimable attitude.

I remembered at once what Mrs. Yglesias had said about local people speaking with innuendo in their voices. Was it possible that in Wimbledon Swinburne had found a place where he could obtain the same services as formerly he had received in St. John's Wood? It would be unlikely that verification could be obtained now. The landlord – that landlord – of the Rose and Crown was probably dead, having taken his secret to the grave with him, and new people would know nothing.

Nevertheless, I had intended visiting the Rose and Crown. I had written five weeks earlier, addressing my letter simply to The Proprietor. I had explained that I was writing a book on Swinburne, enquired whether they had any Swinburne relics, and, since I had not been able to find the inn in the telephone directory, asked if he would be good enough to ring or write to me. I had had no reply.

But, now that I was in the district, I could at any rate see The Rose and Crown. I had spent several hours in the Library at Wandsworth. It was closing, and the inn would be open. I made my way back along the West Hill Road to Putney Hill, and then, as Swinburne had always walked the entire distance, decided myself to walk it. It seemed interminable. At last I came to the cluster of houses which marked the beginning of Wimbledon. Right on the main road, was a house which looked several centuries old, with a white painted and timbered front. From it hung a sign, on which was painted a pink rose, and a crown. I pushed the saloon door.

Inside, it was brightly lit, warm and cheerful. I went to the bar, and said, 'Could I speak with the proprietor?' The barman turned and indicated a lady. Fair haired, immaculately coiffeured, she came up to me and said, 'I'm sorry I didn't answer your letter.'

It seemed as if she had by extra-sensory perception divined my identity.

'So you know who I am?' I exclaimed, surprised.

'I read your letter again this morning,' she said. 'And I reproached myself for not having answered it.'

She had been busy, and she did not know what she could tell me, as she did not know much about Swinburne. She was no relation of the proprietor of Swinburne's day, and had no connection with the management of that time. The inn had changed hands more than once. All she knew was that it was said to be haunted; Swinburne still came to the Rose and Crown. That was the legend.

She led me to look at a print which hung close to the bar. It showed the Rose and Crown from the outside. Before the front door Johnnie Walker (of Johnnie Walker's Whisky) was greeting Swinburne, the figure of Swinburne lightly etched and transparent, to show that it was his ghost. Beneath the design there was lettering:

JOHNNIE WALKER: 'Greetings: Illustrious Poet—we still enjoy your poems and ballads.'

SHADE OF SWINBURNE: 'The inspiration you dispense is more universally enjoyed, I am sure.'

When I had copied this down, she spoke again of the belief in the locality that the inn continued to be haunted by Swinburne. He was

still here. He was always here. Unexpectedly, she said with some firmness 'I believe it.'

The cheerful atmosphere, the gay colours and bright lights, and the
voices of customers chatting, were all against the impingement of
mystery. Yet in spite of myself I looked around the saloon, asking
myself in which corner, if I could make my eyes sufficiently sensitive, I
should discern Swinburne's spectre.

'We still have his chair,' she said. It had been patched, but was
otherwise as when he had sat on it.

'I should love to see it!' I exclaimed. And immediately, I felt that I
had asked too much.

She shook her head. That would not be possible. 'It's in an upstairs
room.'

42

The Voice of Dolores

AND Mary? Gosse regarded her existence as an obstacle to Swinburne studies. In his *Confidential Paper* he explained the obstacles against which his *Life* of Swinburne had been written, of which she was the chief. He tells an odd story. When, in connection with a brief outline of Swinburne's life for the *Dictionary of National Biography*, he wrote to the poet's surviving sister, Miss Isabel Swinburne, she replied fully and helpfully. On the appearance of the *Dictionary*, however, two letters appeared in the *Times* over her signature, denying that she had communicated with him and attacking him in such terms that Lord Landsdowne came up to him in the House of Lords, and said,[1] 'You have indeed struck on a remarkable specimen of *foemina* [*sic*] *furens!*' Gosse was puzzled, because 'Miss Isabel Swinburne was anything but furens.' Later she sent him messages of great kindness. Lord Redesdale, Swinburn's cousin, told Gosse that, as the result of his investigations, he was convinced that Miss Isabel Swinburne had not written the letters (presumably the furious ones) and that they had been written by Mrs. Leith, in conjunction with a Jesuit cousin, Father Bowden. As the latter name does not enter into Swinburne's story, one takes it simply that the *foemina furens* was Mary Leith.

Lord Redesdale, though in his eightieth year, travelled to the Isle of Wight to see Mary, and to try to persuade her to see Gosse, or at least to give him some kind of cooperation, in connection with his proposed biography of Swinburne. He was not successful. Gosse continues, in his *Confidential Paper*:

> Mrs. Disney Leith was quite open in her line of action. She objected to 1) the assumption that Algernon was irreligious, 'he was in communication with the Church of England all his life,' she declared; 2) the suggestion that he drank ('he was never intoxicated in all his life,' she said; and 3) she, and Miss Isabel in her wake passively, were infuriated at what I had said about Swinburne's relations with Adah Isaacs Menken. Mrs. Leith had the naivete to say, to the very great amusement of Lord Redesdale, 'Algernon was

[1] Gosse, *Confidential Paper*, ff. 9–10. British Museum: MSS. Ashley, 5753.

far too well-bred a gentleman ever to *speak* to a woman of that class!'

One is obviously meant to take it from this that Mary was a fool and a snob. There are, however, several things to bear in mind, and the first is that her words come to us through two intermediaries, first Redesdale and then Gosse, and at either stage there may have been a distortion. We cannot be sure they are exactly the words Mary Leith spoke. Then, as to her points, though in his earlier poems Swinburne seemed often blasphemous, there is a certain, deeper sense in which he was not irreligious, but reflecting; moreover, it is probable that on his visits to the Isle of Wight he went with the family to church. One must remember that Mary had never been with Swinburne in Chelsea or Blooms-bury, but only in the Isle of Wight and in Northumberland, always in his parents' home or in that of her own parents, or in the homes of their grandparents, and these were all places in which he would be careful of his behaviour. If she said she had never seen him intoxicated, this might be the truth. That she was aware he stood reproached for excessive drinking may, however, be inferred from her novel *Like His Own Daughter*. On the third point, though she found it needless to avow that she, herself, was Dolores, it must been infuriating to have it supposed that Dolores was somebody else.

That Gosse intended, in his biography, to make Adah Menken the woman in Swinburne's life appears from a note he wrote to Wise, which is in the British Museum:[1]

> I hope you will secure "Dolorida" from Maggs. It has great biographical importance.'

Dolorida was the verse Swinburne had written in Adah Menken's note-book, and Gosse, apparently oblivious that Swinburne had not met her when *Dolores* was composed, was obviously going to make this identification, which was erroneous, central to his book. He was going to say that Adah Menken was Dolores.

This was the situation with which Mary Leith was confronted. She could not say, 'It wasn't her, it's me!' She had to put Gosse off; and, to prevent him from publishing what was false, one phrase may have seemed as good as another to use as a deterrent.

The *foemina furens*, the woman whose temperament Swinburne had celebrated in poetical works, must have been a formidable antagonist.

[1] British Museum: MSS. Ashley, 4378, f. 14.

Had Gosse persisted in writing what he wished of Swinburne and Adah Menken, however false, she could have had no legal redress. But by the sheer fury of her opposition, he was deterred. He had his revenge in the *Confidential Paper*, wherein he represents her as a narrow-minded virago. And yet, after all, the laugh is not altogether on Gosse's side. For he saw in his antagonist only an obstacle, and not the core of the drama.

Left to herself, she could sing about Swinburne. For it is not in her formal memoir, *The Boyhood of Algernon Charles Swinburne*, that she speaks with the throb of her woman's heart; it is in her poems, which nobody reads. While Swinburne lived, she had sung of the 'first white rose,' of the 'wood-dove's note' and the 'first viol,' that was Swinburne's love for her. Now that he was dead, she wrote a poem, which she did not publish until 1920, when she was eighty years old, in *Northern Lights and Other Verses*. It is entitled *Rocket*, and I ask the reader to believe that it is the voice of Dolores hymning Swinburne:[1]

ROCKET

'Creature of air and fire!'
Temper of steel,
Attuned to heart's desire
Of hand and heel.

Hath life of flesh and blood
Held aught more sweet
Than rush of air and thud
Of flying feet?

Comrade of bygone days,
Lightsome and glad,
Now our familiar ways
Seem lorn and sad.

O'er the far downs, aglow
In summer's shine,
Ne'er more with me you go,
Comrade of mine.

[1] Leith, *Northern Lights and Other Verses*, pp. 96–7.

THE VOICE OF DOLORES

You–that with wingéd feet
  Straight as a dart
Sped, while between us beat
  Only one heart.

Life, and its loyal best
  To us you gave,
Your meed but dreamless rest
  In a green grave.

Rest well, my true, my own,
  Where naught shall fret!
Heart that has loved and known
  Ne'er can forget.

Appendix

WATERMARKS IN *THE FLOGGING BLOCK*

Algernon's Flogging	f.5	1887
Note to Algernon's Flogging		1876
Reginald's Flogging	f.1	1881
	f.2	1881
	f.3	1879
	f.7	1879
Epilogue to Reginald's Flogging		1879
Percy's Flogging	f.1	1879
	f.4	1881
	f.5	1881
	f.6	1881
Prelude to Willie's Flogging	f.1	1881
Willie's Flogging	f.3	1879
Charlie's Flogging	f.1	1881
	f.4	1881
	f.11	1881
Frank's Flogging	f.6	1881
		1878 (unfoliated leaf following f.10)
Frederick's Flogging	f.1	1881
Edgar's Flogging		1869 (unfoliated but first folio)

Folios not listed show no water marked date.

Selective Bibliography

Selective Bibliography

BOOKS

SWINBURNE

The Poems of Algernon Charles Swinburne (London, Chatto & Windus, 1904). Six volumes.

The Tragedies of Algernon Charles Swinburne (London, Chatto & Windus, 1905–6). Five volumes.

The Duke of Gandia (London, Chatto & Windus, 1908).

Love's Cross Currents (London, Chatto & Windus, 1905).

A Song of Italy (London, John Camden Hotten, 1867).

Lesbia Brandon, edited by Randolph Hughes (London, Falcon Press, 1952),

The Complete Works of Swinburne, edited by Edmund Gosse and Thomas James Wise (Bonchurch Edition, London, Heinemann, 1925–7). Twenty volumes.

The Swinburne Letters, edited by Cecil Y. Lang (New Haven, Yale University press, and London, Oxford University Press, 1959–62). Six volumes.

'Arthur's Flogging,' 'Reginald's Flogging' and 'A Boy's First Flogging at Birchminster' in *The Whippingham Papers* (London [E. Avery, 1887]).

The Triumph of Gloriana, edited by Edmund Gosse (London, Printed for Private Circulation only for T. J. Wise, 1916).

Undergraduate Sonnets (London, Printed for Private Circulation only for T. J. Wise by Eyre & Spottiswoode, 1918).

The Ride from Milan and Other Poems (Printed for Private Circulation only for T. J. Wise by Eyre & Spottiswoode, 1918).

Ernest Clouet, a Burlesque, edited by Edmund Gosse (London, Printed for Private Circulation only for T. J. Wise, 1916).

A Vision of Bags, edited by Edmund Gosse (London, Printed for Private Circulation only for T. J. Wise, 1916).

The Ballad of Truthful Charles and Other Poems (London, Printed for Private Circulation only for T. J. Wise, 1910).

Juvenalia (London, Printed for Private Circulation only for T. J. Wise, 1912).

Blest and the Centenary of Shelley, etc. (London, Printed for Private Circulation only for T. J. Wise, 1912).

SWINBURNE

Aeolus (London, Printed for Private Circulation only for T. J. Wise, 1914).

Lady Maisie's Bairn and Other Poems (London, Printed for Private Circulation only for T. J. Wise, 1915).

The Italian Mother (London, Printed for Private Circulation only for T. J. Wise, 1918).

SWINBURNE STUDIES

Cassidy, John A., *Algernon Charles Swinburne* (New York, Twayne, 1964).

Chew, Samuel C., *Swinburne* (London, Murray, 1931).

Connally, T. E., *Swinburne's Theory of Poetry* (New York, State University of New York, 1964).

Drinkwater, John, *Swinburne: an Estimate* (London, Dent, 1913).

Gosse, Edmund, *The Life of Algernon Charles Swinburne* (London, Macmillan, 1917).

Hare, Humphrey, *Swinburne: a Biographical Approach* (London, Witherby, 1949).

Hughes, Randolph, 'Commentary' in *Lesbia Brandon* (London, Falcon Press, 1952).

Lafourcade, Georges, *La Jeunesse de Swinburne* (Paris, Université de Strassbourg, Les Belles Lettres, and Oxford, Humphrey Milford, Oxford University Press, 1928). Two volumes.

Lafourcade, Georges, *Swinburne: a Literary Biography* (Oxford University Press, 1932).

Leith, Mary C. J., *The Boyhood of Algernon Charles Swinburne* (London, Chatto & Windus, 1917).

Lucas, E. V., *At the Pines* (London, Privately Printed by Clement Shorter, 1916).

Mackail, J. W., *Swinburne: a Lecture* (Oxford University Press, 1909).

Maupassant, Guy de, 'Notes sur Swinburne' in *Ballades et Poemes de A. C. Swinburne* traduits par Gabriel Mourey (Paris, Albert Savine, 1891).

Mayfield, John S., *The Luck of an Autograph Hunter* (Washington, D.C., The Fraternity Press, 1950).

Mayfield, John S., *Swinburne's Boo* (Washington, D.C., The Goetz Company, 1954).

Nicolson, Harold, *Swinburne* (London, Macmillan, 1926).

Peters, Robert L., *The Crowns of Apollo: Swinburne's Principles of Literature and Art* (Detroit, Wayne State University Press, 1965).

Reuil, Paul de, *L'Oeuvre de Swinburne* (Brussels, Robert Sand, 1922).

306

SELECT BIBLIOGRAPHY

Rutland, William, *Swinburne: a Nineteenth Century Hellene* (Oxford, Blackwell, 1931).

Shanks, Edward, 'Introduction' to *Selected Poems of Swinburne* (London, Macmillan, 1950).

Sitwell, Edith, 'Introduction' to *Swinburne: a Selection* (London, Weidenfeld & Nicholson, 1960).

Thomas, Edward, *Algernon Charles Swinburne: a Critical Study* (London, Secker, 1912).

Watts-Dunton, Clara, *The Home Life of Algernon Charles Swinburne* (London, Philpot, 1922).

SWINBURNE'S CONNECTIONS

LEITH, MARY C. J. *née* GORDON.

The Boyhood of Algernon Charles Swinburne (London, Chatto & Windus, 1917).

Mark Dennis: or, The Engine Driver (London, Rivingtons, 1859).

The Children of the Chapel [with Swinburne] (London, Chatto & Windus, 1910).

The Chorister Brothers (London, J. Masters, 1867).

*The Incumbent of Axhill: a sequel to The Chorister Brothers (1875).

A Martyr Bishop and Other Verses (London, J. Masters, 1878).

Like His Own Daughter (London, Walker Smith, 1883).

*Rufus: a Story in three books (1886).

Original Verses and Translations (London, J. Masters, 1895).

Briskupar: Stories of the Bishops of Iceland translated from the Icelandic (London, J. Masters, 1895).

Three Visits to Iceland, with translations of J. Hallgrimsson's 'Gunar's Holm' (London, J. Masters, 1897).

Iceland, with 12 watercolour illustrations by M. A. Wemys and the author (London, Black, 1908).

Champion Sandy: a Story (Aberdeen, Alexander Murray, and Dumfries, Mann, Scottish Chronicle Office, 1910).

A Black Martinmass: a Story (London, Lynwood, 1912).

Lachlan's Widow (London, Lynwood, 1913).

Northern Lights and Other Verses (London, Arthur L. Humphries, 1920).

* The British Museum copies of these two books were destroyed by bombing in the war, and I have consequently been unable to study them.

SWINBURNE

ROSSETTIS

The Poetical Works of Christina Georgina Rossetti, with memoir and notes by William Michael Rossetti (London, Macmillan, 1904).

Christina Rossetti by Lona Mosk Packer (University of California Press and Cambridge University Press, 1963).

The Rossetti-Macmillan Letters, edited by Lona Mosk Packer (Cambridge University Press, 1963).

Dante Gabriel Rossetti: Poems and Translations (Oxford University Press, 1913).

The Letters of Dante Rossetti, 1835–1870, edited by Oswald Doughty and J. R. Wahl, (Oxford, The Clarendon Press, 1965). Two volumes.

A Victorian Romantic: Dante Gabriel Rossetti, by Oswald Doughty (Oxford University Press, 1960).

Portrait of Rossetti, by Rosalie Glynn Grylls (London, Macdonald, 1964).

Life with Rossetti: or, No Peacocks Allowed, by Gale Pedrick (London, Macdonald, 1964).

Dante Gabriel Rossetti, his Friends and Enemies, by Helen Rossetti Angeli (London, Hamish Hamilton, 1949).

Pre-Raphaelite Twilight: the Story of Charles Augustus Howell, by Helen Rossetti Angeli (Richards Press, 1954).

The Pre-Raphaelite Tragedy, by William Gaunt (London, Cape, 1942).

SIMEON SOLOMON

A Vision of Love Revealed in Sleep (London, Printed for the Author, F. S. Ellis, 1871).

Five Years Dead: a Postscript to 'He Laughed in Fleet Street' with Chapters on Simeon Solomon the Artist and the stolen Gainsborough Portrait by Bernard Falk (London, Hutchinson, 1937).

VICTOR HUGO

Victor Hugo, by André Maurois (London, Cape, 1936).

OTHERS

Memories, by Algernon Bertram Mitford, Lord Redesdale (London, Hutchinson, 1915).

Monkton Milnes, the Years of Promise, by James Pope-Hennesey (London, Constable, 1951).

Adah Isaacs Menken: a fragment of Autobiography by Algernon Charles

308

Swinburne [extracts from Swinburne's letters with an 'Introduction' by X.Y.Z. (London, Printed for Private Circulation only, 1917).

Leaves of Grass by Walt Whitman, edited with introduction by Malcolm Cowley (London, Secker & Warburg, 1959).

Aylwin, by [Walter] Theodore Watts-Dunton (London, Hurst & Blackett, 1899).

Poets and the Renaissance of Wonder by Walter Theodore Watts-Dunton (London, Jenkins, 1916).

A Mid-Victorian Pepys, the letters and memoirs of Sir William Hardman, edited and annotated by Stewart Marsh Ellis (London, Cecil Palmer, 1923).

The Letters of Sir William Hardman, Second Series, 1863–1865, edited and annotated by Stewart Marsh Ellis (London, Cecil Palmer, 1925).

The Hardman Papers, a further Selection, 1865–68, edited and annotated by Stewart Marsh Ellis (London, Cecil Palmer, 1930).

WISE, T. J. (warning concerning bibliographies by)

An Enquiry into the Nature of Certain Nineteenth century Pamphlets by John Carter and Graham Pollard (London, Constable, and New York, Scribner, 1934).

'Two Footnotes to an Enquiry' in *Books and Book Collectors* by John Carter (London, Hart Davis, 1956).

MANUSCRIPTS

In the British Museum

SWINBURNE

Works
Lesbia Brandon, Ashley 5264.
The Flogging Block, Ashley 5256.
Frank Fane, Ashley 5751,
Eton: Another Ode, Ashley 5271.
The Ballad of Fat Madge (translation from Villon, Ashley A.4427).
Letters
To Dante Gabriel Rossetti, Ashley 5074.
To Dante Gabriel Rossetti, Ashley A.3870.
To William Michael Rossetti, Ashley A.4633.
To William Michael Rossetti, Ashley A.294.
To William Michael Rossetti, Ashley A.1926.
To William Michael Rossetti, Ashley A.1964.
To Watts-Dunton, Ashley 5090 (two volumes).
To Watts-Dunton, Ashley A.1400.
To Watts-Dunton, Ashley 1893.

LETTERS TO SWINBURNE

From Dante Gabriel Rossetti, Ashley 4995.
From Dante Gabriel Rossetti, Ashley 5074.
From Dante Gabriel Rossetti, Ashley 1387.
From Dante Gabriel Rossetti, Ashley 1878.
From Dante Gabriel Rossetti, Ashley A.3870.
From Dante Gabriel Rossetti, Ashley A.3870, A.2871, A.3872.
From Christina Georgiana Rossetti, Ashley 1386.
From William Michael Rossetti, Ashley A.1400.
From Simeon Solomon, Ashley A.1754.
From Simeon Solomon, Ashley 1755.
From Simeon Solomon, Ashley A.4273.

APPENDIX

From Simeon Solomon, Ashley 5752.
From Simeon Solomon, Ashley A.1753.
From John Nichol, Ashley 5752.
From John Nichol, Ashley 1941.
From John Nichol, Ashley A.295.
From Mary Leith, Ashley 5752.

GOSSE

Confidential Paper on Swinburne's Moral Irregularities, with attached letters, Ashley 5753.
Letter to Wise, Ashley 1755.
Letter to Wise, Ashley 5752.
Letter to Wise, Ashley 4378.

This is but a very selective bibliography of the manuscript sources in the British Museum; it would be impractical to list all the letters to Swinburne from his many connections, and from these connections to each other, on the many files of the Ashley Library perused.

On the Premises of Messrs Chatto and Windus

The Letter-Books of John Camden Hotten
The Letter-Books of Chatto & Windus.
The contracts between Chatto & Windus and Watts-Dunton as Swinburne's agent.
Memoranda in the hand of Andrew Chatto.
Typescript copy of a hitherto unpublished letter from Swinburne to Watts-Dunton.

In the Wandsworth West Hill District Library

Swinburne and his Poetry by Henry Thomas Mackenzie Bell, a typescript.
Wandsworth Notes, a compilation of newspaper cuttings concerning Wandsworth and persons of note who at any time resided in Putney or Wandsworth.

Index

Rossetti–*cont.*
house with A.C.S., 66, 80–2, 85,
110, 112–13, 177; and Jane Burden
(Morris), 80; 'Chastelard', 92;
A.C.S's epilepsy, 93–4, 166; and
Howell, 111; Hampton Court trip,
120; publication of A.C.S., 123, 154;
and Thomson, 145; A.C.S's private
life, 149, 163; art, 158; *Mahabharata*,
173; A.C.S's parents' anxiety, 180–1;
poetry advice from A.C.S., 183,
189–96; breakdown and rejection of A.C.S., 196–8, 225; and
Watts-Dunton, 199; A.C.S., parodies, 239; death of, 265; and Whitman,
267
Rossetti, Mrs. Dante Gabriel *See*
Siddal, Elizabeth
Rossetti, William Michael, A.C.S.
and Shelley, 26, 30; A.C.S. meets,
59; and Blake, 66; at Cheyne Walk,
81; A.C.S's convalescence letters,
93–4; smoking, 113; 'Dolores', 114;
on flagellation, 144; 'Songs before
Sunrise', 157; A.C.S's 'fit', 166;
D. G. Rossetti's breakdown, 197,
225; 'Erechtheus', 214; Christina's
death, 280–1; edits Shelley, 281
Royal Academy, 177, 236
Ruskin, John, 31, 56, 92, 123
Rutland, William, 217

Sade, Marquis de, Milnes and, 54–5, 59,
148; summarised, 60–2; A.C.S's
reaction to, 62–5, 67, 69–71, 149;
influence on A.C.S's writing, 114–
16, 134, 148; Watts-Dunton's views,
227
St. Aldwyn, Lord, 24
Sark, 224, 239, 261
Scott, William Bell, friendship with
A.C.S., 31, 37, 45, 48, 66; on
'Rosamund', 47; and hermaphroditism, 85; and Christina Rossetti,
138; on A.C.S's private life, 149–50;
and D. G. Rossetti, 265
Sewell, Elizabeth, 24

Shakespeare, William, 18, 23, 57, 87,
245–6, 258
Sheffield, Lord, 113
Shelley, Percy Bysshe, A.C.S. likened
to, 17, 25–6, 30, 52; forged letters,
35; 'Revolt of Islam', 40; influence
on A.C.S., 49, 84; 'Prometheus',
95–6; religious views, 101, 148, 153;
'West Wind', 190; 'Epipsychidion',
238
Shelley, Sir Timothy, 30
Siddal, Elizabeth (Mrs. D. G. Rossetti),
55–7; death of, 57–9; description,
79; A.C.S. and, 179; poems buried
with, 58, 180, 189, 196
Skrimshire, Mrs., 288
Smith, Dr. H. Gordon, 287–8
Solomon, Abraham, 177
Solomon, Simeon, friendship with
A.C.S., 80–1, 175–8; homosexuality,
150, 178, 181, 184–6, 188; flagellation, 175–8, 186–7, 258; as artist,
178, 182–5, 187; letters to A.C.S.,
181–8, 198, 202; poetry criticized,
195; renounced by A.C.S., 202, 234;
decline and death of, 236–7
Spectator, A.C.S's reviews in, 65–6,
68–9, 83, 85; poems in, 109, 120, 122
Spenser, Edmund, 19
Stubbs, Rev. William, 45, 48
Swinburne, Algernon Charles, birth
and family, 17, 21; childhood, 18;
nickname, 18; relations with father,
17, 20–1, 23, 28–30, 77, 129–30, 180,
226; Italian studies, 19, 24; French
studies, 22, 24, 30 n.; schooling, 23–7;
personal appearance, 23–4, 34, 38, 55,
112–13, 287–8; courage, 24–5, 28–9;
flagellation: (at Eton) 25, 144, 272,
(paternal) 30, (in writings) 51, 117,
130, 132–3, 135–7, 256, (in Milnes
correspondence) 67–70, 144, 186,
268, (and Howell) 144, 161–2, 200,
(in Gosse's biog.) 145, (in prostitu-
tion establishments) 145–7, 172, 293,
(and Solomon) 175–8, (Hotten's
publications) 200–1, (Mary Leith's